Historical Problems:
Studies and Documents

Edited by
PROFESSOR G. R. ELTON
University of Cambridge

9

THE CITY IN AMERICAN HISTORY

In the same series

THE CITY IN AMERICAN HISTORY

Blake McKelvey
City Historian, Rochester, New York

LONDON: GEORGE ALLEN AND UNWIN LTD
NEW YORK: BARNES AND NOBLE INC

© *George Allen & Unwin Ltd,* 1969

SBN 04 301017 2 *cloth*

SBN 04 301018 0 *paper*

PRINTED IN GREAT BRITAIN
in 10 *on* 11 *pt Plantin type*
BY WILLMER BROTHERS LIMITED
BIRKENHEAD

EDITOR'S FOREWORD

The reader and the teacher of history might be forgiven for thinking that there are now too many series of historical documents in existence, all claiming to offer light on particular problems and all able to fulfil their claims. At any rate, the general editor of yet another series feels obliged to explain why he is helping one more collection of such volumes into existence.

One purpose of this series is to put at the disposal of the student original materials illustrating historical problems, but this is no longer anything out of the way. A little less usual is the decision to admit every sort of historical question: there are no barriers of time or place or theme. However, what really distinguishes this enterprise is the fact that it combines generous collections of documents with introductory essays long enough to explore the theme widely and deeply. In the doctrine of educationalists, it is the original documents that should be given to the student; in the experience of teachers, documents thrown naked before the untrained mind turn from pearls to paste. The study of history cannot be confined either to the learning up of results without a consideration of the foundations, or to a review of those foundations without the assistance of the expert mind. The task of teaching involves explanation and instruction, and these volumes recognize this possibly unfashionable fact. Beyond that, they enable the writers to say new and important things about their subject matter: to write history of an exploratory kind, which is the only important historical writing there is.

As a result, each volume will be a historical monograph worth the attention which all such monographs deserve, and each volume will stand on its own. While the format of the series is uniform, the contents will vary according to need. Some problems require the reconsideration which makes the known enlighteningly new; others need the attention of original research; yet others will have to enter controversy because the prevailing notions on many historical questions are demonstrably wrong. The authors of this series are free to treat their subject in whatever manner it seems to them to require. They will present some of their evidence for inspection and to help the learner to see how history is written, but they will themselves also write history.

G.R.E.

The rapid and astonishing transformation of America in the last three decades poses a new challenge to historians. Both its unexpected demographic vitality and its almost incredible productivity, as well as several unsuspected weaknesses, reveal the inadequacy of the traditional interpretations of its development. Clearly some hidden forces or poorly recognized circumstances have been significantly operative to account for such dramatic changes. Many scholars are tackling the question, which will of course defy any simple resolution. But a suggestive hint is provided by linking together two of the most remarkable of recent developments—the tremendous growth of national as contrasted with state power, and the widespread emergence of dynamic but somewhat impotent metropolitan communities.

These two seemingly independent developments appear on closer examination to be both closely related and crucial aspects of the contemporary transformation of America. Their convergence suggests the need for a reappraisal of the place of the city in American history. In this effort we will want to look back to see how and in what respects the planting and development of cities influenced and was influenced by the colonial settlement, the achievement of independence, the occupation of the continent, the development of industrial enterprise, the arrival of a heterogeneous throng of newcomers, the challenge of foreign wars, the fluctuations of a dynamic economy, the frustrations of political and social strife in a still imperfect democracy. Numerous historians have already explored one or another of these questions, and scholars in other fields have studied the special civic, geographic, ecological, and economic aspects of urban growth. It is hoped that a review of their findings, supported by a selection of related documents, will shed fresh light on the history of America's development and provide a more adequate interpretation of current transformations in its community structure on both the national and the urban levels.

In the preparation of this summary essay I am deeply indebted to several historians whose major studies have made this review possible. I have cited their volumes repeatedly in the footnotes, but I wish especially to mention here Carl Bridenbaugh, Charles N. Glaab, Constance M. Green, Roy Lubove, John W. Reps, Bayrd Still, and Richard C. Wade whose scholarly contributions have been most helpful to this study. In the last six chapters I have relied heavily on two books of my own, *The Urbanization of America: 1860–1915* and

The Emergence of Metropolitan America: 1915–1966, (New Brunswick, N.J., 1963 and 1968), both published by the Rutgers University
Press, which has generously given consent to this use. I am indebted,
too, to several publishers for permission to reproduce copyrighted
materials in my documentary section. Proper acknowledgements
appear below in the citations of these documents, but I wish here to
thank the following publishers for permission to reproduce materials
from their journals and reports: *The American City,* The National
Municipal Association, The United States Conference of Mayors,
The Advisory Commission on Intergovernmental Relations, The
National Advisory Commission on Civil Disorders and the United
States Government Printing Office. I wish also to thank my secretary Miss Yolanda Ranches for painstaking assistance throughout the
writing of this volume.

                                                   Blake McKelvey
City Historian
Rochester, New York, U.S.A.
October 1968

CONTENTS

INTRODUCTION

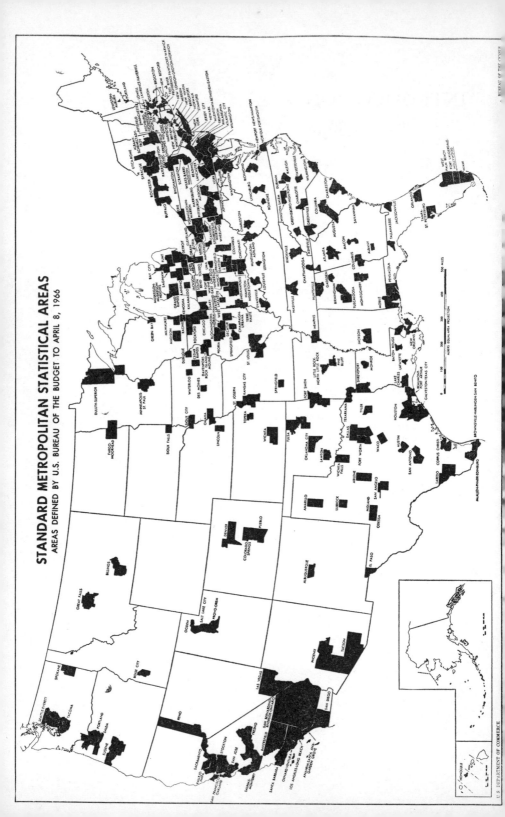

STANDARD METROPOLITAN STATISTICAL AREAS

AREAS DEFINED BY U.S. BUREAU OF THE BUDGET TO APRIL 8, 1966

Colonial Ports—Cradles of Freedom

Conceived and promoted as trading and administrative outposts by the expanding mercantile empires of the sixteenth and seventeenth centuries, a dozen colonial ports became thriving commercial towns by 1700. Scattered from Santo Domingo, the oldest, in the West Indies to Montreal in Canada, they represented the efforts of four rival powers and presented many striking contrasts. More striking, however, than their urban differences were the divergent roles they would assume during succeeding decades in the history of these contending empires. Only the British ports, and only those on the mainland, where this study focuses, became 'cradles of freedom', as one astute observer later described them, and the circumstances that determined that course call for careful study by American historians.

Located in each case at a favourable commercial site, the colonial ports also reflected the urban concepts of their promoters. The Spanish towns, as John Reps has demonstrated, followed a pattern of city planning derived from Greek and Roman experience and promulgated in the Laws of the Indies in 1753.[1] The bastide shape and fortifications of these towns reflected the military character and close imperial controls that differentiated these strongholds, designed to impress and rule the surrounding natives, from the trading centres planted by the British to serve and administer colonies of transplanted Englishmen. The walls erected by the Dutch at New Amsterdam (later New York) and by the French at Quebec and Montreal in Canada were originally designed to ward off attacks by unfriendly Indians. Later fortifications there and at the West India ports, notably Havana and Santo Domingo, marked the efforts of rival kings to defend these strategic outposts from hostile fleets. They revealed the pervasive insecurity that distinguished these island communities from the mainland settlements of the British. The progressive replacement of the natives on the West India plantations by Negro slaves added to that insecurity.

But if walls and imperial ties were less substantial in the mainland ports, the influence of contemporary British town planning and other

[1] John W. Reps, *The Making of Urban America*, Princeton 1965, pp. 26–43.

traditions was clearly evident. The plan for Charles Town, planted in South Carolina in the 1670s, followed that drawn for Londonderry in northern Ireland a few decades before; the more geometric design for New Haven, an offshoot of Boston in 1638, represented an early version of the gridiron pattern proposed for London after its great fire in 1666 and adapted by William Penn for Philadelphia a few years later.[2] Charles Town and some of the other British settlements erected stockades, but most of the proprietors gave more attention to the selection of safe harbour sites; moreover, the designation of choice squares for parks and meeting houses reflected the maturity of their community planning. The ports were planned as commercial, administrative, and residential centres with highways leading out to nearby and distant agricultural settlements in colonies designed to absorb a surplus population of landless and unemployed Englishmen and to produce raw materials lacking in the home country.[3]

Although their original objectives were seldom realized in full, most of the colonial ports developed products and trading functions that contributed to the strength of the British Empire. Charles Town, for example, failed to produce the silks, wines, oils, and olives hopefully anticipated under its 1663 charter, but its shipments of indigo and rice rewarded the promoters and helped to nurture a rich planter class that maintained residences in the city. Boston, the first major British port, founded in 1630, gathered and supplied masts for the Royal Navy, assembled and shipped thousands of pounds of fish, and built and dispatched such an increasing host of large and small ships that it soon dominated the coastal trade. Newport in Rhode Island also built ships, and some of its captains ventured to carry mutton, pork, and other products to the West Indies, and brought slaves on the return voyage to exchange for tobacco in Virginia. New York served as a base for the fur trade and supplied flour to provision the merchantmen that called in increasing numbers at its docks. Philadelphia, with the productive energies of a host of eager settlers developing the rich lands that surrounded it on all sides, bid vigorously to supply the food needs of the West Indies.[4]

But the colonial ports were so far distant from England both in time and space that they progressively assumed new and independent functions. Not only did the colonial merchants compete with the

[2] Reps, pp. 14–15, 128–129, 158–165. See also Anthony N. B. Garvan. *Architecture and Town Planning in Colonial Connecticut*, New Haven 1951.

[3] William A. Williams, *The Contours of American History*, Cleveland 1961, pp. 27–61.

[4] George L. Beer, *The Origins of the British Colonial System*, New York 1908, pp. 53–77 ff.; Carl Bridenbaugh, *Cities in the Wilderness*, New York 1938, pp. 1–5, 22–54, 175–198.

British for the coastal trade and in carrying supplies to the West Indies, but they could not resist the temptation to visit the French and Spanish ports there, where prices were often most attractive. Some boldly sailed to Europe, again defying the mercantile restrictions. During the frequent imperial wars, these clandestine operations generally proved very profitable. Enriched and emboldened by such exploits, some merchants fitted out privateers and engaged in semi-military forays in search of prizes of war that brought additional wealth and prestige to the colonial ports and nurtured their sense of self-reliance.

As some venturesome merchants expanded the colonial markets abroad, others promoted the output of local craftsmen and of neighbouring settlements to fill their holds. Enterprising craftsmen, who had grudgingly been permitted to supply the local needs in each town, found new markets in the interior and began to ship their furniture, silverware, and other articles to more distant ports where they sometimes competed with British products. Artisans of ability appeared in such numbers in Boston, New York, and Philadelphia by the early 1700s that their shops rivalled those of the retailers who had brought supplies from England. In the process they developed a thriving middle class and made the mainland ports more attractive to poor newcomers than those of the West Indies. As the migration continued, each port dispatched groups of settlers to the interior, some to found new market towns, but the great majority to cultivate the land. Only in Virginia and the Carolinas, where the raising of tobacco, cotton, and rice favoured the development of large estates, did the planters rely heavily on slaves imported from the West Indies, and only in Charles Town among the leading towns did the presence of slaves in large numbers check the growth of a sturdy middle class.[5]

The increased independence evident in the marketplace was matched in the civic field. Growth in size and activity had brought additional responsibilities to the colonial ports. The selectmen chosen by the town meetings under the democratic provisions of the New England charters and the municipal councils elsewhere, generally appointed by the governors, often suspended the traditional medieval regulations when their enforcement proved difficult. Thus price controls, licences, class distinctions, and other restraints gradually lost their hold as local authorities turned to the development of regulations more germane to the needs of the community. A succession of 'great fires' in Boston in the 1650s brought ordinances requiring householders to equip themselves with water buckets and with ladders too

---

[5] Bridenbaugh, *Cities in the Wilderness*, pp. 42–44, 190–192; Carl Bridenbaugh, *Cities in Revolt*, New York 1955, pp. 260–280.

in all two-storey houses. Soon the construction of wooden buildings within certain limits was prohibited; a destructive conflagration in 1679 prompted the organization of a volunteer company to operate a hand-driven fire engine ordered from London that autumn.

As the colonial ports facilitated the transit of British customs, they emphasized those that seemed most useful. The services of constables by day appeared in all towns shortly after their establishment, and Boston was the first in 1635 to form a night watch, chiefly as a precaution against fires. New York, with a more diversified population, organized a security patrol in the 1650s. As their inhabitants increased and the visits of trading vessels multiplied, other towns experienced similar disorders. Efforts to enforce the peace by inflicting public floggings and by exposure in stocks proved ineffective, and town after town moved to establish a goal. When attempts to halt the influx of newcomers who lacked appropriate occupations failed, because of the mounting commercial activity, most of the ports opened almshouses to remove orphans and paupers from the streets. The progressive construction of handsome public buildings, churches and other institutions in each town marked the birth, as Constance Green has shown, of a new civic spirit.[6]

Except for the New England towns, where the English for a time predominated, all of the colonial ports developed a diversified population by the close of the century. New York attracted Jews and Swedes and additional migrants from Holland, as well as many from England and its West India colonies. Philadelphia welcomed German, Irish, and Welsh migrants, as well as Dutch and English Quakers. Charles Town received a contingent of Huguenots from France and drew many Scots from northern Ireland as well as Englishmen from the West Indies; the last group brought so many Negroes as slaves that by 1765 fully half of the town's population was of that race. This increased diversity of inhabitants produced a comparable diversity of customs and institutions. Only in Boston was one sect, the Puritans, able to retain full control throughout the seventeenth century, partly by expelling Roger Williams and other dissidents to Rhode Island. Newport became, in contrast, a centre of religious diversity, a haven for Baptists, Quakers, and Jews who also found entry to New York and Philadelphia.

After 1700 the clergy and practitioners of medicine and law formed, with the established merchants in the North and with resident planters in the South, an *élite* class that began to assume the prerogatives of an aristocracy. Some of them welcomed the royal governors and other British representatives sent over to strengthen imperial ties, and many

⁶ Bridenbaugh, *Cities in the Wilderness*, pp. 55–85; Constance M. Green, *The Rise of Urban America*, New York 1965, pp. 43–44.

even in Boston and Philadelphia hastened to join the Church of England, the favourite of the English upper class. This shift created a rift among the leaders in some towns and, as Carl Bridenbaugh has shown, eventually resulted in the estrangement of the more pretentious adherents of the aristocratic tradition, forging still another link in the chain of forces promoting independence.[7]

Several urban circumstances, however, curbed the influence of the nascent aristocracy. The increased diversity of religious institutions in the cities made a united front among the clergy precarious. When the Rev. George Whitefield brought the Wesleyan revival to America, many who deplored his emotional zeal could at least support his criticisms of the Church of England, which seemed too formal and pretentious. The limited influence exerted by the 'better classes' through their church schools and other institutions was less evident in the taverns, which provided the meeting place for residents of all ranks and supplied shelter and entertainment to the numerous travellers who thronged into towns large and small. A few hostelries in each city catered to the rich and decorated certain rooms for their balls and other functions, but generally the taverns maintained a boisterous atmosphere that fostered a democratic spirit. The tavern was one of the first urban institutions to carry its influence out to every cross-roads hamlet in the land.[8]

Equally important in this respect was the successful launching of several small weekly newspapers. Boston, which produced the first in 1704, had three within two decades, and Philadelphia soon equalled that accomplishment. All the other leading towns quickly launched papers, and these four-page sheets, edited and published by self-taught journeymen printers, gave the rising middle class of artisans and small tradesmen a voice in community affairs. The accomplishments of the most famous of these publishers, Benjamin Franklin, in establishing lending libraries, debating clubs, and other societies for his fellow craftsmen contributed in still another way to the mounting spirit of self-reliance and independence.[9]

With continued growth in the eighteenth century, all the colonial ports assumed additional responsibilities. Muddy streets were improved and extended; Boston by 1720 had a street system that excelled any in the colonies and, as Bridenbaugh has shown, rivalled all but London's in England. Its drainage sewers and its new public market, a gift by Peter Faneuil in 1742, were likewise outstanding. But a move by the selectmen, endorsed by the town meeting, for a bridge over the Charles River failed to secure the approval of the Governor's

---

[7] Bridenbaugh, *Cities in Revolt*, pp. 332–372.
[8] Bridenbaugh, *Cities in Revolt*, pp. 150–171.
[9] *Ibid.*, pp. 179–192, 385–393.

council. In similar fashion, inadequate powers and limited resources often checked the efforts of the officials in other towns to expand their services. Householders in each place had to sweep the streets in front of their properties, dispose of their garbage and night-soil, and hang lanterns over their doors if they wanted street lights. Philadelphia was the first in 1750 to secure authorization for a public system of street lamps and won acclaim two years later as the best lighted city in the Empire. Each such accomplishment added to the self-confidence of the colonial ports.[10]

The varied cultural provisions of the leading ports were similarly important. Although the colonists, as Thomas J. Wertenbaker has demonstrated, 'continued to look to England for guidance in cultural things', local conditions in each town produced varied adaptations. In Boston and other New England towns, concern for an educated ministry supported the development of both Harvard and Yale and of many lesser schools, as well as of bookshops and circulating libraries. They also fostered church and instrumental musicians, portrait painters, and other skilled artisans. Philadelphia quickly matched Boston in its support of both bookshops and libraries, surpassed it in the profusion and performance of its artisans, and developed an interest in science that constrasted with the more academic intellectual activity in Boston. Charles Town, with its wealthy resident planters cultivating Britain's more aristocratic tastes, introduced the theatre, concerts, sumptuous dining and dancing, and an elegance of display in dress and equipage that none of the other ports could match. The planters of Virginia endeavoured to emulate those of South Carolina by importing some of this elegance to their estates; many flocked to Williamsburg, the new capital of the colony established in 1699, for a season of gaiety and entertainment during the Assembly meeting each winter. New York achieved the most cosmopolitan blending of these varied cultural trends and, because of its enduring Dutch heritage, gave them an independent un-English flavour.[11]

The town officials everywhere secured ready support for dock improvements and for the construction of market buildings and other aids to commerce. Philadelphia and New York rivalled Boston in these respects and, by the mid-century, in the private construction of other urban facilities. Although the Bay City had previously held the lead in population, all its old rivals enjoyed more rapid gains, and several new competitors appeared, each bidding for a share of the coastal trade and for shipments abroad. Indeed Boston's stagnation, after reaching a population of 16,000 in the 1740s, was due in part to

---

[10] *Ibid.*, pp. 3–36.

[11] Thomas J. Wertenbaker, *The Golden Age of Colonial Culture*, New York 1949; Bridenbaugh, *Cities in Revolt*, pp. 36–42.

the rise of Salem as a fishing and ship-building centre to the north, and of Newport, Providence, and New Haven on the Sound. Boston, however, had practically exhausted the potentials of its limited tract and was already spilling over into Roxbury, Charleston, Cambridge and other adjoining towns. Philadelphia and New York, better able to extend their borders, attained populations of 40,000 and 25,000 respectively by 1775, yet both saw new towns emerging on the outskirts. Newport witnessed the rapid rise of Providence in its vicinity, and Charles Town lost part of its southern trade to Norfolk in Virginia and Annapolis in Maryland.[12]

These developments had several important consequences. The growth of towns swelled the number of urban residents in fifteen places of 2,500 or more to nearly 100,000 by 1765, but the population of the thirteen colonies as a whole had grown more rapidly and exceeded 2,200,000 that year. Their products and demands had expanded accordingly and presented opportunities to urban merchants and craftsmen that even the most aggressive ports could not fully grasp. New towns were springing up inland—Albany and Baltimore with easy access to ocean shipping, Lancaster and Hartford on good interior routes. There was ample trade for all, especially in the war years when the demand was brisk for military supplies to equip and provision armies and fleets sent against the French in Canada and in the West Indies. But trade routes were often disrupted, and established merchants, such as John Hancock in Boston, sometimes suffered losses that made them resentful of British restraints.[13]

The appearance of new interior rivals awakened some coastal merchants to the opportunities for inland commerce. Townsmen as well as rural settlers demanded highways, and improved roads were opened in these decades to connect all of the northern ports, from Salem to Philadelphia; other roads were extended westwards from Boston, Philadelphia, and Charles Town to tap the interior regions. Merchants with funds to invest, but dismayed by the foreign hazards in wartime, turned with increased interest to speculation in western lands. Craftsmen with idle apprentices encouraged some of them to try their skills in new western hamlets. Thus, as Glaab and Brown have suggested, the opening of a new frontier for urban enterprise in the west strengthened the feeling of autonomy and self-reliance already developing in the old ports.[14]

[12] Charles N. Glaab & A. T. Brown, *A History of Urban America*, New York 1967, pp. 10–14; Green, *The Rise of Urban America*, pp. 31–46.
[13] Bridenbaugh, *Cities in Revolt*, pp. 5, 216–217; Evarts B. Greene, and V. D. Harrington, *American Population Before the Federal Census of 1790*, New York 1932, pp. 6 ff.; N.S.B. Grass and Henrietta Larson, *Casebook in American British History*, New York 1939, pp. 61–73.
[14] Glaab & Brown, p. 15; Bridenbaugh, *Cities in Revolt*, pp. 48–58, 264–267.

Improvements in inter-city communications reached a milestone in 1756 when the colonial postal service, first instituted by coastal vessels in 1693, finally reached overland to Charles Town. This facility was only one of several contributions to the mounting sense of colonial unity. Several of the older towns had cooperated in raising and provisioning expeditions during the French and Indian Wars, and all had assumed responsibility for the safety of their own ports. When, on the return of peace, the King endeavoured not only to reinforce old restraints against foreign trade but also to collect part of the war's cost from the colonies, merchants and lawyers in every town protested. Even Williamsburg, one of the least of the towns, focused the grievances of planters unable to liquidate their debts. Craftsmen, stimulated to increased production by wartime demands, were as dismayed as the merchants by export restrictions. Emboldened by the indignation against the stamp tax voiced by the weeklies that numbered almost a score in the 1760s, artisans and merchants in numerous towns formed a chain of clubs, known as Sons of Liberty, that extended throughout the colonies. John Hancock, provoked in 1768 to the point of smuggling a shipment of '100 pipes of wine from the Madiera Islands' into Boston at night, rounded up a mob of 500 Liberty boys who vainly endeavoured to prevent the customs officials from seizing the ship appropriately named the 'Liberty'.[15]

Similar protests were voiced in the British West India colonies, but townsmen there were fewer in number and more dependent on the favour of the King and on the protection of British troops and warships. Even in Kingston, former capital and largest city in Jamaica, more than half the approximately 5,000 inhabitants were Negro slaves, and the constant fear of uprisings among them or among the still more numerous Africans who had long since replaced the Indians on the surrounding plantations made the outnumbered whites as loyal in the British West India ports as the French were in their turn at St Françoise, their chief port in Hispaniola (Haiti), and the Spanish at Havana, or in the much larger mainland cities of Lima and Mexico City where the Indians outnumbered the whites by five or more to one. In Quebec and Montreal the British after 1763 maintained a still more precarious hold over the French settlers who, however, had no love for the rival ports to the South.[16]

These diversions and fears were less in evidence in the thirteen British colonies on the mainland. There a diversified population of

---

[15] Bridenbaugh, *Cities in Revolt*, pp. 289–291, 362, 388–391; Constance Green, pp. 47–51; Grass and Larson, pp. 73–74; Williams, *Contours of American History*, pp. 61–117.

[16] Edmund Burke, *An Account of the European Settlements in America*, Dublin, 1762, I: 225, 257, 289; II: 16, 27, 77, 86, 112.

nearly 2,000,000 transplanted Englishmen plus more than a half million from Scotland, Ireland, Germany, Holland, and Sweden, with some 400,000 Negro slaves, had achieved a productive, self-sufficient economy centred in a dozen thriving cities and towns. Despite active rivalries and sharp differences in their social character, the leaders of these towns had developed inter-colonial bonds that enabled them, when Britain challenged their sense of autonomy, to assert and maintain a bid for national independence.[17]

Thus the colonial ports, designed to serve as dependent administrative and trading centres in an expanding mercantile empire, developed, in the course of a century and more of turbulent growth, a degree of autonomy that enabled them to assume a role of leadership in the struggle for independence. As centres of colonial trade, the ports provided the focus and leadership for a separate if not an independent economy, and as emergent urban centres they harboured social and cultural institutions that developed inter-colonial ties and nurtured a sense of national integration. In sharp contrast to the bi-polar social structure of the rival ports to the north and to the south, the British ports in the thirteen colonies had developed from diverse ethnic and cultural ingredients a homogeneous urban society that achieved a sense of separate national identity and provided, as Carl Bridenbaugh has put it, 'the essential prelude to independence'.[18]

---

[17] Green & Harrington, pp. 7 ff.; Ellen Chase, *The Beginnings of the American Revolution*, New York, 1910.
[18] Bridenbaugh, *Cities in Revolt*, p. 418.

2

Cities in the Early Federal Period: to 1825

If the colonial ports played an important role as cradles of freedom, the limited extent of their influence became apparent during the Revolution and continued into the early decades of Independence. No one city achieved undisputed dominance or supplied indispensable leadership. Yet the fact that old rivalries persisted while new ones appeared probably helped to strengthen the federal character of the new nation. As their common interests supported the move for a more perfect union, their corporate jealousies promoted the search for a new and undeveloped site for the national capital, and their competitive eagerness to enlarge their economic sway speeded the westward extension of the interior settlements. They developed sufficient enterprise and diversity of function to hold the widely dispersed states and territories together and to provide the country with a viable economy. They absorbed the first arrivals of a fresh stream of newcomers from abroad and nurtured the new nation's aspirations for an autonomous if not an indigenous culture.

Few if any of these urban accomplishments, celebrated at receptions for General Lafayette staged at a score of cities in 1824 and 1825, had even been dreamed of fifty years before. Aside from the confident inhabitants of the colonial ports, only a few observant travellers and an occasional official visitor from England had expressed high opinions of their attainments, comparing some of them favourably with provincial towns at home. But the King's apparent expectation in the 1770s that he could subdue the colonies by occupying the rebellious ports proved false. New towns had appeared in the interior and together with the older ports they developed a system of communications sufficient to carry on the struggle. The major effect of the British occupation at Boston, New York, and Philadelphia was to drive the Patriots inland, reducing the populations of these cities to an estimated 3,500, 5,000, and 20,000 respectively and leaving ample space to house the troops. Norfolk escaped that fate when its

Patriot defenders, unable to withstand a siege, burned it to the ground to deny facilities to the British.[1]

Trade everywhere was disrupted, but many of the refugees found useful jobs in other towns. Some, for example, built privateers in Salem and Providence; others produced munitions for the Continental Army at Springfield, Massachusetts, and at Fredericksburg, Virginia. When the British shifted their forces from one port to another and finally withdrew entirely, evacuating several thousand Loyalists in the process, many former residents returned and others joined them in reviving the cities. Merchants hastily launched new trading ventures; craftsmen resumed and expanded their enterprises; and, in addition to the Bank of North America, chartered by the Congress at Philadelphia in 1781, investment groups in Boston and New York secured the establishment of their first banks. Yet neither Boston nor Philadelphia fully recovered its former primacy; even New York, which soon captured the lead, could not match the rate of growth of the rising new city of Baltimore. The most striking urban gains of the eighties occurred in the smaller towns, yet the population of the twenty-four places of 2,500 or more inhabitants, according to the first Federal Census of 1790, was only 201,655 or 5.1 per cent of the nation's total.[2]

The achievement of independence brought varied fortunes to the different ports. Boston, because of its large share in the colonial trade with Britain, suffered more than the others when the imperial preferences were withdrawn. When France and Spain also closed their West India ports to the Americans, Yankee traders suffered another blow, especially at Norfolk which was energetically struggling to rebuild its houses and wharves. Each port had its special interest in the creation of a stronger national leadership, and when the plight of Norfolk's merchants prompted James Madison to initiate the call for a Constitutional Convention, the delegates of the principal cities became active proponents of a federal union.

The battle over the Constitution was not, of course, an urban-rural controversy. Outnumbered twenty to one, the cities could not have won such a contest. Nor were they united in their stand on all issues. Yet their leaders, such as the ageing Franklin and the youthful Hamilton, were able to rally sufficient support from the delegates of all districts to secure the adoption of a federal system and to give the

[1] Thomas J. Wertenbaker, Norfolk: Historic Southern Port, 2nd edition, Durham 1962, pp. 48–72; Green, Rise of Urban America, pp. 50–53; Evarts B. Greene, The Revolution Generation: 1763–1790, New York 1943, pp. 273, 354–356.
[2] Bray Hammond, Banks and Politics in America From the Revolution to the Civil War, Princeton 1957, pp. 40–72; Bureau of the Census, Current Population Reports, Population Characteristics, Series P 23, No. 1, p. 14.

central government specific powers to coin money, levy tariffs, maintain an army and a navy, and thus to make a strong stand in foreign affairs. The ports were equally interested in banning internal tariff barriers and in empowering Congress to regulate banks and to provide for the general welfare. Recent scholarship has discredited Charles Beard's thesis that the economic interests of creditors, and especially of speculators in state notes, determined the character of the Constitution and manipulated its adoption. But if no simple alignment of interest groups is possible, as Forrest McDonald maintains, his analysis of the positions taken by the various delegates to the convention and to the ratifying conventions that followed does reveal that the more highly developed states, containing the more aggressive urban centres, experienced a greater desire for a stronger national union.[3]

Yet no state or city was ready to submerge local interests to a national government. Just as the desire of the restless inhabitants of all states for equal opportunities in the western territories forced the secession of the trans-Appalachian lands to the Confederation and assured the development there of new self-governing states to broaden its limited authority, so the jealousies of the rival cities prevented the designation of any one of them as the national capital and led to the selection of a new central site for that purpose. And when Alexander Hamilton, as Secretary of the Treasury under President Washington, arranged for the adoption of his economic program, including an assumption of the depreciated state notes, by supporting the campaign of Washington and Jefferson to locate the federal capital in the predominately rural Potomac valley, he not only pleased many of his New York friends by denying that prize to Philadelphia, but he also strengthened the commercial and investment interests of all the older towns.

The location of Washington, as the new capital was named, on an undeveloped site had several important consequences for America's urban developments. It removed the federal legislators and administrators from the incessant bustle and the corroding influence of city life deplored by Jefferson; it also freed the business interests of the larger towns from the close surveillance and increasing involvement of government that might otherwise have occurred. If the effects of this spatial separation were intangible in both respects, they were nevertheless real and would persist for many decades. In the meantime, the planning and building of the new federal city focused the attention of many venturesome men on the opportunity to plant and develop other new towns throughout the land.[4]

[3] Forrest McDonald, *We The People*, Chicago 1958, pp. 349–417.
[4] Morton and Lucia White, *The Intellectual Versus the City*, Cambridge 1962, pp. 12–20.

Despite his antipathy to cities, Jefferson took a keen interest in the planning of Washington. Not only did he draft two tentative sketches for a city 1,200 to 1,500 acres in size, but when the President engaged Pierre Charles L'Enfant to prepare a more detailed plan, Jefferson cooperated by collecting street plans from noted cities abroad for his assistance. As the grand design evolved for a spacious city with radial avenues and circles superimposed on an expandable grid, the vision of a magnificent capital appeared spread over an area of 5,000 acres and affording numerous sites for notable public buildings in well-chosen settings. No city in America and few abroad approached these dimensions or rivalled it in design. And when the President secured an agreement by the property owners to convey alternate lots to the federal government for £25 an acre, the prospective returns on their sale promised to cover the cost of public buildings and other improvements. Unfortunately the demand for lots was sluggish and construction even more so. Scarcely 600 dwellings dotted the landscape when Jefferson strode down from a nearby boarding house for his inaugural in March 1801. John Adams, who as second president had first occupied the Executive Mansion for a few months that winter, was glad to get back to Quincy, Massachusetts, where the neighbourhood was more settled.[5]

Quincy, a rural hamlet near enough to Boston to enable the ex-President to participate in its unrivalled civic and cultural activities, was, however, sufficiently detached to escape the speculative virus that had already invaded such Boston suburbs as Cambridge and would soon infect the new city of Washington. That place was in fact described in 1801 by the recently launched *National Intelligencer* as the fastest growing town in the country, yet its increase to 8,208 by 1810 could not compare in numbers to that of several established cities. Philadelphia and Boston had each added approximately 10,000 during the decade, and Baltimore 20,000, while New York, which had attracted 36,000 newcomers, was approaching the 100,000 mark. New York had in 1807 adopted an official street map that followed a modified form of the gridiron pattern of Philadelphia and extended it northward over most of Manhattan to present 155th Street. Its purpose, of course, was to expedite real estate developments, not to create a beautiful city. Indeed, except for a few paper plans for new towns, such as that of Joseph Ellicott for Buffalo, and an abortive plan for the expansion of Philadelphia, which also reflected L'Enfant's

[5] Reps, *Making of Urban America*, pp. 240–262; Elizabeth S. Kite, *L'Efant and Washington*, Baltimore 1929, pp. 7–26 ff. Saul K. Padover, ed., *Thamas Jefferson and the National Capital*, Washington, 1946, pp. 1–57.

influence, the gridiron pattern prevailed in most new towns where speculation was rife.[6]

Yet the sustained growth even of some large cities justified their optimism. New York and Baltimore had each trebled in population since 1790, and both Albany and Richmond, newly designated as state capitals, enjoyed comparable gains, exceeding 9,000 by 1810. Other rapidly growing places in the east—Portland in Maine, Brooklyn and Troy in New York, Newark in New Jersey, and Kensington in Pennsylvania—would reach that size in another decade or so. The growth of these and other towns was sufficient to check the decline in the urban-rural ratio, which had slipped to 1:20 in 1790, and to start it on an upward course by 1820.[7]

The shift in population trends reflected the increased stability of the older urban centres of the east and marked the successful launching, largely through their efforts, of an indigenous American economy. Hamilton's economic program pumped some needed currency and confidence into the commercial groups at Boston, New York, and Philadelphia, where most of the depreciated state notes had accumulated. The Bank of the United States, chartered by Congress in 1791, was located at Philadelphia, which also served as the temporary capital until 1800. But like its predecessor, the Bank of North America, it could not, even with the opening of eight branches in other cities, forestall the establishment of independent banks in many places. New York and Boston each already had such a bank, and the contributions they rendered to local enterprises there prompted commerical and investment groups in Baltimore, Providence, and New Haven as well as Philadelphia, to establish similar institutions to supply community leadership in this field. New York's second bank opened in 1798 on Wall Street, a street already chosen by a group of bankers in 1791 as the site for a curb market; the New York Stock and Exchange Board soon located its rooms there too.[8]

These developments underlined and strengthened the federal and diversified character of the American economy. The Bank of the United States provided many coordinating services and endeavoured to restrain inflationary note issues by independent banks, but it could not establish full national control. Local groups, organized as boards of trade or chambers of commerce in several towns, supported the

[6] Reps, pp. 263–265, 294–300; Constance M. Green, *Washington: Village and Capital, 1800–1878*, Princeton 1962, I: 3–30.

[7] Glaab & Brown, *A History of Urban America*, pp. 25–27; U.S. Census (1850), p. lii.

[8] Hammond, pp. 114–137; J. Van Fenstermaker, *The Development of American Commerical Banking: 1782–1837*, Kent, Ohio 1965, pp. 6–7, 111 ff. Cleveland Rogers and R. B. Raskin, *New York: The World's Capital City*, New York 1948, pp. 31, 134–136.

efforts of state chartered city banks to promote new enterprise. Merchant traders in Boston and New York developed new markets in South America and the Far East. Merchant craftsmen in both of these cities and more especially in Philadelphia stimulated handicraft and factory production. Philadelphia in fact was becoming an industrial city. Its traders, turning from the sea to inland routes, faced increased competition in that direction from Baltimore, which enjoyed more direct contact with settlements in the Susquehanna Valley and with those on the Ohio.[9]

Each of these and the lesser ports experienced a revival of trade with the West Indies and with England after the outbreak of war in Europe in 1792. The shipbuilding industry boomed, and American merchantmen captured a large share of the carrying trade to Europe. Among the lesser ports, Norfolk especially shared in this prosperity. But as the struggle in Europe grew more bitter, both English and French warships endeavoured to curb trade with the enemy. The resultant infringements on American rights prompted an attempt by Jefferson and Madison to correct the situation by peaceful means. All the ports suffered new losses when the Embargo and Non-Intercourse acts of 1807 and 1809 again curbed trade with Europe. But a division had by this time appeared in several cities between those interested both in the export of staples and the import of finished goods and, on the other hand, those interested in home industries. The additional impetus given, as Madison predicted, to handicraft production sustained urban growth and contributed to the increased independence of the American economy.[10]

When conciliatory measures failed to avert a second conflict with Britain, the Atlantic ports again faced the uncertainties of war. Too strong now for easy occupation, they could not, however, escape the effects of a blockade by the British fleet, which proved especially frustrating at New York. A British force did land and capture the new city of Washington, reducing its unfinished public buildings almost to ashes, but an attack on Baltimore was turned back and that on the recently annexed city of New Orleans at the mouth of the Mississippi was soundly defeated.

The Peace of Ghent had many repercussions on American cities. The British, despite their greater power and many victories, had brought the war to an end partly to enable their merchants and indus-

---

[9] Kenneth Sturges, *American Chambers of Commerce*, New Work 1915, pp. 11–41; Hammond, pp. 130–169; William A. Sullivan, *The Industrial Worker in Pennsylvania: 1800–1840*, Harrisburg 1955, pp. 1–27; Sam B. Warner, *The Private City: Philadelphia in Three Periods of Its Growth*, Philadelphia 1968, pp. 3–22.

[10] Wertenbaker, *Norfolk*, pp. 81–110; Fenstermaker, pp. 3, 18–19.

trialists to invade the American market. Many of the ships that sailed from British ports on the return of peace headed to New York to dump their cargoes at prices sufficiently reduced to undercut American products. They chose that port chiefly because of its central location, but they continued to favour it also because of the prompt action of its leaders in securing the adoption at Albany of a law authorizing and regulating auction sales.

As Robert G. Albion has shown, New York became the great entrepôt as a result of its eager exploitation of every advantage. Its auction rooms attracted merchants from rival cities. The lively market thus created spurred New York's ocean traders to organize the Black Ball packet line, which established the first regular schedule of shipments back and forth across the Atlantic. New York benefited more than its rivals from the introduction of steamboats after the successful trial of Fulton's *Clermont* in 1807. Their use on the Hudson increased rapidly during the next decade, and steamboats spread onto Long Island Sound after the withdrawal of the British fleet. None of the other eastern ports had such extensive and sheltered routes; moreover New York in 1817 also gave its support at Albany to a state scheme to build a canal connecting the upper Great Lakes with the Hudson.[11]

Each of the other port cities responded in its own way at the return of peace. Philadelphia bankers, after a five-year delay, secured the establishment in 1816 of the Second Bank of the United States. That accomplishment prolonged the period of its leadership in banking matters, but in the turbulent years since the expiration of the first federal bank's charter many other banks had appeared in towns large and small, some even lacking state charters, and the new central bank's efforts to reform and stabilize the currency brought it near the brink of disaster during the depression of 1819. Its conservative policies won support, however, from leading banks in the larger cities and effected a resumption of specie payments in most places by the end of that year. The total number of banks reached 327 by 1820, with two or more competing for business in every city and in many growing towns, yet the Bank of the United States was able, partly because of its role as fiscal agent for the federal government, to restrain most of them from making excessive issues of bank notes and to check the export of specie during the early twenties.[12]

The state-chartered city banks took the lead in local and regional

[11] Robert G. Albion, *The Rise of New York Port*, New York 1939, pp. 7–15, 20–37, 410.
[12] Walter B. Smith, *Economic Aspects of the Second Bank of the United States*, Cambridge, Mass. 1953, pp. 56, 99–143, 236–240; Fenstermaker, pp. 11–14, 21–23, 42, 69–73; Hammond, pp. 191–196, 251–285.

promotions. Thus seven Philadelphia banks, with other groups of townsmen, gave increased attention to manufacturing activities; local merchants began to develop a flow of hard coal from the upper Delaware and Lehigh Valley region and pressed the state for improved road connections to the west. They could not, however, match the enterprise of similar groups in Baltimore, which as a result of river and road improvements up the Susquehanna and west-ward to the Ohio River, was supplanting Philadelphia as the leading mart for grain and other food products. Baltimore was also contesting with Norfolk for the coastal trade of the Carolinas. Richmond grew as a milling centre and as an exporter of tobacco and soft coal. Charleston, as the leading southern port had been renamed, turned its back on the sea and preened itself as the capital of an expanding cotton kingdom. Savannah, a lesser rival about a hundred miles to the south, was likewise absorbed by interior trade prospects.[13]

Several New England ports vied with Baltimore and New York for the cotton export trade of Charleston and Savannah; two in particular developed special links with that economy. New Haven on the Sound was the home of Eli Whitney, whose cotton gin (invented in 1793) had made possible the expansion of the cotton culture; as the base for his cotton gin factory and for the development of other ingenious applications of his new principle of interchangeable parts, the Connecticut port became an industrial specialist. Providence, in nearby Rhode Island, profited even more substantially as the spinning loom, first introduced there by Samuel Slater on his arrival from England in 1790, made it for a time the leading producer in America of cotton yarn. Boston, while not abandoning its share in the foreign trade, especially that with China, was struggling to maintain its dominance over the coastal trade of New England and to restore its contacts with the Carolinas and extend them into the Gulf; it was likewise promoting local industrial activities. Boston capitalists established a dozen incorporated banks before 1824 and supported the handicraft production of shoes at Lynn, of cotton cloth by the newly developed factory system at Waltham, and of similar ventures at water-power sites along the Merrimac, Fall River, and other turbulent streams.[14]

So many Bostonians were striking out to promote industrial and other urban functions in nearby and distant towns that its slow

[13] Albion, pp. 80, 102, 108, 134–142; Green, *The Rise of Urban America*, pp. 58–59; Fenstermaker, pp. 18–19, 80–81, 96–99, 169–171.
[14] Albion, pp. 122–135, 390–393, 402–404; Green, *Rise of Urban America*, pp. 59–61; Oscar Handlin, *Boston's Immigrants, 1790–1865*, Cambridge, Mass. 1941, pp. 3–16; Fenstermaker, pp. 139–143; American State Papers, *Finance* II: 433.

population growth would have been still more retarded had it not attracted a renewed stream of newcomers from across the Atlantic. Boston began to receive an influx of Irish shortly after the return of peace and in 1821 saw 827 arrive plus another 525 from Canada, some of them also Irish. Its old boast of being the most English of all American ports was forgotten, yet even at the start of this new migration it did not rival New York as the chief entrepôt. Proportionately, however, more of its newcomers took up permanent residence, so that Boston by 1825 had developed, in its North End and Fort Hill District, an Irish neighbourhood comparable in some respects to the earlier Germantown in Philadelphia and to emerging Irish, German, and Jewish colonies in New York.[15]

Some of these newcomers landed or stayed at Philadelphia and Baltimore but few sought refuge further south except at New Orleans. After the importation of slaves was terminated in 1808, slave markets developed in several southern cities, even at Washington, to auction off the surplus slaves of the coastal regions to buyers from the expanding cotton plantations of the Deep South. The earlier practice of granting a faithful slave his freedom after many years of service, or the freedom of his children, was progressively abandoned as the market value of such chattel improved. Yet the number of free Negroes, most of them living in cities, had mounted rapidly, increasing 80 per cent in each decade before 1820, by which date most slaves in the North had been freed and manumission in the South was checked. Baltimore in 1820 contained the largest colony of free Negroes, over 10,000, and more than double the number of its slaves; it was followed by New Orleans where, however, as in other Southern cities, they were greatly outnumbered by the slaves. Inevitably the presence of this plentiful supply of relatively unskilled labour checked the influx of poor newcomers from abroad.[16]

All Southern cities had as a result a dual rather than a multiple population base. Charleston, over 55 per cent Negro, had no distinctly coloured district, however, since most of the slaves lived at the rear of the premises of their masters, and the free Negroes, only one-tenth of the total in 1820, found lodgement in scattered quarters. Indeed, mounting fears of possible Negro uprisings brought the imposition of new curbs on their activities and forestalled the development of Negro sub-communities. At Norfolk, where 3,260 slaves and 600 free Negroes comprised almost half the population, as in other Southern towns where the ratios were somewhat comparable, the vitality of the handi-

---

[15] Handlin, pp. 29–30, 36–44; Albion, pp. 336–338, 418.

[16] U.S. Census (1850), pp. xlvi, liv; Constance M. Green, *The Secret City*, Princeton 1967, pp. 13–33. Although most Negros in New York State were free, the law of 1818 abolishing slavery there did not take final effect until 1827.

craft and other enterprise was retarded. Of all Southern cities, only Baltimore, where as we have seen the free Negroes greatly outnumbered the slaves and where together they comprised less than a fourth of the population, escaped this retarding influence, and its progress, as we have noted, was in commercial rather than industrial directions. The dramatic success of the gas lights, first installed in its streets in 1821, made it a symbol of municipal progress.[17]

No city could rival New York's drive in the early twenties. Not only did the value of its exports and imports as well as the number of its immigrants exceed the combined totals of its three leading rivals for the five-year period, but its advantage in each field was increasing and the progressive construction in these years of the Erie Canal strengthened its self assurance. Yet the building of the canal also revitalized several struggling villages and cities along its 363-mile route across the state and gave birth to a dozen new towns. Albany at its eastern terminus surged ahead of both Richmond and Washington and became the seventh city in size in the nation by the mid-twenties. Troy, Schenectady, and Utica on the eastern division each exceeded 6,000 by that date, while, farther west, Rochester and Buffalo, mere hamlets at the start of construction, reached 5,000 by the official opening of the canal in 1825. More important, however, than the number of their inhabitants, was the variety of their economic activities. Already the iron foundries and machine shops of Troy, the salt vats of Syracuse, and the lumber and flour mills of Rochester were supplying a diversified economy to the Empire State and compelling its great port to assume larger metropolitan responsibilities.[18]

Yet the evidences of population growth and economic progress everywhere apparent were not the only urban contributions to national stability. The pride displayed in the late colonial period at Boston in its educational as well as its religious institutions, at Charleston in its theatre and other sophisticated forms of culture, and at Philadelphia and New York in a mingling of these attainments, was now shared in varying degree by the residents of a dozen cities. Local associations of interested citizens maintained libraries, staged musicals, held assemblies and literary meetings, and backed the efforts of ambitious teachers to establish academies and even colleges, two score of which were in operation by 1825.[19]

---

[17] Richard C. Wade, *Slavery in the Cities*, New York 1964, pp. 325–330; Ward Harrison, *Street Lighting Practice*, New York 1930, p. 28.

[18] Albion, pp. 84–91, 266, 390–391, 418; Blake McKelvey, 'The Erie Canal, Mother of Cities,' *New York Historical Society Quarterly*, January 1951, pp. 55–71.

[19] Merle Curti, *The Growth of American Thought*, New York 1943, pp. 204–224.

C

General Lafayette, who had returned for a triumphal tour of America the year before, observed with delight the transformations he found on every side. He responded as might be expected to greetings at Independence Hall in Philadelphia: 'My entrance into this great and superb city . . . awakens in my heart the remembrance of all those feelings which I experienced fifty years ago. It is here, in this hall, consecrated by the councils of sages, where the independence of the United States was boldly proclaimed. . . . Here commenced a new era for the civilized world, the era of social order founded on the rights of mankind—the advantages of which are every day exemplified in the peace and happiness of your republic.' He never tired, as he journeyed by stage, horseback, carriage, river and canal boat on three great circle tours through the interior. He visited and admired more than a score of large towns and cities and many villages; he responded to the greetings of their officials and received innumerable delegations from local literary as well as benevolent societies, associations of workmen as well as professionals, asylums for lunatics as well as for orphans, and churches of many denominations. The stage was properly set for him, but his comments were often revealing, as for example when he noted on leaving Troy, after observing the burgeoning canal trade in July 1824: 'The inhabitants of Troy are no less remarkable for their love of literature and science than for their manufacturing activity and intelligence. They have three newspapers in their city, four printing offices, five large libraries and many schools.'[20]

Historians, political scientists, and other commentators have traditionally stressed the contributions of the states in the formation of the federal union. Yet their jealous rivalries were no more real and seldom as vividly expressed as the rivalries between their leading cities. Indeed a sense of a community of interests was developing in many urban centres, even in new towns of modest size, such as Troy, which had not only lofty aspirations but substantial cultural attainments. Thus the wide diffusion of urban centres reinforced the basic federal checks and balances, strengthened the inter-state trade and cultural bonds, and fostered the development of an autonomous national society.

[20] A. Levasseur, *Lafayette in America in 1824 and 1825*, New York 1929, pp. 116, 135 ff.

3

The First Urban Frontier: to 1835

Lafayette's tour in 1825 took him on a vast swing through the West, where he was saluted by booming cannon and given official receptions at a score of cities and towns that had made their appearance since his departure four decades before. Almost 130 years later, an able historian, Richard C. Wade, would describe several of these cities as 'spearheads of the frontier'. But behind the spears were the spear throwers, and the full significance of the urban frontier can only be grasped by considering its relation to the outward thrust of expansive metropolitan communities in the east and its impact on their economic and political structure.[1]

The planting of new towns in the West was in some respects a replication of the establishment of the colonial ports two centuries before. This time, however, the movement was greatly accelerated both in the speed and size of urban growth and in the consequent development of regional autonomy. Not only did the land companies that originally planned the establishment of Pittsburgh, Cincinnati, Louisville and other western towns give way more quickly to local leadership, but the more rapid settlement of the surrounding territories created urgent import and export demands that forced the growth of cities at unprecedented rates and brought self-reliant civic and cultural communities into being. Now, instead of imperial restraints, a federal union was ready to welcome these territories to equal state-hood. And, in the economic field, expanding metropolitan centres in the east were competing for their trade. Yet the skies were not alto-gether bright, for the uneven growth of the frontier, national, and international economies brought frequent crises and spurred the struggle of the new western cities for internal improvements and other advantages.

Each of the new urban centres had its particular assets and its special problems, yet all shared in the surging advance of the west-ward movement. Although the wide-spreading French empire had

[1] Levasseur, *Lafayette in America* II: 89–222; Wade, *The Urban Frontier*, pp. 1 ff.

established trading posts and fortified settlements at Detroit on the upper Great Lakes in 1701, at Mobile and New Orleans on the Gulf during the next two decades, and finally in 1764 deep in the interior at St Louis, few permanent residents had arrived before the advancing American frontier pushed westward to absorb these outposts. The first French post to fall was Fort Duquesne, established in 1754 but captured four years later by the British and renamed Fort Pitt. Indian hostilities and the British attempt to hold the restless colonists east of a Proclamation Line, drawn for that purpose in 1763 along the Appalachian divide, retarded further developments until the Revolution successfully eliminated both restraints. Located at the point where the Allegheny and Monongehala Rivers joined to form the Ohio, Fort Pitt guarded the natural gateway to the West, and William Penn's heirs dispatched surveyors to its site in 1784 to lay out the town of Pittsburgh.[2]

Venturesome frontiersmen, such as the score or more who had already settled around Fort Pitt, had also pushed west in 1779 to found Louisville at the falls of the Ohio and Lexington, sixty miles to the south astride an overland route through the mountains. Both of these pioneer settlements secured land grants from the Virginia Assembly, much as several New England towns had done in colonial days. In contrast, hastily chartered land companies founded Marietta in 1787 and Cincinnati a year later, both on the north bank of the Ohio. The promoters of each of these frontier towns adopted Philadelphia's gridiron street pattern, adjusting it where necessary to their particular sites, and each aspired to become the commercial metropolis of the West.[3]

Though that goal proved elusive, each of these and several additional towns performed significant roles in the westward movement. Lexington, because of the heavy overland migration from populous Virginia to the rich bluegrass regions in Kentucky, the first western state admitted to the Union, became a thriving market town with 1,795 residents at the turn of the century when it already boasted two newspapers, a library, and an academy that ambitiously assumed the name of Transylvania University. Pittsburgh, its leading rival with 1,565 inhabitants in 1800, saw an even larger flood of migrants stream through its portals; in an effort to supply their material needs it quickly became both an entrepôt for merchandise from the East and a thriving centre for artisans and boat builders. Farther west, Cincinnati and Louisville had served at the start as provisioning depots for the

[2] Wade, pp. 3–12; Reps, *The Making of Urban America*, pp. 204–207. See also Document 10.

[3] Wade, pp. 13–35; Reps, pp. 218–227; Green, *American Cities*, pp. 41–45. See Document 11.

military units assembled to combat the Indian menace; when that hazard disappeared, after the Battle of Fallen Timbers in 1794, these towns became provisioning centres for the migrating settlers who scattered throughout the valley, increasing the population west of the mountains to some 400,000 by 1800.[4]

Several other frontier settlements had appeared by this date and acquired more positive urban status in the next decade. Nashville (1784) and Knoxville (1792), both in Tennessee, had likewise served as military posts and provisioning centres and now became regional trading depots on the Cumberland and Holston Rivers respectively. St Louis, near the junction of the Missouri and Mississippi Rivers, would enjoy a rebirth after the Louisana Purchase in 1803 when American fur traders rushed in to make it a base for expeditions into the mountain west. Yet the great distances that separated them, the slow and tedious means of travel, and the intervening Indian settlements kept these frontier towns on the periphery of the westward movement throughout this decade. Even New Orleans at the mouth of the Mississippi, though already an established city, numbering 10,000 inhabitants at the time of its annexation, communicated more actively with the West Indies and Europe than with the Ohio Valley towns. It was a port of transhipment for western produce, yet it would not seem an integral part of the Union until after Jackson successfully defended it from British attack late in 1814.[5]

The War of 1812 was but one of several historic events of the period that transformed the character and functions of the Western cities and influenced the direction of America's urban developments. With the Embargo and Non-Intercourse Acts that preceded it, the war disrupted commerce, creating a glut of exports at every port and a shortage of merchandise, particularly army supplies. Like Philadelphia and other manufacturing centres in the East, Pittsburgh prospered as an industrial town specializing in ironmongering and glass making and produced numerous other finished products. The Iron City, as it was now designated, finally surpassed Lexington which, however, developed rope walks and hemp factories to employ its numerous slaves in making twine, bagging, and similar articles in great demand on the frontier. A manufacturer of steam engines at Pittsburgh supplied millers and other regional processors in western

[4] Wade, pp. 7–35; Catherine E. Reiser, *Pittsburgh's Commercial Development*, Harrisburg 1951, pp. 1–9.

[5] Green, *American Cities*, pp. 66–72; U.S. Bureau of the Census *Statistics of Cities* (1885) II; 213–251, Earl F. Niehaus, *The Irish of New Orleans: 1800–1860*, Baton Rouge, La. 1965, pp. 3–14.

cities with a substitute for water power and encouraged industrial enterprise to take up the slack in trade.[6]

The War of 1812 accelerated another transformation in western urban life. Originally hostile to banks, because of their location in the East, several western towns had relied for a time on the financial resources of other local incorporations, such as the Kentucky Insurance Company at Lexington and the Miami Exporting Company at Cincinnati. As the need for currency mounted, however, eight state banks and two branches made their appearance in western towns before 1811 when Congress, by refusing to renew the charter of the first Bank of the United States, cleared the way for a multiplication of state banks. The western towns acquired a dozen new banks before the end of the war, and their unrestricted note issues supplied an abundance of paper currency to promote industrial ventures and ease the flow of trade.[7]

Yet only New Orleans, which because of its French and Spanish heritage retained trading privileges with their West India ports, enjoyed an expanding commerce in these troubled years. So busy in fact were its docks that an influx of several thousand refugees, white and black, from Cuba in 1809 was readily absorbed in a city and suburban population that reached 24,000 by 1815, slightly in excess of the total of all contemporary urban settlements in the West. With three banks and numerous other institutions it acquired metropolitan proportions and began to collaborate with the half-dozen lesser cities and numerous hamlets in serving the urban needs of the 1,500,000 settlers now scattered throughout the western states and territories.[8]

The rapid rise of New Orleans, even in the flat-boat era, was but a forecast of its growth following the introduction of the steamboat on the Mississippi. First demonstrated experimentally on the lower river in 1812, steamboats did not push north to the Ohio River until after the close of the war, but they multiplied rapidly during the late teens and numbered sixty-nine by the close of the decade. With the possibility of transhipping merchandise from Europe and the East up the river to balance the flood of western products coming down, New Orleans prospered. Its population in 1830 approached 50,000, more than half of them Negroes, which won it fifth place among American cities at the Fourth Census.[9]

Several of the up-river cities did not immediately fare so well.

[6] *Statistics of Cities* (1885) II: 220–251.
[7] Wade, pp. 69–70; Fenstermaker, *American Commercial Banking*, pp. 112–183.
[8] *Statistics of Cities* (1885) II: 220–251.
[9] George Taylor, *The Transportation Revolution*, New York 1951, pp. 63–64; Niehaus, pp. 14–26.

Pittsburgh, which built most of the western steamboats of this period, was hard-hit by the renewed flow of cheap British goods from the East and now also from New Orleans. With its industries paralysed, its traders faced a new hazard as the completion of the National Road from Baltimore to Wheeling in 1818 threatened to make that town, ninety miles down the Ohio, the principal depot for river shipments. More migrants than ever before pushed by without stopping, and in the depths of the post-war depression, when many of its residents joined the trek to the West, the Iron City lost a thousand inhabitants. Yet its recovery was only a matter of time. The last stretches of the Pennsylvania turnpike connecting Pittsburgh with Philadelphia were finally completed in 1820, providing a route that was superior in many respects to the National Road. And although many local merchants protested when the Pittsburgh branch of the Second Bank of the United States endeavoured to enforce retrenchment in 1819, similar branches in four other western towns were applying pressure too, and within a few years Pittsburgh would profit as much as any of them from the increased stability.[10]

Each of the several western cities made a characteristic response to the hard times. Lexington, with its hemp markets undercut and its overland trade routes antiquated by the fast-moving steamboats, suffered more permanent injury than the others and saw even rival Louisville pull ahead. Relying almost exclusively on trade, the Falls City largely escaped the ravages of the depression and, rebuilding its docks to accommodate the improved steamboats, recorded 1,000 such visits in 1819. Cincinnati, 105 miles up stream, petitioned frantically for the construction of a canal around the falls at Louisville, but its merchants had to content themselves with control of the trade of the upper river, docking their steamboats, some now built at local yards, at the Kentucky port for transhipments. Fortunately the Porkopolis of the West, as Cincinnati now proclaimed itself, had increasing quantities of its own and regional products to ship and, after a brief panic among its bankers late in 1819, recovered to reach the 10,000 mark a year later, surpassing Pittsburgh in the process.[11]

Steamboats had varied impacts on other western towns. They brought St Louis more actively into the economy of the Midwest by facilitating communications with this formerly isolated town, by affording it easier access to the lead mines along the upper Mississippi (which, for example, enabled its lead merchants to supply Pittsburgh glass makers with the means for recovery) and by extending its fur trading activities farther up the Missouri River, thus permitting its

[10] Reiser, *Pittsburgh*, pp. 75–82, 160–165; Fenstermaker, pp. 54, 87; Hammond, *Banks and Politics*, p. 256.
[11] Wade, pp. 161–220.

fur companies to gratify Europe's demand for pelts also shipped by way of Pittsburgh. Its residents probably exceeded 5,000 at the time of Lafayette's visit and rejoiced to hear of his refusal to pass them by in order to oblige the impatient Tennesseans, who had to wait their turn to carry him 400 tortuous miles up the Cumberland to Nashville. There another western town had successfully recovered from the depression by developing a line of shallow-bottomed steamboats that made it the commercial centre of the state and swelled its population to 4,000, one in every four a slave. Farther southwest Natches, though on the more navigable Mississippi and formerly the chief port above New Orleans, was now a way station awaiting the growth of regional trade with its back country. More than a third of its 3,000 inhabitants were slaves, which gave it the same size and proportions as Mobile. That Gulf port, captured and annexed by the Americans during the war, was now developing with the aid of steam packets into a trading centre for the pioneer cotton planters of Alabama.[12]

Adequately supplied with shipping facilities and, except for St Louis, with an abundance of slave labour to man the docks, these peripheral towns had little interest in industry. Content like New Orleans with commercial functions, they established banks and, despite the limited settlement of their hinterlands, erected markets to facilitate trade. Their modest size, aside from New Orleans, was due in part to the slow growth of their territories, although all were granted statehood by 1821, when Missouri was admitted as the twenty-fourth state. Yet even when the populations of their regions began to mount in the late twenties, that of the trading towns, especially those with high percentages of slaves, failed to keep pace. Merchants from New York and other distant ports eagerly supplied the carrying trade, designating local merchants as their agents.[13]

In the Ohio Valley, however, competition was brisk, and enterprising leaders in every town eagerly exploited their industrial and cultural opportunities. Cincinnati finally pressed its campaign for a canal around the Louisville falls to a successful conclusion in 1830 and in the meantime vigorously increased its exports of meat and other products. The iron and glass factories of Pittsburgh were again in full blast, boosting its city and suburban population to over 22,000 by the close of the decade, only a few thousand less than that of the Queen City, as Cincinnati was now called. Louisville, relying on commerce, was scarcely half as large, and Lexington, having failed to surmount its drawbacks in both commerce and industry, was valiantly striving to hold its own as a cultural centre. Even that goal was lost when dis-

---

[12] U.S. Census (1850), pp. lii; Levasseur, Lafayette, II: 95–97, 128–139, 164–170.
[13] Wade, Slavery in the Cities, pp. 3–9.

sension over the educational policies of President Horace Holley of Transylvania University prompted his withdrawal a few years before a disastrous fire, in 1829, reduced its buildings to ruins. That event encouraged Nashville 180 miles farther south to redouble its efforts to make Cumberland College, renamed the University of Tennessee, the leading college in the West. Cincinnati likewise aspired to Lexington's title of Athens of the West, and vigorously pressed its claims in the next decade.[14]

Cincinnati and Pittsburgh had other challenges to meet, too, for a new frontier was opening to the north. The completion of the Erie Canal to Buffalo in 1825 not only brought rapid growth to that town, transforming it into a city of 8,500 by the end of the decade, but the successful operation of the new waterway also spurred the multiplication of steamboats on the upper Great Lakes. Detroit was suddenly jolted from its dormancy and Cleveland received a new infusion of vitality, while new settlements appeared at a half dozen places, notably at Toledo and Sandusky before the end of the twenties. These were all trading towns and, west of Buffalo, none exceeded the 2,222 inhabitants found at Detroit by the 1830 Census; yet their growth had only commenced and their establishment threatened to divert trade, both east and west, from the middle and southern routes to the newly developing route in the north. Cincinnati responded with plans for an Ohio state canal to link it with Lake Erie at Toledo, and other canal projects were soon launched to tap the northern trade route farther east—but still bypassing Pitsburgh and its near neighbours.[15]

Pittsburgh, of course, was not the only city threatened by the Erie Canal and its western extensions. Both Philadelphia and Baltimore observed the mounting tonnage on the water-level route with envy and alarm. Both were losing out in the contest with New York for the coastal trade with New Orleans, and the prospect of also losing the rich trade over the mountains was sobering. Improvements in the Pennsylvania turnpike and the National Road would not suffice. Philadelphia, prodded by Pittsburgh in 1827, persuaded the Pennsylvania legislature to undertake the construction of a joint canal and railroad line across the state. As work on this ambitious project commenced, Baltimore merchants boldly launched a privately chartered, but city and state backed railroad, the Baltimore & Ohio, the longest yet projected in America. The Pennsylvania state canal and railroad system reached Pittsburgh in 1835 and helped to sustain its commerce and to promote its industrial growth. Philadelphia's rewards were not so evident, however, since the mixed system permitted an

---

[14] Wade, *Urban Frontier*, pp. 195–202, 231–248, 330–336; Sullivan, *Industrial Workers in Pennsylvania*, pp. 13–17, 21–24.
[15] Wade, *Urban Frontier*, pp. 328–330.

entry and discharge on the eastern end at many points even including Baltimore, which was meanwhile pressing the westward construction of its railroad with great vigour.[16]

New trade arteries might solve the problem for some groups in western as well as eastern cities, but they would create new problems for other men in the same cities and elsewhere. The leaders of Pittsburgh were well aware of this situation, for while some pressed for an improved trade artery, others petitioned for the adoption of tariffs to check the importation of cheap foreign goods. Cincinnati also supported state and national internal improvements and at the same time petitioned for protective tariffs. Lexington pressed eagerly for federal aid for a turnpike to Maysville on the Ohio, and, when President Jackson vetoed that bill in 1830, its indignant leaders turned more positively to the support of Henry Clay's policies. While support for the Kentucky senator was divided in every town, as was that for President Jackson, Clay's more successful opponent from Tennessee, it seemed quite fitting that both of these national leaders should be western men with close ties respectively to rival Lexington and Nashville.

By the mid-thirties, when the population of the ten western states had reached 5 million—a larger growth in a half century than the thirteen colonies had enjoyed in 150 years—a dozen cities of 5,000 or more inhabitants supplied regional leadership in economic and cultural affairs and, with a host of smaller towns, afforded outlets for the social and political energies of a region that had become an integral part of the larger national society. If many of the economic services were managed and in part supplied by the expansive metropolitan centres back east, the urban leaders of the West had a vigorous sense of autonomy and, by their practice of playing one eastern city against another, strengthened the metropolitan rivalry that already distinguished American from English or other European societies.

But the new western cities, dependent as in most cases they were on the charters granted by the still younger territorial and state legislatures, experienced some of the limitations as well as the vitality of the frontier. The remarkable rapidity of urban growth in the West accentuated the speculative aspects of the newly emerging American economy and gave a boisterous quality to its democracy. But the booming cities, which developed civic needs more rapidly than their rural neighbours, generally appealed without success for adequate fiscal and charter powers. As a result, many of the relatively stable traditions of colonial cities, when not lost in the process of migra-

[16] James W. Levingood, *The Philadelphia-Baltimore Trade Rivalry: 1780–1860*, Harrisburg 1947; Reiser, pp. 43–46, 85–108.

tion, were neglected and soon forgotten amidst the frantic excitement of western growth. Not only did the village greens and town commons tend to disappear, west of the mountains, but the reliance on town meetings and on a well recognized group of city fathers gave way to a more individualized pattern of community action. The rapidity with which the builders of the new western cities reproduced the private structures and institutions of eastern cities, while neglecting to supply public facilities, reinforced the new pattern of American private enterprise.[17]

[17] Wade, pp. 270–326.

4

Nurseries of Enterprise and Havens for Newcomers: 1830-1860

The prospect of developing commercial ties with vast provinces in the West was only one of the exciting challenges that stirred the leaders of eastern metropolises in the second quarter of the nineteenth century. While many businessmen in New York, Philadelphia, Baltimore, and Boston were busy constructing new transport arteries and other communication lines into the West, others in each of these and several additional cities were developing industrial specialities to meet the needs of the country's expanding economy. Foreign capitalists, who in earlier decades had been absorbed in land deals, now became interested in transport and urban investments. An increasing influx of immigrants supplied an abundance of labour and new skills and swelled the populations and the consumer needs of the cities, which now multiplied in number until by 1860 America had forty-five cities over 20,000 in population scattered in twenty-three of its thirty-four states and in addition fifty-seven other towns of 10,000 or more inhabitants.

The grand strategy of America's urban and economic advance was ably described by Michael Chevalier in 1839. 'The works which... chiefly occupy the attention of statesmen and businessmen in the United States are those designed to form communications between the East and the West.'[1] Of the four principal Atlantic ports, New York enjoyed the greatest advantage, partly because its centrally located ice-free harbour and its water-level route to the interior over the state-built Erie Canal attracted an influx of enterprising newcomers from other cities and states and made it the focal entrepôt for an increasing flood of immigrants from abroad. Its spectacular growth from 202,589 in 1830 to 813,669 three decades later was exceeded in rate by the increase of its suburbs from 40,000 to 350,000 and also by the upsurge of several of its interior distribution centres.

[1] Michael Chevalier, *Society, Names and Politics in the U.S.*, Boston 1839, p. 230 ff. See Doc. 12.

Although the natural advantages of its site freed New York from some of the initial burdens faced by rival ports, the progressive development of its potentialities and the production of sufficient goods and services to sustain a metropolitan population, which surged over a million in the mid-fifties, made New York by the mid-century the undisputed leader of the new world in commerce, industry, and banking.[2]

If its chief rivals were forced after the mid-twenties to concede New York's superior advantages, each was determined to maintain its economic autonomy by capturing a share of the western trade. Baltimore made the most forthright bid when in 1827 it chartered the Baltimore & Ohio Railroad and pressed forward with its construction, despite many obstacles, to reach the Ohio River in 1853. Philadelphia, spurred by Pittsburgh, had responded to this challenge and built the privately financed Pennsylvania Railroad across the mountains and reached that city the year before. Baltimore surged ahead of Philadelphia numerically in 1850, but only because of the failure of its northern rival to annex its suburban outflow, as the Maryland metropolis repeatedly did. When in 1854 Philadelphia, responding to a desire to strengthen its internal police controls, absorbed its Northern Liberties, Kensington, and several other suburbs, boosting its population to 565,529 by the end of the decade, Baltimore with 212,000 was left far behind. Yet the southern metropolis, by bridging the Ohio at Wheeling in 1857, linked its railroad with two in the Ohio valley that stretched westward to rapidly growing Cincinnati and St Louis, making Baltimore their most direct eastern port and assuring its commercial vitality.[3]

Philadelphia and Boston were less single minded in their enterprise. Both promoted a number of radiating lines to integrate the economy of their regions. Boston built short railroads to Lowell, Worcester, and Providence in the thirties and extended these and other lines to reach Portland, Montreal, and Albany as well as New York by the mid-century when it boasted the most extensive rail network in the country. Philadelphia built railroads at a more leisurely pace in the forties to the coal fields near Scranton and Reading and to Newark on the Hudson and Baltimore on the Bay, and after reaching Pittsburgh in the early fifties established links over other roads with Cleveland and

[2] Chevalier, pp. 231–237; U.S. Census (1910), Pop. I: 80–81; see comparative tables in Albion, The Rise of New York Port, pp. 389–419.
[3] Taylor, The Transportation Revolution, pp. 77–78; Albert Fishlow, American Railroads and the Transformation of the Ante-Bellum Economy, Cambridge, Mass. 1965, pp. 9–10, 50, 100; Albion, pp. 378–384; Livingood, The Philadelphia-Baltimore Trade Rivalry.

Chicago by 1860.[4] Yet the most vigorous men in each of these metropolises were absorbed in other enterprises. Some at Boston were promoting industrial ventures in an inner ring of surburban towns stretch-
ing from Lynn on the north side to Dorchester on the south side. Others
were reaching out to build factories in Lowell, Lawrence and Salem,
or in Brockton and more distant towns in the second most industrialized region in the nation in the late forties. Even Philadelphia, despite
the leadership it achieved in heavy industry, challenged only by Pittsburgh and its satellites, could not at the mid-century equal the Boston
area in the number of factory employees or in the value they added
to its products. By the close of that decade, however, Philadelphia
would finally achieve second place, surpassing Boston in industry,
Baltimore in population and commerce, and rivalling even much larger
New York in industrial employment.[5]

South of Baltimore, Richmond, Charleston and Savannah each had
its railroad projects though none of them acquired major importance.
Richmond, with the longest line, extending deep into the interior
and reaching the Mississippi at Memphis by 1860, became the leading
industrial city in the South, but the 7,500 employed by its tobacco
processing and iron-mongering concerns, as well as in the flour and
cotton mills, depended less on the interior rail line than on the coastal
waters for raw materials and markets. All the other southern ports,
from Charleston to New Orleans, were ports of transhipment; New
Orleans in fact ranked first in exports for a decade after 1834 and then
stood second only to New York, while Mobile moved into third place
after 1847. Despite occasional attempts to establish processing industries to employ slave labour in slack seasons, none of the southern
cities achieved an industrial rating comparable to its population rank.
Even Baltimore, which stood fourth in size, ranked eighth in manufacturing, while New Orleans, though sixth in size, was seventeenth in
industrial production.[6]

Except in the Deep South, however, urban growth in the pre-Civil
War decades fostered an increasing amount of local industrial enter-

---

[4] Taylor, pp. 78–85; Albion, pp. 380–386, 417.
[5] U.S. Census (1850), *Statistical View of the U.S.* Washington 1854, pp. 129,
179–181; Taylor, pp. 274–278; Sullivan, *The Industrial Worker in Pennsylvania*,
pp. 3–27; U.S. Census (1860), *Reports, Statistics of the U.S.*, Washington 1866,
pp. xviii–xix; Albion, pp. 391–392; 401–404. Warner, *The Private City*, pp.
63–98. See Doc. 12.
[6] Wade, *Slavery in the Cities*, pp. 12–13, 33–54; U.S. Census (1860), *Reports,
Statistics of the U.S.*, p. xviii. Except for Richmond and Louisville, the Southern
cities had higher ranks in population than as industrial centers; Baltimore 4th
and 8th, New Orleans 6th and 17th, Charleston 22nd and 85th, Mobile 27th
and 79th, Memphis 38th and 74th, Savannah 41st and 65th. See Albion, p. 390,
for their export ratings.

prise. Commercial towns established at a break in the natural flow of trade, such as Louisville at the falls of the Ohio, became processors of regional products. St Louis displayed the most dramatic advance as enterprising men launched industrial ventures to provide the implements and materials in demand in its vast hinterland and to process the increasing flow of regional products. Its growth to 160,773 by 1860, with an industrial output valued at $21,772,000, placed it eighth in population, just behind Cincinnati and New Orleans, and well ahead of the latter in manufacturing. Even Chicago, with 264 per cent growth in the fifties, did not quite match the river port's population increase and trailed far behind in industrial output.[7]

Regional products, such as hogs and tobacco in the case of Louisville or wheat and lumber at Rochester, could give a town a vigorous start provided it had adequate power resources and attracted sufficient labour. Both of these cities met these requirements and enjoyed a thriving development, yet their growth was not as spectacular as that of Cincinnati where a more diversified flow of regional products—cattle, grain and lumber in particular—stirred metropolitan aspirations. Its meat packers, tanneries, shoes, leather, and candle factories were unsurpassed in the West, as were its flour mills, breweries, and distillers, its furniture factories and boat builders, and, most enterprising of all in the fifties, its clothing establishments. With more than $17,855,000 invested in manufacturing by 1860, it gave employment to almost 30,000 artisans whose output, valued at $46,500,000, exceeding that of Boston proper and of all other cities except New York and Philadelphia.[8]

New York's comfortable lead in the value of manufactured products reflected the size of its population, not its industrial concentration, for it was still predominately a trading centre; indeed the mounting flood of its commerce, with imports rising from $118 million in 1836 to $233 million in 1860 and exports from $18 million to $126 million, played a decisive role in the economic development of its hinterland. Except for Troy and Rochester, none of the cities on its water-level route into the interior attained an industrial rank comparable to its population standing. Of the eight cities scattered west from Albany, the tenth largest in the nation in 1850, Buffalo early took a decisive lead only to be passed by Chicago before the close of the decade as their combined steamboat and rail traffic boosted them into

---

[7] U.S. Census (1860) *Manufacturers* III: 310–312; Ibid., *Statistics of the U.S.*, Washington 1866, p. xviii. See also Doc. 15.

[8] U.S. Census (1860) *Manufacturers*, III: 453–457; *Statistics of the U.S.* (1866) p. xviii; Louis L. Tucker, 'Cincinnati, Athens of the West, 1830–1861' *Ohio History*, Winter 1966, pp. 16–17; Blake McKelvey, *Rochester The Water Power City: 1812–1854*, Cambridge, Mass. 1945, I: 205–241.

tenth and ninth places respectively. Rapidly growing Detroit, Milwaukee, and Cleveland trailed eighteenth place Rochester in size and much more distantly in industrial activity.[9]

Rochester's industrial growth, like that of Lowell and several other New England towns, was based on the abundance of its water power. The four successive falls of the Genesee within its borders supplied power for more than a score of large flour mills and for numerous saw-mills and other wood- and metal-working shops. As the world's leading flour producer in the 1840s it attracted accessory trades—coopers, blacksmiths, wagon and carriage makers, and boat builders. Several attempts to develop textile mills to take advantage of its water power proved disappointing, possibly because shipments of raw cotton up the canal were pushed aside by more urgent cargoes bound for the upper Great Lakes. Yet among others heading west were thousands of newcomers, many of whom stopped off at Rochester, some to find jobs at their trades, others to purchase clothing, shoes, and other supplies before continuing their journey. These demands gave birth to new industries, which the stream of immigrants helped to man, and by the late fifties, when flour milling was moving west, a diversified production had taken its place.[10]

Troy at the eastern end of the canal not only stood, like Pittsburgh, at a gateway to the West but also enjoyed easy access to regional iron deposits and became an iron-mongering centre. Its output was more comparable to that of Richmond than that of Pittsburgh, however, and although it lacked the tobacco processing function that chiefly accounted for Richmond's growth, and the glass making enterprise and skills that helped sustain Pittsburgh, Troy's diversified production gave it an industrial rating well above its population rank. Troy, moreover, shared some of its industrial and most of its commercial advantages with nearby Albany, the New York State capital, which still outranked Washington in size as well as all other capitals except Boston.[11]

Boston was of course a major port, second in imports throughout the period; it was also a centre of the mushrooming textile industry, the nation's most productive and most progressive industry. But Boston capitalists, as we have noted above, were developing many of their cotton factories at nearby or distant water power sites—at Lowell, Fall River, and Chicopee among other places. Lowell became

---

[9] *Statistics of the U.S.* (1866), p. xviii; Albion, pp. 391, 398, 401; McKelvey, *Rochester*, I: 321–334; II: 4–21.

[10] McKelvey, *Rochester*, I: 321–334; II: 4–21; U.S. Census (1860) *Manufacturing*, III: 377–379.

[11] U.S. Census (1860) *Manufacturers*, III: 394–396, 492–495, 616–617; *Statistics of the U.S.* (1866), p. xviii.

the model in more than one respect. A promotion of the Boston Associates, who constructed the dam and the first mills and built many of the dormitories that housed the young women who comprised most of its employees during the thirties and forties, it combined some of the features of a well-designed community with some of the limitations of a company town. The abundance of its water power attracted other textile mills and some machine industry, giving the city a measure of diversity, while an influx of French Canadian workers in the late forties and of Irish workers in the fifties lessened the town's reliance on unmarried young women and relaxed restraints formerly maintained over its dormitory residents. Lowell was in 1860 the tenth city in industrial output, far ahead of many more substantial places; its female employees were almost twice as numerous as the male workers, a circumstance rivalled only at Manchester, N.H., another predominately textile city, yet that fact reduced its growing power and, together with the narrow bonds of its speciality, limited its capacity for development.[12]

Yet if Lowell and some of the other textile towns appeared too specialized to enjoy major growth, they had because of their need for equipment spurred the development of machine shops within their borders or nearby, and thus promoted the growth of such tool-making centres as New Haven, Providence, and Springfield as well as much larger Philadelphia. Scores of blacksmiths and small machine shops in scattered cities backed the efforts of local inventors to produce ingenious devices that sometimes led to the formation of productive new industries. Thus in 1831 Ichabod Washburn, adapting a device borrowed from the textile industry, developed at Worcester a machine to produce wire, and made that city the centre of its manufacture in volume and at a price sufficiently reduced to make possible the extension of telegraph wires from city to city after Professor Samuel F. B. Morse perfected that invention in New York a few years later. In similar fashion, progress in the textile industry spurred efforts in many places to develop a sewing machine, and when Elias Howe got his patent in 1846 and launched production at New York, other inventors introduced improvements that adapted it to the making of both clothing and shoes and drew these widely dispersed handicrafts into urban factories in a half dozen cities by the early 1860s.[13]

---

[12] W. Chambers, *Things as They Are in America*, Philadelphia 1854, pp. 220–224; U.S. Census, *Statistics of the U.S.* (1866), xvii; Glaab, *The American City, A Documentary History*, pp. 130–144; Fishlow, *American Railways*, pp. 251–261; Marvin Fisher, *Workshops in the Wilderness*, New York 1967, pp. 87–109.

[13] George S. Gibb, *Saco-Lowell Shops: Textile Machinery Building in New England 1813–1949*, Cambridge, Mass. 1950, pp. 168–179; Rostow, *The Economics of Take-off into Sustained Growth*, New York 1963, pp. 50–53; Bur-

D

If the wants of growing cities sometimes inspired new inventions, the spirited rivalries between them often assured ready backing for local ventures. Few if any of the new industrial enterprises relied on foreign investors, yet the heavy contributions the latter made to the building of American railroads in the 1840s and, through the purchase of state bonds, of canals as well, promoted technological advances that were reflected in the new industries. The combination of new and growing cities and new investments from abroad also fostered a wider use of the corporate organization, which proved especially suitable for new industrial ventures. Enterprising businessmen established banks in every city and in many towns, over 1,500 of them by 1860. Their formation accelerated with the spread of the free banking system after the mid-forties. The free incorporation clauses inserted in the constitutions of a dozen states at this time greatly facilitated their growth. Among the first corporations chartered in many cities were insurance companies, and by 1860 a partial list for seven states included 300 such companies. In New York, where the largest number appeared, several of their leaders came together in 1820 and formed the New York Board of Underwriters to spread and stabilize the risk, and the underwriters at six other metropolises established similar boards in these decades. A more typical form of business cooperation was the board of trade or chamber of commerce organized in Buffalo and Pittsburgh, in Cincinnati and Chicago, as well as in New York, Philadelphia, and Boston. In addition to supplying useful services to their commercial members, these organizations, which also appeared on a less permanent basis in several other cities, provided a means of focusing the business community's demand for state and national legislation. Several supported protective tariffs as well as internal improvements and helped to give direction to the emerging free enterprise system.[14]

The growth of cities, which reached its highest rate in the forties and fifties, represented the convergence of two population movements —that of rural residents to the towns and that of immigrants from

lingame, *Engines of Democracy*, pp. 168–169; Ed. W. Byrn, *The Progress of Invention in the 19th Century*, New York 1900, pp. 15–22, 183–194; Courtney R. Hall, *History of American Industrial Science*, New York 1954, pp. 13–14. See also Doc. 13.

[14] Leland H. Jenks, *The Migration of British Capital to 1875*, New York 1938, pp. 73–108, 169–710; Reisner, *Pittsburgh's Commercial Development*, pp. 186–188; Baldwin, *Pittsburgh*, pp. 292–296; Albion, pp. 265, 272–274; Lloyd Graham and F. Severance, *The First Hundred Years of the Buffalo Chamber of Commerce*, Buffalo 1945, pp. 16–60; Bessie Pierce, *Chicago*, I: 159–162; II: 77–78; U.S. Census (1860), *Statistics of the U.S.*, pp. 291–294; George H. Evans, *Business Incorporations in the U.S., 1800–1943*, New York 1948, pp. 10–30.

abroad. After an increase of 63·7 per cent in the thirties, the urban growth jumped to 92·1 per cent in the forties and held strong at 75·4 per cent in the fifties. These rates more than doubled the national growth rate and increased the proportion classed as urban (resident in towns of 2,500 or more) from 10·8 to 19·8 per cent of the total. Most of the 6,216,518 urbanites of 1860 were native born, but the mounting stream of newcomers from abroad, which brought almost 5 million to America between 1835 and 1860, contributed at least half of these migrants to the cities. A census table showing the number of foreigners resident in forty-three of the principal cities of 1860 reveals that they ranged from a low of 15 per cent at Portland, Maine, to a high of 61 per cent at St Louis. They also comprised over half the population at Chicago, Milwaukee, and San Francisco, and approached that ratio in other rapidly growing interior cities, such as Buffalo, Detroit, Cleveland, Cincinnati, and New Orleans, as well as at New York City where the great majority of them landed. As the migration into the Midwest mounted, New Orleans, with its cotton and grain exports commanding first place in outbound ships, received a mounting flood of immigrants on their return voyages and became in 1837 the second port of entry; moreover it retained a sufficient number to give it the largest contingent of foreign born in the South. Over 50,000 newcomers settled there in the thirties, most of them Irish who, by the close of the decade, outnumbered Negroes in the Mississippi River port. San Francisco on the west coast became in 1850 the third most popular port of entry during the height of the gold rush.[15]

These multiple trends had important effects on the history of the nation. Not only did the cities by their increased number, size, and productivity, sharply reduce America's reliance on European manufactures, which were overshadowed five to two in value by the nation's industrial output in 1860, but because of their increased heterogeneity they acquired a character that clearly differentiated them from the British provincial towns with which they had often been compared. The heterogeneity of the big cities became so striking, in fact, and presented such a sharp contrast with the rural and small town pattern, that it provoked a reaction in the form of the American Party, which campaigned in the mid-fifties for the exclusion of foreign-born residents from public office.

The anti-foreign reaction had, of course, an earlier origin, particularly in the cities that received the largest influx, and produced a significant response. Smarting from the unexpected rebuffs, the Irish,

---

[15] U.S. Census (1860), *Statistics of the U.S.*, Washington 1866, pp. lvii–lviii; Albion, p. 418.

who comprised the largest minority in such ports as Boston, New York, and New Orleans and in Albany among other inland cities, acquired a new sense of nationality as their old loyalties to native counties gave way in the new and tumultuous urban setting to the more inclusive Irish identity. Their Hibernian societies and other associations rallied to the support of Daniel O'Connell and the Repeal Movement in the early forties and later to the relief of famine sufferers in the homeland. They contributed from their modest resources huge sums to bring thousands of refugees to America, thus increasing the fears of urban as well as rural nativists.[16]

The Know Nothings, as the nativists were sometimes called, because of their reluctance to publicize their objectives, wished also to check the growth of the Catholic Church to which most of the Irish and many of the German immigrants belonged. Yet, by the end of the decade, imposing Catholic Churches had appeared in all of the principal Northern cities, and the hostility their members had experienced there in earlier years was overshadowed by the mounting contest over slavery and would be forgotten during the Civil War when Protestant and Catholic, native and immigrant, fought side by side to preserve the Union.[17]

A more lasting consequence of the rapid influx of newcomers from Europe was appearing in many cities where the crowding of many poor refugees from famine and enclosure in Ireland and Britain and from wars and upheavals on the continent was transforming the social and economic structure of the American society. The labour shortage that had characterized many cities during the first quarter, assuring fair wages to most artisans and stirring the envy of their fellows abroad, disappeared during the depression of the late thirties and never became so pronounced in the succeeding years, partly because a mounting influx from Europe inundated the cities. Refugees of peasant background predominated, coming both from Ireland and from Germany, and their competition for unskilled jobs was intense; in New Orleans the Irish Paddies even pushed the Negroes, both slave and free, out of the carrying trade and other menial jobs. Artisans from England and Germany, however, also found themselves in

[16] Handlin, *Boston's Immigrants*, pp. 140–144, 157–167; Niehaus, pp. 3–26, 71–97; Nathan Glazer and D. P. Moynihan, *Beyond the Melting Pot*, Cambridge, Mass. 1964, pp. 219–250; William E. Rowley, 'Albany: A Tale of Two Cities: 1820–1880,' MS Thesis Harvard University, Cambridge, Mass., pp. 256–369.
[17] Robert Ernst, *Immigrant Life in New York City: 1825–1863*, New York 1949; Handlin, *Boston's Immigrants*, pp. 128–221; McKelvey, *Rochester* I: 229, 306–307, 343, 351–354; II: 45–46, 90; *Historical Statistics of the United States*, pp. 544–546; Niehaus, pp. 37–58.

surplus supply at some eastern cities and eagerly sought opportunities at the new towns springing up in the West.[18]

But the spirited development of urban communities that encouraged businessmen to form corporations and boards of trade also prompted craftsmen and professional workers to organize to promote their interests. Thus skilled workmen had formed trade unions at Philadelphia, Boston, New York, and a few other cities in the mid-thirties, and although the depression snuffed out most of these bodies before the end of the decade, several reappeared in the middle fifties in these and such other industrial cities as Pittsburgh, Cincinnati, and Rochester. Everywhere the old American pattern of the apprentice becoming a master craftsman and then possibly an independent entrepreneur was giving way to a division of the population into labourers, artisans, merchants, professional workers, and capitalists, although the last term had not yet come into general use.[19]

Yet numerous opponents of this trend appeared in many cities. The Workingmen's parties that formed in New York and several other towns in the late twenties persisted in varied forms as a third party movement for over two decades. They received their chief support from craftsmen but they also attracted adherents from dissident elements of other groups including some merchants and professional men. Their chief issue was opposition to privilege and monopoly, and they quickly rallied to the side of Jackson in his battle against the Bank of the United States, centred at Philadelphia, but later split with the Democrats when Van Buren sought to give special advantages to the New York banks; instead they supported the free banking and free incorporation proposals of the Whigs. Although the reforms they jointly effected in the forties swept away some of the privileges previously enjoyed by favoured groups, thus clearing the way for a more democratic free enterprise system, the New York bankers, because of their easier access to and more vigorous use of foreign capital, were able to achieve a commanding leadership among the numerous state and private bankers scattered throughout the cities of America.[20]

New York's leadership acquired some of the attributes of domina-

---

[18] Ernst, *Immigrant Life*, pp. 25–36, 61–121; Fisher, pp. 135–140; Rowland E. Berthoff, *British Immigrants in Industrial America, 1790–1950*, Cambridge, Mass. 1953. See also Niehaus, pp. 37–162, for a graphic account of the Irish invasion and the resulting adjustments in that leading southern city.

[19] Sullivan, pp. 85–158; Ernst, pp. 99–121; Walter Hugins, *Jacksonian Democracy and the Working Class*, Stamford 1960, pp. 51–80; Berthoff, pp. 62–89.

[20] Douglas T. Miller, *Jacksonian Aristoctacy: Class and Democracy in New York: 1830–1860*, New York 1967; Hugins, pp. 11–10; 131–224; Sullivan, pp. 159–208; Taylor, pp. 225–288; Warner, pp. 125–156.

tion, in the eyes of many of its competitors, but enterprise was the key factor in the newly evolving American system, and any city that displayed it had a chance to share in the nation's increasing bounty. Thus at Rochester when a number of men who had invested modest sums in numerous telegraph lines, built from city to city in the early fifties by their enthusiastic neighbour, Henry O'Reilly, became impatient for some returns on their stock, one of their number, Hiram Sibley, devised a scheme to draw these scattered lines into the Western Union system equipped to serve the nation's vast interior. O'Reilly, pushed aside by the emerging giant, cried out against the formation of America's first great trust and organized an anti-monopoly league in New York to promote his cause.[21]

But O'Reilly's voice was only one of many that were criticizing various aspects of the emerging urban society. An undertone of anti-urbanism had persisted since the 1790s when Jefferson had characterized cities as 'pestilential' and warned his countrymen against them, yet his vision of a rural America had given way amidst the excitement of building new cities. Most critics now focused their attention on specific ills, for which they were ready, like O'Reilly, to propose hopeful remedies. John Griscom, for example, urged the acceptance of a public health program in New York to correct the sanitation deficiencies of that great city. Andrew J. Downing proposed public parks there to supply 'ventilation' and breathing spaces. Joseph Tuckerman of Boston urged an organized community effort to care for the needs of the poor. Horace Mann promoted an acceptance by the states of full responsibility for the education of all their children, but in most states only the cities responded. These and other reforms would ultimately be advanced for the nation as a whole, but their first application was in the cities where they found their chief support.[22]

Several of the leading cities were developing new standards of excellence in both civic and cultural fields. Philadelphia, New York, and Boston each expanded and dramatically improved its water system under public control in the thirties and forties, and a dozen other major cities launched similar projects by the middle fifties. New York and Boston now equipped their policemen with uniforms and began to transform them into an organized service. Several cities also made attempts to standardize the fire fighting service by introducing some paid officials among the volunteers. But the most dramatic innovation in the municipal services was the development, again at New York, Boston, Philadelphia, Cincinnati and a few other cities, of horse car

[21] McKelvey, *Rochester*, I: 322–333; II: 20, 69–70.
[22] Glaab and Brown, *A History of Urban America*, pp. 53–81.

companies to facilitate the movement of traffic within the expanding metropolises. These companies reported a total of 402 miles of track in 1860, a slight foretaste of things to come.[23]

The major eastern ports and Cincinnati likewise took the lead in cultural improvements. These five, together with several others, boasted well-established colleges, libraries, museums, and concert halls, and Cincinnati, which now preened itself as the 'Athens of the West', acquired an observatory in 1845, the first in the nation open to the public. Citizen associations of varied types supported these efforts and brought lecturers and entertainers to their platforms; they also formed local orchestras, choirs, and theatrical groups to support the visiting artists. And if few communities rivalled the cultural provisions now available at Boston and New York, and if only limited portions of their inhabitants fully shared in these urban luxuries, a dozen other cities scattering from New Haven in New England to Charleston in the South and St Louis in the West had made positive strides in some cultural fields, while numerous towns in every state boasted their academies, library companies, and even in 204 cases a college. Moreover the newspapers, which now included 385 dailies, reported a circulation of almost 1,500,000 daily, plus 7,500,000 once a week, enough to reach all urban residents and to alert them to the larger opportunities and responsibilities soon to appear.[24]

Yet stirring as these accomplishments appeared to most observers, to an increasing number of critics, they left much to be desired. The Jeffersonian school of proponents of the unspoiled frontier had found a new and more eloquent spokesman in Henry D. Thoreau, but his moving call for a retreat to the solitude of the woods had little relevance to the problems of the emerging cities that troubled the more pragmatic critics such as the Rev Joseph Tuckerman and his fellow Unitarian William E. Channing, both of Boston, who called for a renewal of religious and moral influences in the cities. Still a minor strain in the cacophony of urban growth, their views were destined to play an increasing role in the history of cities.[25]

---

[23] Nelson Blake, *Water for the Cities*, Syracuse 1956, pp. 265–271; U.S. Census (1860) *Statistics of the U.S.*, p. 332; Warner, pp. 99–123.

[24] U.S. Census (1860) *Statistics of the U.S.* (1866), pp. 321–322, 505–510; Tucker, 'Cincinnati, Athens of the West,' pp. 19–25.

[25] Glaab and Brown, pp. 53–106; Morton and Lucia White, *The Intellectual versus the City*, Cambridge, Mass. 1962, pp. 24–94.

5

Urban Reconstruction and Diffusion: 1860-1890

In the three decades following 1860, most American cities doubled or trebled in size, increasing the non-rural population to a third of the nation's total. The enterprise engendered by the pre-Civil War cities transformed their character, constructed new arteries of trade, and scattered almost a thousand new urban places throughout the land. Natural and man-made waterways and an agrarian landscape continued to dominate the scene, but cast-iron store fronts, iron piers, and expanding grids of steel rails, copper wires, and lead pipes, both intra- and inter-city, gave the nation a new structural unity and strength. The older Americans, who had previously supplied leadership in town building, found themselves surrounded and in some cases challenged by newcomers from abroad who brought fresh skills as well as problems to the cities and played an increasing role in their development. Thus, as the cities grew in number and size and cast a larger shadow over the land, they also gave rise to internal frictions that contributed a new tension to American history.

Inter-city rivalries, though muted somewhat during the Civil War, acquired a new intensity after the return of peace. New York City resumed its spectacular growth though much of it was now diverted to Brooklyn, Jersey City, and other booming suburbs. Philadelphia and St Louis each added more than 100,000 residents in the sixties, but the rising city of Chicago, with an increase of 189,000, experienced the most rapid gain (173·6 per cent) during the decade.

As the leading railroad centre in the nation (and indeed in the world), Chicago pointed the way for other aspiring metropolises. St Louis, its old rival but primarily a river port, discovered the merits of rail connections in the sixties, too late to check Chicago's more rapid advance. St Louis had suffered along with other borderland and southern cities from the blighting effects of the war, yet the rapid extension of rail lines into the Far West, spurred by federal land grants, restored its vitality. The federally incorporated and backed

Union Pacific, constructed westward from Omaha, Nebrasks, in the middle and late sixties, was not an urban project, though it did give Omaha and Oakland a great boost, but both Chicago and St Louis in the Midwest and Denver, Portland, Seattle, and Los Angeles in the Far West hastened to build connecting roads to draw the transcontinental trade to their doors.[1]

In every town, enterprising promoters and business leaders competed in projecting these essential urban tentacles. In many places, they sought and procured municipal subsidies to supplement the state and federal grants as well as the investments of distant capitalists and thus assured a local connection. Rival cities, such as Cincinnati and Louisville, eager to expand their trading areas, bid frantically for control of railroads to the South through Chattanooga and Nashville to Atlanta and Birmingham. A similar rivalry in the late sixties enlivened the contest between Kansas City and Omaha for the western trade.[2]

The rapid extension of rail lines in that and the succeeding decade, and the equally rapid settlement of the Great West in their wake gave a powerful impetus to its leading trade centres. Omaha, Minneapolis, and St Paul each experienced a two-fold increase during the eighties, while Kansas City, Denver, and Portland were close on their heels, and much smaller Seattle and Los Angeles shattered even these records. In the South, Memphis, Atlanta, and Nashville enjoyed renewed growth largely as a result of the opening or extension of regional rail links.[3]

Each community gave enthusiastic support in the early years to its corporate offspring, yet divergent interests soon appeared. When, as frequently occurred, the railroads increased their rates as the traffic improved, or diverted their trains to more lucrative routes, towns that had loyally backed their construction cried out in protest. And when some roads, seeking to terminate unprofitable rate wars, formed pools, as the Baltimore & Ohio, the Pennsylvania, the Erie, and the New York Central did in 1877, leading merchants in towns adversely affected demanded a curb on such monopoly practices. Bitterly conflicting interests appeared even in the most dramatically growing cities. Thus it was the Board of Trade in Chicago and the Board of

---

[1] Wyatt W. Belcher, *The Economic Rivalry Between St. Louis and Chicago: 1850–1880*, New York 1947; Glenn C. Quiett, *They Built the West: An Epic of Rails and Cities*, New York 1934.

[2] N. S. B. Gras and H. M. Larson, *Casebook in American Business History*, pp. 373–385; John F. Stover, *The Railroads of the South: 1865–1900*, Chapel Hill 1955.

[3] Blake McKelvey, *The Urbanization of America: 1860–1915*, New Brunswick, N.J. 1963, pp. 25–29; Charles N. Glaab, *Kansas City and the Railroads*, Madison 1962.

Trade and Transportation in New York that took the lead in moves for state regulation of railroad rates and services in the late 1860s and 70s.[4]

As the spreading rail systems, assisted by telegraph networks, drew widely distant cities into the same commercial basin, local industrialists as well as merchants found themselves threatened by the transport monopolies. Manufacturers of regional products, such as the flour millers of Rochester and the meat packers of Cincinnati, had in the sixties faced the mounting competition of western centres of wheat growing and cattle raising with confidence because of their lesser freight costs. But their advantages soon disappeared when the rival railroad systems, competing fiercely for the trade of Chicago and other key western centres, announced long-haul rates that sometimes actually undercut the short-haul charges from cities lacking competing outlets. Their pleas for relief had to be carried beyond the state level and contributed to the creation of the Interstate Commerce Commission in 1887. In the interim, however, many of the trade assets and industrial specialities of the cities of the old West suffered a decline. St Louis and Chicago had by 1870 outstripped Cincinnati and New Orleans, even Baltimore and Boston, in population and would soon surpass them all in industrial output as well.

Yet several of the older cities quickly replaced outworn specialities with promising new industries. Cincinnati for example became a clothing, shoe, and brewing centre after the slaughtering trade moved west; Rochester likewise developed a reputation in these fields as well as for nursery plants to replace its vanishing millers. These and other cities profited from the skills brought by immigrants who established new firms, such as the Bausch & Lomb Optical Company in Rochester, that progressively reduced the demand for finished products from abroad. Other cities profited from the development of new sources of fuel, notably oil in the vicinity of Pittsburgh and Cleveland, or of new mineral resources, as the iron fields of northern Michigan and central Alabama, which gave a boom to Milwaukee as well as to Cleveland and Birmingham. Technological improvements in the production of steel at Pittsburgh, and of a host of other products there and elsewhere, speeded urban industrial developments and boosted the value added fivefold in the three decades following 1860, so that by 1890 the American industrial output exceeded the value of all imports by a ratio of five to one.[5]

[4] Lee Benson, *Merchants, Farmers and Railroads: Railroad Regulations and New York Politics: 1850–1887*, Cambridge, Mass. 1955; McKelvey, pp. 30–32.

[5] Charlotte Erickson, *American Industry and the European Immigrant: 1860–1885*, Cambridge, Mass. 1951; Bayrd Still, *Milwaukee, The History of a City*, Madison 1948, pp. 329–332; Bessie Pierce, *Chiacgo* II: 89; McKelvey, *Rochester* II: 106–107, 227–243; McKelvey, *Urbanization of America*, pp. 35–41.

The transformation in the American economy wrought by this urban industrial growth was matched by an equally dramatic transformation in the physical structure and social character of cities large and small. Old European patterns, as embodied in the colonial ports, and the promotional adaptation practised on the frontier alike gave way as the horse cars and the steam railroads refashioned pedestrian towns into cities with clearly distinguished commercial and industrial districts. The successive waves of immigrants, some with language and other cultural traits that encouraged their cohesive settlement, further segmented the larger cities into ethnic neighbourhoods. These special characteristics of American cities, evident at New York and a few other places in the 1850s, became typical of most cities in the North and West by 1890, when even small towns had their poor districts 'beyond the tracks' where the most recent immigrants found shelter.

Brick and stone had long since replaced wood in the more densely built-up portions of most American cities, but, except for a few public buildings and an occasional hotel, few structures erected before the Civil War had exceeded three or four stories in height. With the development of cast-iron fronts and the introduction of iron piers and supporting beams, the reconstruction of the more prosperous districts was hastened. Imposing business blocks of six or more stories began to appear in the sixties at busy downtown street intersections in several cities. By the close of that decade, after hydraulic elevators had been developed, a number of venturesome builders began to add an extra story or two on blocks erected with iron piers and cast iron fronts. Although the Chicago fire of 1873 shattered the fire-proof claims of these cast-iron structures, the city's urgent need for new and more substantial buildings encouraged architects to erect still taller structures thus giving birth to steel-frame skyscrapers that exceeded twelve stories in a few cases at Chicago, St Louis, and New York by 1889 when the first electric powered elevator was installed in one on Broadway.[6]

These structural triumphs were made possible only by a combination of related technological improvements, each the product of a group of ingenious inventors centred in one city or another. Without the development of gas heaters and hot-water furnaces in Philadelphia in the 1860s, without the production of metal and tile piping for water, gas, and sanitary uses, without the perfection of the telephone at Boston in 1876, of electric generators at Cleveland, and of incandescent lights at Menlo Park a few years later, even these skyscrapers

---

[6] Siegfried Giedion, *Space, Time and Architecture*, Cambridge, Mass. 1954, pp. 193–209, 366–385; McKelvey, *Urbanization*, pp. 80–85.

would have been impracticable. Louis Sullivan, with other inspired builders chiefly in Chicago, St Louis and St Paul, supplied a fresh architectural design for these new structures that gave them a unique grace and identity. Their wider utility and later expansion depended on the perfection of the electric trolley in the late eighties and the construction of rapid-transit elevated lines in New York, Chicago and a few other cities. While many cities benefited from the introduction of these and other improvements, a few prospered through the manufacture of the new equipment—Philadelphia, Pittsburgh, and Chicago from the fabrication of trolley cars, for example.[7]

Yet each of these technological advances, though loudly hailed on their first introduction in each town, presented new hazards and knotty problems to the municipal authorities. Thus the water and gas companies needed franchises permitting them to lay pipes through the streets; the telephone and electric companies required authorization for the erection of poles; and successive transit companies sought public consent for an extension of the grid of iron rails. Local or out-of-town promoters were ready to pay huge sums for these often lucrative franchises, and the conflicting pressures sometimes corrupted the part-time councilmen empowered to govern the city. Unfortunately the pressure did not let up after the grant of a charter, since demands for and against its extension or cancellation or for the licensing of a competitor appeared at frequent intervals in every town and complicated successive political contests. Competition soon proved a futile safeguard of the public interest in the utility field, as city after city became frustrated when a newly chartered company tore up the streets a second or third time only to sell out to the monopoly when its demands were met. New York City secured authority in 1875 to create a Rapid Transit Commission to supervise the operation of these lines, but the attempts of several towns to enforce the standards and rates prescribed in their franchise grants proved disillusioning.[8]

The common councils, which shared responsibility for the government of most cities with a popularly elected mayor, were ill prepared to cope with the new urban problems. Their committees on roads and buildings had a long experience to draw upon, and the committees on public health, the water works, and the schools were frequently amenable to expert advice from recognized authorities. But aldermen charged with the supervision of the rapidly growing utilities, with the direction of the police, or with the administration of relief had to make decisions under pressures that were sometimes overwhelm-

[7] Roger Burlingame, *Engines of Democracy*, New York 1941, pp. 95–125; McKelvey, *Urbanization*, pp. 75–84.

[8] John A. Fairlie, *Municipal Administration*, New York 1922 ed.; McKelvey, *Urbanization*, pp. 86–92.

ing. The urgent need for action in expanding cities hastened the rise of the party boss, as in New York where Boss Tweed became a symbol of corruption because of the huge sums he extracted in the course of rushing necessary improvements, or in Minneapolis where 'Doc' Ames acquired a similar reputation by exacting payments from the degenerate inhabitants of the saloons and brothels that flourished in its boom period. In some cities the state legislatures intervened and placed the police, public buildings, and other municipal programs under state-appointed commissions.

Citizen protests against the bosses, and against the erosion of local authority under these commissions, appeared in several cities, notably at Philadelphia where a Committee of One Hundred, formed in 1880, launched an attack on the gas ring that was soon taken up by similar groups in Cincinnati, Milwaukee, and elsewhere. St Louis adopted the first home rule charter in 1876, and Brooklyn a strong mayor system in 1882. But these were isolated and transient achievements in an era of municipal misrule, that prompted Lord Bryce to declare that 'the government of cities is the one conspicious failure of the United States'.[9]

The rapid urban growth was, of course, a major cause for many civic ills. Pressure for an extension and improvement of the streets called for huge outlays in every city, but the successful introduction of asphalt paving at Washington and Buffalo in 1882 supplied promising innovations. In similar fashion, vast outlays on the water and sewer systems produced some hazardous situations until the application of scientific precautionary measures imported from Europe opened an advance in the field of sanitation—as Philadelphia and Boston among other cities demonstrated. The recreation needs of the teeming throngs in the leading metropolises were widely neglected, but a few cities followed New York's example in acquiring park lands and other open spaces, though none was as impressive as the vast Central Park opened in New York in the late fifties. The bond issues required to finance these developments sunk the cities deeply into debt and intensified the desire of many bankers and other substantial citizens for fiscal and political reforms.

The reformers soon found themselves embroiled in an uneven controversy with the leaders of ethnic groups that had invaded and occupied major portions of most northern cities. Tammany Hall, an Irish and Democratic club in Manhattan, was not only the most notorious but also the most influential of these bodies, and its hold was firmly based on the friendly concern displayed by its chieftains for

[9] James Bryce, *The American Commonwealth*, New York 1910 ed., I: 642, II: 379–405; McKelvey, *Urbanization*, pp. 92–96. See Doc. 18.

the poor and struggling inhabitants of their precincts. Residents eager
to avoid penalties for minor, even major, infractions of unwanted or
imperfectly understood regulations, or grateful for a timely relief
basket in a period of crisis, were not inclined to support reformers
who openly blamed corruption on the hoards of immigrants that
were flooding the cities.[10]

The immigrant tide was steadily mounting in these decades and
averaged a half million annually during the eighties, more than double
that of the sixties. An increasing portion of these newcomers settled
in the cities, and although no place was 50 per cent foreign-born in
1890 (as three had been in 1860) their declining proportion was due
to the swelling number of their American-born children who now
approached a third of the urban total. Moreover foreign-born adults
exceeded native-born adults in eighteen of the twenty-eight cities over
100,000 in 1890, and, although not all were naturalized, they strongly
influenced their political life.

No southern city, large or small, attracted many immigrants in
these post-war decades. Except for the border cities of Baltimore,
Louisville and Wheeling, no town in the South reported as many
foreign-born as Negro residents in 1880 and, in spite of the increased
application of discriminatory practices, the non-whites outnumbered
immigrants five or ten to one in most southern towns by the end of
that decade. Even New Orleans, now that the Irish migration had
subsided, was more dependent on the rural South and saw its Negro
residents outnumber the foreign-born four to three in these years.
The slow recovery of most cities of the old South, evident in their
sluggish population growth and in their retarded industrial progress,
reflected their denial of civil and political rights and their neglect
of the productive potential of the Negro residents who comprised
from 25 to 55 per cent of their totals.[10b]

Most of the northern and western cities, on the other hand,
welcomed or at least attracted immigrants in great numbers and responded in varied ways to their influence. The Germans, who outnumbered the Irish in most cities by the late 1860s, hailed from many
different and often jealous principalities but like the Irish before them
they acquired in the strange American cities a new national identity.
Drawn together by linguistic ties, they established a host of social and
relief societies to free themselves from dependence on others and
swelled with a new sense of pride over the unification of Germany

[10] Harold Zink, *City Bosses in the United States,* Durham 1930; see also
Documents 17 and 18.

[10b] Rupert B. Vance, *All These People: The Nation's Human Resources in the
South,* Chapel Hill, N.C., 1945, pp. 14–18, 31–36; U.S. Census, *Social Statistics
of Cities* (1880) Part III.

in 1870. In the religious field most of the open hostility to Catholic and Jewish newcomers, evident in many cities before the Civil War, had disappeared during that struggle as northern communities achieved a new sense of unity. In the late sixties when Protestant churchmen in the cities began to consider the plight of the poor working-men; Episcopal clergymen, discovering that many were former Church of England men, launched a drive to win them back to the church. An Evangelical Alliance, organized in 1867 with branches in several cities, spurred the formation of other bodies that soon spread evangelical and philanthropic work so vigorously that Catholic and Jewish leaders, fearful of proselytism, launched programs of their own. By the early 1880s the plight of urban immigrants had prompted the establishment of some thirty missions, one or more in each of the leading cities of the Northeast, and had awakened their religious leaders to an awareness of urban problems.[11]

Prominent among the new problems that now commanded attention were unemployment, housing, and education. The industrial revolution, accentuated in the post-war years as the improved railroad network and new manufacturing devices drew many handicraft operations into urban factories, increased the productivity of those employed, but threw thousands more out of work. Many migrants, both native and foreign, flocked to the cities where the new factories and railroads centred, and in greater numbers than the cities could employ or shelter. In earlier periods of imbalance and hard times, the destitute had headed for a new frontier or found shelter on the land, but by the mid-seventies the mechanization of farming was sending a host of displaced agrarians to the cities to swell the number of the unemployed. The concentration of this misery in poor urban areas made it more visible and stirred new welfare efforts by humanitarian citizens and religious groups, giving birth to a new movement for organized charity at Buffalo and Boston among other cities. But a similar movement for the organization of craft and trade unions suffered a severe setback in many places.[12]

Perhaps the major achievement of the new humanitarian groups was their discovery of the urban housing problem. Although congestion and poor housing had been described by health officers in plague-infested cities before the war, public concern over these social ills was seldom expressed until alerted by the charity visitors of the mid-seventies. In New York City, a Board of Health survey in 1866 had

[11] Aaron I. Abell, *The Urban Impact on American Protestantism: 1865–1900*, Cambridge, Mass. 1934; McKelvey, *Urbanization*, pp. 156–165.

[12] Frank D. Watson, *The Charity Organization Movement in the United States*, New York 1922, pp. 175–245; McKelvey, *Urbanization*, pp. 143–154. See also Doc. 16.

prompted the enactment a year later of the first Tenement House Act, but its ban against windowless bedrooms had helped to create the standardized dumbell flats with narrow and sunless airshafts that spread over most of Manhattan and into other rapidly growing cities. Repeated complaints against the wretched housing conditions encountered by charity workers in Boston, New York, and several other large cities in the 70s prompted the appointment of housing inspectors at Chicago and a few other places by the close of the decade. Although most of these efforts soon subsided, a new aspect of the city had been identified and would command increased attention as the years progressed.[13]

The mushrooming cities, their new industrial functions, and the polyglot character of their populations combined to demand new services from the schools. The memory work and routine drill in the 'three R's', that had provided a literate introduction to advanced classical studies in pre-Civil War decades, no longer sufficed. Several talented educators—Edward A. Sheldon in Oswego, William T. Harris in St Louis, and Francis W. Parker in Chicago, all cities where the schools were thronging with immigrant children—evolved new techniques for object teaching, new courses in elementary science, and new programs for handicraft and mechanical instruction that progressively made the public schools vital urban institutions. As their educational functions reached down into the kindergarten age, first at Boston and St Louis, and advanced to the high school level in these and other cities, the urban schools, now widely backed by compulsory attendance laws, not only effectively removed children from the streets but hastened the absorption of diverse ethnic groups and also prepared their members for participation in the increasingly urban society.[14]

Although the concept of America as a great Melting Pot had not yet appeared, the teeming cities were assuming the creative social function of formulating a new society. As important ingredients in the educational innovations noted above were derived from European antecedents, and as basic aspects of the industrial technology developed in American cities were also borrowed from England, so a host of cultural attitudes and talents were imported from the Continent both by steerage passengers seeking new homes and, on the top deck, by Americans returning from a Grand Tour with new concepts of refinement. As German and Italian opera companies and British and French theatrical stars packed the galleries of an increasing

[13] Edith E. Wood, *The Housing of the Unskilled Wage Earner*, New York 1919; Robert W. DeForest and Lawrence Veiller, eds., *The Tenement House Problem*, New York 1907; McKelvey, *Urbanization*, pp. 78–79, 118–120.

[14] Elwood P. Cubberly, *Public Education in the United States*, Boston 1934, pp. 385–392, 563–574; McKelvey, *Urbanization*, pp. 168–175.

number of urban theatres, they stirred a creative response from travelling minstrel troupes, local stock companies and ethnic cultural clubs. The dramatic fare was as eclectic as the riot of architectural details that adorned the new and more substantial mansions and commercial blocks erected in New York, Chicago, St Louis and a score of other expanding cities. Philadelphia's great Centennial Exposition set the proper tone in 1876, introducing Moorish as well as Gothic and Renaissance touches that found their way not only into the street façades of many cities but into the new art museums opened in the seventies at Boston, New York, and Baltimore, as well as at Philadelphia and Washington, and in the next decade at Cincinnati, Chicago, and several other cities. Art institutes boasting ties with the schools of Düsseldorf and Paris, as well as those of London and Rome, nurtured the talents of native as well as immigrant artists in Providence, New Orleans, and San Francisco.[15]

Choral societies and orchestras in Rochester and Milwaukee eagerly endeavoured to match the performances of the more professional symphony orchestras of New York, Philadelphia, Boston, Cincinnati, and Chicago. Each had special characteristics, derived in part from the ethnic composition of the city's population, and each jealously guarded its reputation and welcomed expressions of approval from foreign visitors, such as Cincinnati for example won from Henry Irving in 1884, and San Francisco received from a long succession of visitors including the British suffragist, E. Catherine Bates, who pronounced it in 1887 the most attractive city in America and one in which she would not hesitate to settle if a few of her friends would join her, for it had, she declared, many qualities of the best cities in Europe.[16]

Yet observant foreign visitors also noted some qualities peculiar to American cities. Their incessant bustle and the sharp contrasts between commercial and residential districts, between rich and poor neighbourhoods, and among their several ethnic communities differentiated them from most European cities and frequently attracted comment. Travellers, such as George A. Sala back for a second visit in the late seventies, were sometimes surprised at the increased sophistication they found and the greater appreciation of the leisurely arts. They were as surprised by the softening of manners as by the forest of tall poles bearing a tangled web of telephone and other electric wires high above the streets of the leading American cities. And those who like Willard Glazier ventured into the stock exchange

[15] Christopher Tunnard and Henry H. Reed, *American Skyline*, Boston 1955, pp. 137–186; Giedion, pp. 358–360; Oliver Larkin, *Art and Life in America*, New York 1949, pp. 265–317; McKelvey, *Urbanization*, pp. 115–121, 207–214.
[16] McKelvey, pp. 196–205; Louis C. Elson, *The History of American Music*, New York 1925 ed.

E

in New York, the department stores of Philadelphia, or the stock yards of Chicago, were impressed by the new technological devices—the ticker tape machines, the cash registers, the overhead butcher trolleys and other ingenious devices that gave America cities an atmosphere of innovation, of living in the future. Only in their comments on women and children did the foreign visitors find groups fully enjoying the present—the women with an engaging freedom of expression, the children with an assertiveness that appalled most visitors. It was in the cities that foreign commentators saw the emergence in the 1880s of a new America—a nation that was both more cosmopolitan and more tumultuous as well as more sooty and much more pretentious and materialistic than the pre-Civil War society it had displaced.[17]

[17] George A. Sala, *America Revisited*, London 1883; H. H. Vivian Swansen, *Notes on a Tour in America*, London 1878; Joseph Hatton, *Henry Irving's Impressions of America*, London 1884; Willard Glazier, *Peculiarities of American Cities*, Philadelhpia 1886.

6

Cities in the Progressive Movement: 1890-1910

Many foreign visitors in the late eighties and nineties were appalled by the materialism and debauchery that had tarnished the American dream. Not all agreed with English journalist G. W. Steevens, who saw the quest for dollars as the dominant concern in New York and other cities, but several, echoing Lord Bryce, were amazed at the evidence of corruption in urban affairs. William Archer, however, saw much to admire in America cities, particularly the critical appreciation of their problems he found in Chicago among other places.[1] The protracted depression of the mid-nineties had disclosed many urban deficiencies. In Chicago and elsewhere the first short-term relief efforts quickly gave way to ambitious economic programs that eventually brought not only a measure of recovery but also an outburst of industrial growth that produced a surge of monopoly power and created a widespread demand for social control and reform. But the progressive movement that swept through the cities at the turn of the century was more than a campaign for municipal reform; it was equally a response to the changing character of the urban population and an effort to assimilate the cultural heritage the newcomers had brought.

Despite their economic blemishes and their social and cultural deficiencies, the cities continued to grow in number and size and more rapidly than the nation at large. Although the depression cut the urban growth rate from 56·5 per cent in the booming eighties to 36·4 per cent in the nineties, it also slowed the rural gains and cleared the way for a new urban upsurge in the first decade of the twentieth century when the addition of 12 million urbanites increased the number of cities over 100,000 to fifty, eight of them exceeding a half million each. As in the case of New York, which in 1900 absorbed Brooklyn and

---

[1] G. W. Steevens, *The Land of the Dollar*, New York 1897, pp. 300–307, and passim; William Archer, *America Today*, New York 1899, pp. 24–48, 109–114.

three other suburban boroughs, the dramatic growth of the metropolitan giants reflected the reannexation of many suburban migrants. But the most spectacular increases in these decades occurred in such rising new cities as Los Angeles and Seattle on the West Coast and Birmingham and Atlanta in the new South.

The tumultuous street life, both in the booming new cities and in the teeming metropolises, revealed sharp contrasts between wealth and poverty, between refinement and depravity, and between native and foreign traditions. And although these dichotomies were not closely matched, the recurrent attempts in many cities to establish ethnic societies often produced an anti-foreign reaction and helped to confine the strange newcomers in ghetto-like settlements that had made their appearance in most large American cities. Because of their initial poverty or the exhaustion of their resources in the act of migration, most immigrants were generally glad to share the modest quarters of relatives and fellow countrymen who had arrived earlier, and, by crowding in, helped to transform these settlements into congested slums.[2]

Although the squalor and destitution evident in many dark urban alleys was not new, the easy confidence that these evils could be eradicated by an application of charity and a conversion to temperance disappeared in the mid-nineties. Most of the earlier efforts continued, of course, and with redoubled energies, as the Charity Organization Societies of the late seventies became Associated Charities in some places and United Charities in others. They promoted the spread of humane societies, day nurseries, rest and recreation centres, and employment bureaus, and they called for more realistic measures for public relief, but they were no longer so self-assured. Even the newly developed settlement houses, inspired in the late eighties by Toynbee Hall in London, which now made their appearance in a dozen cities scattered from Boston to Chicago, experienced new challenges. Their self-appointed task of bridging the gap between the rich and the poor, the native and the immigrant, became more complex as depression swept the land. Some, following the example of Jane Addams at Hull House in Chicago, made their social halls available for neighbourhood forums at which controversial issues such as socialism were heatedly debated; a few, including Robert Woods at Andover House in Boston, provided space and encouragement for union organizing drives. Among the new institutions sponsored by these settlement houses was the Women's Trade Union League of 1903, formed by Lillian Wald and others at Henry Street Settlement in New York; a

[2] John Higham, *Strangers in the Land: Patterns of American Nativism: 1860–1925*, New Brunswick, N.J. 1955, pp. 39–87; McKelvey, *Urbanization*, pp. 61–71.

few years later it would prod President Theodore Roosevelt to establish the Federal Children's Bureau—the first hesitant step by the
national government in the welfare field.[3]

Ethnic and denominational societies were performing similar functions for still larger numbers of urban dwellers. The prosperity of
some nationality groups in the 1880s, particularly the Germans and the
Jews, had prompted the creation of a host of rival societies; each
represented a particular city or province in the Old Country, and all
strove to preserve ethnic traditions in their new neighbourhoods.
When the onset of the depression highlighted their relief functions,
some of these societies drew together to maintain asylums, placement
bureaus, and other forms of relief for their fellow countrymen. Like
the Irish and the Germans before them, the Poles, the Eastern European Jews, and the Italians among others were discovering their
broader ethnic identity and were endeavouring to assume their responsibilities in the urban community. Many ethnic societies had religious
affiliations and received added support as a result.

While urban Catholics and Jews promoted a number of 'combative
benevolences' as these ethnic societies were characterized, the Protes-
tants, who had few ties with the major immigrant streams, forged a
new social gospel to meet the challenges of the slums. Washington
Gladden at Springfield in Massachusetts and later at Columbus, Ohio,
developed a warm approach to the urban poor and an understanding
of the needs and aspirations of working people that enabled him in the
early nineties to conduct pioneer labour-management conferences at
Columbus and Toledo. Some Protestant clergymen, among them
W. D. P. Bliss of Boston, aligned themselves with the more radical
labour groups and founded the Society of Christian Socialists, while
Walter Rauschenbusch at Rochester, though shunning the materialism
of Marx, learned enough from a survy of the city's social conditions
in 1904 to see the future of the urban church and of urban society
generally as linked with the welfare of the labouring classes. His
seminal volume, 'Christianity and the Social Crisis,' published in 1907,
gave religious sanction to the progressive movement.[4]

But the progressive movement had somehow lost contact with the
basic economic issue of the nineties—the dilemma of unemployment
in the midst of technological advance and economic progress. Despite
the glamour and excitement that surrounded the annual conventions
and rallies of the old Knights of Labor, its fortunes declined in the

[3] Robert H. Bremner, *From the Depths: The Discovery of Poverty in the United States*, New York 1956, pp. 50–85; McKelvey, *Urbanization*, pp. 147–155. See also Doc. 21.

[4] Abell, *Urban Impact*, pp. 55–94, 166–193; McKelvey, *Rochester III:* 130–135; McKelvey, *Urbanization*, pp. 160–167.

early nineties as the more prosaic Federation of Labor pressed its campaign for business unionism and modest contract gains. Neither body had an answer to the depression, but the bread-and-butter philosophy of the Federation proved more enticing as the depression receded in the late nineties. Even the demise of the Knights did not assure victory to the Federation, however, for an open-shop movement, spreading in the smaller industrial cities, labeled all unions as foreign-dominated and subversive, and organized the National Association of Manufacturers in 1895 to combat them. Valiant conciliatory efforts by the National Civic Federation, formed at Chicago in 1900, moderated the conflict between business and labour groups in some cities and brought civic leaders such as the former Mayor Seth Low of New York into friendly association with Samuel Gompers of the AF of L and John L. Mitchell of the Mine Workers Union. But almost the only tangible results were the creation of a Federal Conciliation Service in 1903 and the exclusion of unions from the Sherman Antitrust restraints.[5]

That exemption of labour unions from the anti-monopoly restrictions revealed much as to the philosophy of the progressives. They were pragmatists, or at least practical reformers, who saw some combines as constructive, and therefore good, and others as constricting and therefore bad monopolies. Many were small business men who felt the dominance of the great transport and utility combines but had little contact with unions, though they could sympathize with the hardships some workers suffered from monopoly control. The progressive business leaders, like their professional colleagues among educators and clergymen, saw the restoration of competition as their chief objective. Except in cities such as Detroit and Dayton where the efforts of labour unions to organize the rising new industries stirred an open-shop movement, the progressive business leaders were sometimes tolerant of unions as their religious colleagues were of denominational rivals. Their interest in civic, social, and educational reform overshadowed these differences.

The movement for municipal reform sprang from varied conditions in the different cities. In some it was the low state of public morality as civic officials, at Philadelphia for example, distributed franchises for personal profit; in others, such as Minneapolis, it was the evidence of widespread debauchery; in still others it was the failure of the schools to answer the dual needs of the diversified population

---

[5] Marguerite Green, *The National Civic Federation and the American Labor Movement: 1900–1925*, Washington 1956, pp. 1–106; McKelvey, *Urbanization*, pp. 134–142. See also Robert H. Wiebe, *Businessmen and Reform: A Study of the Progressive Movement*, Campridge, Mass. 1962, pp. 16–41, 157–176, for a full discussion of the varied points of view of businessmen.

and an industrial technology. Tax-conscious business groups took the lead in Baltimore, anti-vice crusaders in Detroit, but everywhere they needed to rally wider support. That necessity brought an eager response when, in 1893, the Municipal League of Philadelphia, backed by the City Club of New York, invited reformers from other cities to attend a Conference on Good City Government at its headquarters. The delegates from twenty-nine similar organizations in a score of cities who gathered at that first conference promptly moved to organize the National Municipal League to promote their multiple causes.[6]

Reports of that conference in a friendly press spurred the organization of municipal leagues and varied reform clubs in cities across the land. Each annual conference enrolled new affiliates and broadened the debate over a Model Program, which the delegates finally drafted and approved at the meeting in Columbus, Ohio, in 1900. Incorporating much of the experience of preceding decades, it favoured a large measure of home rule but under state administrative supervision, a clear separation of powers betweeen the council and the mayor with the latter in full charge of administration and of appointments under a civil service board, percentage limitations on taxing and bonding powers and time limitation on franchises, and finally a secret ballot.

The logical merits of the Model Program won adherents in many places, but the vitality of the progressive movement sprang more directly from the work of a number of strong mayors. Seth Low in Brooklyn, Josiah Quincy in Boston, Sam Jones in Toledo, Hazen Pingree in Detroit achieved records in the nineties that inspired reformers in other cities. Improved methods of street paving, garbage disposal, fire fighting, and police supervision netted practical gains and promoted stable and efficient administrations. These achievements, coupled with a free hand in educational reform, satiated the zeal of the good government leaders in some cities, but in others, where the expanding empires of out-of-town monopolies were absorbing the local utilities, a new burst of vitality revived the movement. Leaders such as Tom Johnson in Cleveland, Louis D. Brandeis in Boston, and Henry George in New York helped to clarify the issue for local or state regulation of utility rates and services and supplied the progressive forces with a major legislative goal.[7]

The discovery by Lincoln Steffens and other journalists of the

[6] Frank M. Stewart, *A Half Century of Municipal Reform*, Berkeley 1950, pp. 1–49; McKelvey, *Urbanization*, 99–114; see Documents 20 and 22. See also Wiebe, pp. 16–23.

[7] Frederick C. Howe, *The Confessions of a Reformer*, New York 1925; Brand Whitlock, *Forty Years of It*, New York 1914; Richard S. Childs, *Civic Victories*, New York 1952; McKelvey, *Rochester*, III: 73–113; see Documents 22 and 23.

colourful and exciting drama behind these developments gave the movement added appeal in the early 1900s. The sensational accounts of urban corruption published by the muck-rakers in the leading magazines alerted many citizens who had been unmoved by the sober advocates of charter revisions. Their disclosures helped to set the stage for the adoption of electoral reforms such as the initiative, the referendum, and the secret ballot, and for the passage of regulatory measures in the fields of public health and public utilities. The leadership in each case came from a group of dedicated local reformers headed by such men as Joseph W. Folk in St Louis, Charles Evans Hughes in New York, and Judge Ben Lindsey in Denver who, after careful study of specific examples of corruption, were able to rally support for the adoption of state incentives for municipal programs. When state regulatory boards failed to meet all of their demands, the progressives moved to create federal bureaus and commissions to collect statistics, set standards, and restore a measure of competition as a democratic safeguard for the public welfare.[8]

The need for factual data and reliable statistics to support demands for reform had led to the formation of a number of local agencies for the collection of civic information. One of the first was the City Club of New York which participated, as we have seen, in the call for the first Conference on Good City Government late in 1893 and aggressively took the lead in organizing a score of good government clubs throughout the metropolis to support the cause. Yet the primary purpose of its founders, early in 1892, had been to undertake 'the study of honest, efficient municipal government;' and unlike many other reform groups, which specialized in forums and debates, it endeavored to maintain an information bureau and to assemble pertinent documents. Its president, James C. Carter, formerly a member of a commission named by Governor Tilden to recommend improvements for the government of cities, was the unanimous choice for president of the National Municipal League formed at Philadelphia in 1894; assisted by Clinton R. Woodruff of the Philadelphia league as secretary he supplied able leadership throughout its first decade.[9]

The City Club's practice of appointing citizen committees to investigate various subjects supplied a pattern for the national league and for many local leagues as well. But the relevant data were not always easily available and in some cases required the talents of expert investigators. Thus in 1906, when the Citizen's Union in New York, an outgrowth of its earlier reform efforts, experienced difficulty in uncovering the facts, its president R. Fulton Cutting created an

[8] Lincoln Steffens, *The Shame of the Cities*, New York 1904; Steffens, *Autobiography*, New York 1931; McKelvey, *Urbanization*, pp. 99–113.

[9] Steward, pp. 26–44, 147.

independent research bureau to compile the appropriate data for its reform campaigns. The Bureau of City Betterment, as it was originally called, was soon renamed the New York Bureau of Municipal Research and became the model for other bureaus established at Philadelphia, Cincinnati, and Chicago in the next two years, and in many other cities as the years advanced.[10]

The civic awakening also found expression in a revived interest in city planning. Inspired by the spectacular character of the Chicago World's Fair, which sent millions of Americans home with new and glamorous visions of a more pleasing urban environment, the new planners were caught up in a City Beautiful movement. An Architectural Club in Cleveland hastened to propose a civic centre for that city to be built around an artificial lagoon as at the White City. Charles M. Robinson of Rochester prepared Beaux-Arts designs for several cities. Daniel Burnham, chairman of the architects responsible for the Columbian Exposition, served after 1900 in a similar capacity on the new planning commission for the restoration of L'Enfant's design for the capital city at Washington, and several years later headed the much larger commission that prepared a master plan for Chicago. Civic minded groups in a dozen cities engaged planners to design civic centres and lay out street plans that stirred a flurry of excitement in many places. Unfortunately these paper plans, lacking a sound political and economic base, were soon relegated to the archives; almost their only contribution was to spur the revival of classical and renaissance architectural designs.[11]

The City Beautiful movement, like the Chicago Fair, turned its back on the new functional architecture of Louis Sullivan and the other designers of the early Chicago skyscrapers. No doubt the depression, by drying up the resources for such construction, was chiefly responsible for the decline of the new style, but when at the turn of the century a new crop of skyscrapers began to appear in every metropolis, their builders felt it necessary to adorn them with classical pillars and cornices or with Gothic arches and towers. A similar eclecticism characterized the façades of the new music halls, theatres and galleries that arose in a score of cities in the early 1900s, as a renewed burst of prosperity enabled their business and social leaders to establish the cultural institutions they had learned to admire on frequent trips abroad.

But if the American cities in the progressive era were ready to emulate and adopt in the best that European cities had to offer, both

[10] Norman N. Gill, *Municipal Research Bureaus*, Washington 1944; McKelvey, *Urbanization*, pp. 108–111.
[11] Tunnard & Reed, *American Skyline*, pp. 179–190; McKelvey, *Urbanization*, pp. 121–126.

in art and science and in municipal government, they were also, by absorbing a great host of newcomers, acquiring staggering problems of poverty and dislocation. Charity workers in Boston, troubled by the shortage of lodging rooms for working men, discovered that the inner city had a floating population in 1895 of 54,000 boarders, many more than its lodging house facilities could properly handle. A wider survey revealed that many cities faced similar problems, though only San Francisco rivalled Boston in the proportion of such lodgers to its total population. In Cleveland as well as Chicago, in Denver as well as New York, thousands of homeless detached males, drifting from one cheap rooming house to another and relying on the saloons for entertainment as well as food, represented an urban backwash from the successive waves of newcomers. Having failed to find a secure foothold in the promised land, they were contributing to the mounting problems of vice and crime, and by transforming sections of the inner city into a jungle they were promoting the exodus of former middle class residents to the suburbs. That movement, initiated by the earlier development of ethnic colonies in the older residential district, was threatening to abandon the central cores of the great metropolises to the poorest and most disadvantaged residents.[12]

Warnings of the development of slum areas were sounded in many places. New York and Boston had received earlier warnings, but few had heard them prior to the publication in 1890 of the vivid reports by Jacob A. Riis in his dramatic book *How the Other Half Lives*. An investigation of the slums of all cities over 200,000, ordered by Congress in 1892, was sharply abbreviated when the appropriation was cut from $150,000 to $20,000, and the Commissioner of Labor's findings on limited districts in the four metropolises investigated tended to minimize the danger except in New York and Boston. A succession of tenement house investigations in these cities, however, amply established the gravity of the problem, and the writings of Robert A. Woods, head of Andover House settlement in Boston, and of Lawrence Veiller, organizer and secretary of the New York Tenement House Commission in 1900, helped to demonstrate its expanding dimensions. These and other leaders in New York, Boston, and Philadelphia rallied the support of philanthropists who backed the efforts of the Association for the Improvement of the Conditions of the Poor in New York, the City & Suburban Homes Company, and other groups to build model apartments for the poor. A count in

[12] John Lloyd Thomas, 'Washington's Hotels,' *Municipal Affairs* (1899) III: 73–94; Albert B. Wolfe, *The Lodging House Problem in Boston*, Cambridge, Mass. 1913.

1910 found such accommodations for some 3,500 families in New York, more than in all other cities combined.[13]

But the achievements of philanthropic investors were insignificant when contrasted with the construction activity of the speculative builders. In recognition of this fact, Lawrence Veiller and his colleagues gave their major attention to an effort to upgrade and enforce tenement house standards. The improvements they incorporated in the New York Law of 1901 included the creation of a Tenement House Department, of which Veiller became the initial chief, and provided a pattern for adoption in other alert cities. Yet the enforcement even of limited standards of light, space, and other sanitary requirements proved difficult and raised questions in some quarters concerning the adequacy of the progressive's philosophy of regulatory reform. A few fleeting accounts of the Garden City movement, launched by Ebenezer Howard in England in the early 1900s, appeared in American journals, but the promising developments at Letchworth attracted less attention than the discouraging flaws revealed at Pullman, Gary, and other new industrial towns in America.[14]

The progressive's emphasis was on the reform and improvement of the American city and the broader society. The continued growth of cities large and small demonstrated their attractive power and justified the effort to make them more wholesome abodes. One proposal that attracted quick approval in many cities was the creation of playgrounds to take children off the streets, and although the cost of acquiring the necessary tracts retarded such developments in crowded districts where playgrounds were most needed, the movement gained momentum and reached eighty cities by 1910. As an upsurge of recreational activity backed that reform, so the deepening intensity of the social gospel movement promoted a renewed effort to draw the Protestant churches together for a united attack on the social problems of the cities. The formation of the Federal Council of Churches in 1908 and the endorsement it gave to the intensive social survey of Pittsburgh, conducted by Paul U. Kellogg for the newly formed Russell Sage Foundation, constituted a high point in the accomplishments of the progressive era and heralded the opening of a new and more analytical approach to the problems of the city.[15]

In short, the cities not only supplied the most compelling challenges to the progressive reformers but also engendered the most hopeful responses. The same polyglot populations that overcrowded and over-

[13] Jacob A. Riis, *How the Other Half Lives*, New York 1919 ed.
[14] Roy Lubove, *The Progressives and the Slums*, Pittsburgh 1962; R. W. DeForest and L. Veiller, eds., *The Tenement House Problem*, New York 1903.
[15] See Document 22.

burdened the aged districts of many large cities, creating harsh social conditions that fostered the development of corrupt politics, also supplied the inspiration and the vital energies for a rejuvenation of the entire urban community. Challenged by the desperate plight of their fellow citizens, as revealed by the hardships of the depression of the mid-nineties, business and professional leaders, churchmen and educators discovered and accepted new social responsibilities. The actual achievements of their housing reforms, their neighbourhood settlements, their institutional churches and evening schools, were modest compared with the extent of the urban needs, yet they created a sense of community involvement and gave a new direction to civic politics.

7

The Emergence of Metropolitan Regionalism: 1910-1920

Since the symbolic closing of the western frontier in 1890 is no longer regarded as a major turning point in American history, partly because of the continued formation after that date of new towns and cities in that region, the search persists for a development that will separate the middle and modern periods of the nation's history. It can perhaps be found in the emergence, during the second decade of the twentieth century, of a new metropolitan regionalism, which not only brought to fruition both the western migration of settlers and the planting of new towns and cities across the land, but also opened a new era of technological advance and civic challenge on the urban frontier. Migrations continued and in fact accelerated in number in the early teens, but they were no longer predominately east-west in direction. And while new towns broke into the census tables (400 reached 2,500 in the second decade) most of them arose on the outskirts of expanding metropolises. They represented, not potential trading centres for regional farmers, but satellite offshoots of industrial and commercial cities. And they posed, in conjunction with some 2,000 other suburban settlements, new civic and cultural dilemmas that have now become deeply meaningful in contemporary American life.

For the first time in its history, the nation's urban growth fell below 30 per cent for the decade, but this fact was overshadowed in significance by the changing character of that growth. Fortunately the census takers shared the increased urban awareness these changes brought and displayed it by a more careful definition of urban categories. In 1910 all places of 2,500 or more residents were classified as urban, and all places of 200,000 or more as metropolitan. By 1920, the census was ready to take a closer look at the rural population and to recognize that a startlingly large segment of it, two-fifths in fact, could properly be described as rural-nonfarm. These were residents of villages of less than 2,500 inhabitants, or of unincorporated suburban towns; and, 20 million in number, they were also potential recruits for the expanding metropolises on whose borders many in fact resided.[1]

As in the past, both the cities and their suburban fringes attracted many in-migrants who comprised more than half of their gains, but by the close of this decade the source of these newcomers had shifted. In place of the million or more immigrants absorbed annually in the early teens, the cities, with their foreign supplies partially blocked by the war, had to develop new sources in the Deep South and in the rural mountain areas. Again, the slower pace of the new influx was less significant than the changing character of the social adjustments it called for. The concluding scene in the dramatic relationship between the American city and successive waves of immigrants was yet to come, but already the migration of Negroes from the South was transferring the focus of attention from the city to the metropolis, for only that broader entity could encompass the reverberations their arrival created.[2]

The attractive power of the larger cities, which drew newcomers to their cores and scattered older residents into the suburbs, reflected a combination of economic forces that provided the chief incentive to metropolitan growth. All major rail lines had long since been completed and the principal trading centres and commercial metropolises had been identified, but a number of less favoured industrial cities, by exploiting regional resources and promoting the inventions and skills of their inhabitants, were also acquiring metropolitan status. By extending a network of inter-urban electric lines out to tap the trade and productive resources of neighbouring towns and farming regions, cities such as Indianapolis achieved unexpected growth and metropolitan character. But in this decade the cities that experienced the most rapid growth were those that specialized in the manufacture of automobiles, notably Detroit, or auto parts as at Akron and Youngstown in Ohio, or motor fuels as at Los Angeles, Dallas, and Houston —all among the top eight in rates of growth. These and other city-building industries, including iron and steel fabrications as at Chicago, Milwaukee and Buffalo, and electrical appliances as at Schenectady and Cleveland, also encouraged a diffusion of plants into industrial satellites located within easy reach of the metropolitan district's core city.[3]

Generally the boards of trade or chambers of commerce of the

[1] *U.S. Census* (1920), 1:50, 53, 64–75; Warren S. Thompson and P. K. Whelpton, *Population Trends in the U.S.*, New York 1933.

[2] Blake McKelvey, *The Emergence of Metropolitan America, 1915–1966*, New Brunswick, N.J. 1968, pp. 15–23; Niles Carpenter, *Immigrants and their Children*, U.S. Census Monograph VII 1927, pp. 158–168, 205–209, 385–397.

[3] McKelvey, *Urbanization*, pp. 239–242; McKelvey, *Metropolitan America*, pp. 4–9.

central cities drew a sufficient number of the business leaders of neighbouring towns into their programs and deliberations to achieve a sense of metropolitan community in the economic field. Most of the major cities had by 1910 achieved a measure of economic integration in the utility fields, with one transit company, one gas and electric company, one telephone company serving the entire metropolitan district or sharing it with one or more rivals that were seldom genuine competitors. The public service commissions and other regulatory devices promoted by progressive leaders in city and state assemblies afforded some protection from monopoly practices but still required extensive refinements.

The major concern of urban progressives in the early teens, however, was for the development of a more adequate banking system. Protests against the necessity of clearing loans and other transactions in the central banks of New York had been heard for decades among the leading bankers of many cities, and the grant of some central banking powers to Chicago and St Louis had only moderated the complaints. The development of local clearing houses had supplied local accommodations and a measure of control in 140 cities by 1910, but the voluntary character of their operations made the issuing of loan certificates in times of financial stress, as in 1908, most precarious. Widespread demands for a revision of the banking system finally prodded Congress to adopt the Federal Reserve System. The new plan, by creating twelve central reserve districts, answered the demand for a wider distribution of banking control but stirred an intense rivalry among the varied contenders for district leadership. New York, Philadelphia, Boston, Chicago, St Louis and San Francisco were obvious choices, but Richmond, Atlanta and Dallas in the South and Cleveland, Minneapolis and Kansas City in the Middle West, each faced jealous and powerful rivals. Some were appeased when designated as branch headquarters, and the clearing houses in others, notably Baltimore, assumed larger powers. Investment brokers in Pittsburgh, Detroit, Los Angeles and a score of other cities established independent stock exchanges to accommodate their industrialists and assure their regional leadership.[4]

Other economic trends contributed to the growth of metropolitan regions. Although many labour groups had by 1910 developed stable national unions, in practice the local labour market retained priority; in the teens, however, with the extension of daily transit facilities into the suburbs, the labour market acquired metropolitan dimensions. Central trades councils welcomed the participation of locals from

[4] Laurence Laughlin, *The Federal Reserve Act, Its Origin and Problems* New York 1933; Henry P. Willis, *The Federal Reserve System*, New York 1923; McKelvey, *Urbanization*, pp. 246–251.

industrial suburbs and included them in their promotional coverage with such success that trade union membership more than doubled during the decade. Labour-day parades in the central city and labour picnics at area parks enhanced the sense of belonging to a broad metropolitan community. Moreover, the advantages to be derived by management from skills shared by a large labour force, and from informational pools among the executives, fostered the development of specialties in several metropolitan centres, such as brewing at Milwaukee, photography at Rochester, insurance at Omaha and Hartford, and both men's and women's shoes in the greater Boston area.

These were examples of internal economic development, but distant commercial decisions and general technological advances likewise supported the metropolitan trend. Thus rapid developments in mechanical refrigeration after 1912 brought new methods of processing and preserving foods and greatly expanded the dimension of practicable milk basins and fresh-vegetable market areas. And in 1914, when improvements in electric typewriters permitted, the Associated Press chose eight cities as press depots and installed the new teletype machines to make them regional information centres. Most cities of any size became information centres for adjoining regions, however, as their more aggressive dailies absorbed weaker rivals and, with the development of photographic printing, distributed weekly rotogravure editions into the suburbs to capture wider attention for their advertisers and newscasters. Washington became a news centre in still another sense, partly as a result of the increased activity of the new administrative bureaus established by the progressives, but more dramatically because of the leadership functions it assumed with the outbreak of the first World War.[5]

America's entry into the war created a demand for military supplies that revived the economy of many cities and fostered the development of metropolitan districts. When the Ordinance Depot, overwhelmed by the task of distributing a long list of contracts among a host of competing firms, received an offer from a group of business leaders in Cleveland to coordinate the capacities of small and large companies in that area in order to permit them to make joint bids for large orders, a Regional War Industries Board was set up there under the chairmanship of Charles A. Otis. His success soon made it a model for similar boards in nineteen later twenty-one ordinance districts, each centred around an industrial metropolis whose business leaders assumed the task of integrating the productive capacities of the entire district. Impressed by the efficiency of the regional system, other wartime agencies—the food and fuel administrators as well as the scrap-

[5] H. H. McCarty, *Industrial Migration in the United States: 1914–1927*, Iowa City 1930, pp. 65–76; McKelvey, *Urbanization*, pp. 231–246.

metal and war-bond directors—adopted similar decentralization schemes and took advantage of the inter-metropolitan rivalries that resulted.[6]

The patriotism engendered by the war found its greatest outlet in volunteer efforts, and these proved especially adapted to the metropolitan setting. Whereas rival civic authorities hesitated to assume responsibilities beyond their borders, private welfare agencies and other volunteer bodies readily expanded their commitments. Thus pleas for relief funds for the Belgians, the British, and other allies spurred on the organization in several metropolises of combined war-relief drives and brought a fusion of these efforts with other charitable drives into community-wide war chests that grew into permanent Community Chests after the war. In similar fashion the Chambers of Commerce and other central-city organizations, especially the civic clubs, broadened their membership base and assumed larger tasks. The chambers, for example, promoted Americanization programs for immigrants in many cities and established employment agencies in a few places to direct enemy aliens into non-sensitive urban jobs or rural employment. These volunteer bodies readily surmounted civic boundaries and helped to draw the entire metropolitan district into one cooperating community.

But the war had in some respects an opposite effect. By checking the influx of immigrants it created labour shortages in some cities that prompted industrialists to look to the South for unskilled workers. A sizable migration of Negroes resulted, bringing tens of thousands north to staff the heavy industries of Chicago, St Louis, Pittsburgh, and Philadelphia, among other cities. As these newcomers sought cheap accommodation in the old central districts, they inevitably crowded the poor residents there, generally the latest group of immigrants, and stirred hostilities that culminated in a series of race riots at East St Louis, Chicago, and elsewhere.[7] These outbreaks hastened the migration of inner-city residents to the suburbs and heightened the contrasts between the decaying slums of the old central cities and their more salubrious suburbs.

Such contrasts invited study and inspired efforts both to ameliorate their effects and to eradicate their causes. A number of social surveys, patterned after that of Pittsburgh, endeavoured to delineate the problem areas and to describe conditions in a score of cities ranging from Springfield, Illinois, to Cleveland, Ohio. A group of social scientists,

---

[6] Charles A. Otis, *Here I Am*, Cleveland 1951, pp. 122–123, 162; McKelvey, *Metropolitan America*, pp. 23–27.

[7] Elliott M. Rudwick, *Race Riot in East St. Louis, July 2, 1917*, Carbondale, Ill. 1964; Chicago Commission on Race Relations, *The Negro in Chicago: A Study of Race Relations and a Race Riot*, Chicago 1922.

F

headed by Robert E. Park at the University of Chicago, commenced a more objective study of the city as embodied in that metropolis. The directors and residents at a number of settlement houses cooperated with other melioristic bodies in an endeavour to salvage and restore the human values of depressed neighbourhoods. Indeed, in addition to the emerging concept of the metropolis that dominated the teens, a fresh interest in neighbourhoods characterized the period. The social centre movement, born a few years before at Rochester, inspired Clarence Perry and others to promote a wider use of the schools as centres for adult as well as adolescent neighbourhood life and prompted an effort at Cincinnati to reorganize all welfare services on the neighbourhood unit level.[8]

Although most of these efforts were swept aside by the hostilities engendered by the war and by the mounting racial strife, they made a significant contribution to early housing and planning leaders. These again were chiefly volunteer in character as alert citizen groups in a dozen places launched non-profit housing projects to supply homes for working-men. The influence of the social centre movement was evident in the neighbourhood design of several of these projects, and in those the federal government, under the pressure of war, launched as wartime housing at several shipbuilding ports and other key production centres. Frederick Law Olmsted, Jr, and the other planners who participated as dollar-a-year men in that wartime effort were also inspired by the Garden City movement in England, but most of the assignments they received in these years from official city planning commissions called for the preparation of street maps and plans for the location of civic centres and other public facilities, including intown parks and playgrounds. In a few cases, however, volunteer groups, such as the Greater Dayton Association, engaged planners to draft wider metropolitan plans. Thus Cleveland, after some difficulty, secured the passage of a special law creating a metropolitan park commission to plan its regional park and related highway developments.[9]

The urgent needs of New York and the other great metropolises for water works, sewers, and port developments had prompted the creation in earlier years of a dozen special authorities. Since these state-appointed bodies had taxing and operational powers independent of the elected officials, they seldom retained the full endorsement of the more progressive mayors. Yet although John P. Mitchell of New

[8] Maurice R. Stein, *The Eclipse of Community: An Interpretation of American Studies*, Princeton 1960, pp. 13–31; McKelvey, *Metropolitan America*, pp. 27–30.

[9] Clarence A. Perry, *Housing for the Machine Age*, New York 1939; McKelvey, *Urbanization*, pp. 253–267; McKelvey, *Metropolitan America*, pp. 9–15.

York, Rudolph Blankenburg of Philadelphia, and Newton D. Baker of Cleveland each supplied civic leadership for a term or two as mayor, none was able to influence developments in the suburbs. And the traditional practice of expansion by annexation was now blocked as the mushrooming suburbs developed independent facilities as well as exclusive qualities and moved to safeguard their privileges. Civic reformers such as Richard S. Childs, long an advocate of home rule and the short ballot, had no ready solution. With many other urban reformers, Childs shifted into Federal service during the war but hastened, after its conclusion, to resume the attack on local civic problems. The National Municipal League, which had struggled valiantly to maintain its activities during the war, now enjoyed a revival and called for a review of its model civic program[10]

Although the war had diverted and absorbed the energies of some urban progressives and disillusioned others, it had also given additional purpose to local bodies such as bureaus of municipal research which increased in number and in technical proficiency. The detailed and objective character of their reports helped to dispel the emotional quality of the reformers and to cast their efforts in a more practical light. They developed methods of measuring and describing the traffic problem, the smoke nuisance, and other municipal problems that now commanded attention, and if their solutions were often tentative they at least avoided controversy. One example of the new approach was the adoption of the first comprehensive zoning ordinance in New York City, in 1915. Its bold attempt to prescribe height, area, and use standards attracted keen interest in other cities and prompted the National Municipal League to devote a full session two years later to this problem.[11]

National conferences had in fact become the favourite means for communication and promotion in the civic field. Both the planners and the housing reformers had by 1910 organized national associations to conduct annual conferences. A new category of urban executives, the city managers, hired by the city councils to manage their governments, held the first national Conference of City Managers at Springfield, Ohio, in 1914; the secretaries of the leading City Clubs and research bureaus organized a Civic Secretary's Association for the same purpose in 1917.

The oft expressed hopes of these men was the eventual triumph of their programs through democratic processes. The fact that residents of cities finally outnumbered the nation's rural inhabitants,

---

[10] Richard S. Childs, *Civic Victories*, New York 1952.
[11] S. J. Makielski, Jr., *The politics of Zoning*, New York 1966; Gill, *Research Bureaus*, pp. 12–29; McKelvey, *Metropolotan America*, pp. 11–13.

in the late teens, lent support to this view, but observant urbanites could not help remarking that, although rural majorities had disappeared in thirteen states by 1910 and in three more by 1920, the legislative apportionment of their state bodies gave rural representatives a clear majority in all but the state of Rhode Island.[12]

This, however, was regarded as an example of cultural lag and called for a vigorous reappraisal of metropolitan culture. Fortunately no artificial boundaries limited the expansive opportunities for urban cultural expression. Moreover the natural disagreements that persisted on both high and low levels merely emphasized the community's metropolitan diversity. Volunteer associations established and maintained at least one art gallery or science museum in every city of 200,000 and in some of smaller size; several metropolises boasted two or more exhibit halls and private galleries catering to groups and individuals with varied tastes. The range of standards was even greater in the field of music, where a dozen metropolises supported symphony orchestras and scheduled annual opera seasons at the same time that they and their lesser rivals harboured music and dance halls of a more popular character where the new jazz bands vied with the more traditional entertainers for public favour. The freedom of choice for both auditors and performers in this field was characteristic of the options the great metropolises afforded in many lines—in entertainment where several legitimate theatres competed with variety houses and the new cinemas for patronage; in the sports arena where professional teams vied for fans with the amateurs and with a miscellaneous group of participation programs; and in the field of print where public and private libraries, serving every city over 50,000, supplied unprecedented opportunities to readers who were also served as never before by a voluminous daily press and a varied assortment of weekly and monthly magazines. No resident of any of the major metropolises could experience and savour all of its potentialities, but few could escape a sense of involvement and participation in a large and dramatic community. Many shared an identity with the ball team, the orchestra, the ragtime band, or some other aspect of metropolitan culture that they had never known in earlier and more constricted settings. At least in the cultural fields a new metropolitan regionalism was confidently emerging.[13]

Thus the cities, responding to their new technological facilities and to current historic challenges, were developing a new societal pattern of profound significance for the nation at large. Not only had the automobile, the telephone, and the metropolitan daily finally breached

---

[12] H. D. Hamilton, *Legislative Apportionment: Key to Power*, New York 1964.
[13] McKelvey, *Urbanization*, 268–285.

old municipal boundaries to create broader areas of day-to-day activity and communication, but changing economic and demographic trends had also presented the emerging regional communities with fresh problems and opportunities that posed the basic dilemmas for the next half century of the nation's growth.

8

The Metropolis in Prosperity and Depression: 1920-1940

The prospects of metropolitan regionalism appeared bright in the early twenties, partly because of the regressive mood of the federal and state governments. Washington's haste in surrendering its war powers and liquidating its commitments at home as well as abroad inspired similar restraints at the state capitals. Yet the economy, though briefly checked by the change of pace, quickly recovered and enjoyed several years of technological development and material expansion. Based as it was on a decentralized urban industrial and commercial system, the nation's prosperity enhanced the regional character of that system and gave increased vitality to its metropolitan centres. Many cities experienced a dramatic growth in population and a diversification of functions, but their attempts to acquire adequate powers and commensurate jurisdictions were repulsed by the rural-dominated state legislatures. And when, at the close of the decade, the uncontrolled economic boom exploded, the cities, after heroic efforts to avert a collapse, turned in desperation to the federal government for aid in combating the depression. In that long drawn out struggle, the cities, bypassing the states, forged a new relationship with Washington that would have a profound effect on the history of America.

Americans first exceeded 100 million in number during the late teens, yet their gains of that decade, though sharply curtailed by the war, had occurred chiefly in the cities, which now comprised well over half the total. The cities continued to absorb the major portion of the slightly renewed growth of the twenties. Indeed they attracted most of the resurgent influx of immigrants, who jumped from a low of 110,000 in 1918 to 805,000 in 1921 when Italy alone sent 222,000 to the American shores. The flood of newcomers coincided with an outbreak of labour agitation that created a Red scare and enabled a group of nativists of rural background or orientation to press successfully for the passage of an exclusionist act, which sharply reduced the influx the next year and set the stage for the adoption in 1924 of a quota system designed to maintain the existing ethnic character of the population.[1]

The new act effectively reduced the flood of immigrants but failed to curb the growth of cities. As the migration from Southern and Eastern Europe declined in the late twenties, the demand for unskilled labour from the rural South increased. Over 600,000 southern Negroes moved to northern and western cities during the twenties. Not only did the Black Belt in Chicago extend southward to the border of Woodlawn near the University, but its residents, who numbered 234,000 by 1930, comprised the second largest Negro settlement in the world and exerted a powerful voice in the city's politics. Only Harlem in New York outranked it in size and, as the Negro's cultural capital, in influence, attracting the top-flight jazz bands and the leading Negro dancers, artists, and writers as well as their outstanding sportsmen and churchmen. A dozen other industrial cities of the North, scattered from Hartford to St Louis, acquired sizable colonies of Negroes, while several southern cities, including Durham and Memphis, based their economic growth in large part on Negro labour. The Negro colonies of Baltimore, Washington, and New Orleans as well as of Philadelphia and Cincinnati, each with its influential editors, educators, and clergymen, vied with those of New York and Chicago in sophistication. In some industrial cities on the other hand, notably at Detroit, the influx of Negroes was so rapid that the competition for housing and other accommodations became acute and erupted in violence. The Detroit riots of September 1925 prompted the organization there, and in a score of other cities both north and south, of interracial committees that endeavoured to assure Negro residents separate but equal accommodations.[2]

Innovations and accommodations became more feasible as the rate of urban growth accelerated. Except for Detroit, all the most rapidly growing cities of the twenties displayed new bursts of vitality and together they decisively outraced the front runners of the teens. Miami with a 234 per cent increase and Los Angeles with 133 per cent not only broke all growth records for cities of their size during the previous half century, but captured first and second place because of their attractions as resort towns. No longer would industrial or commercial functions alone sustain a growing city, and even such specialized industrial centres as Pittsburgh and Milwaukee improved their metro-

---

[1] John Highan, *Strangers in the Land*, New Brunswick, N.J. 1955, pp. 264-330; McKelvey, *Metropolitan America*, pp. 37–39.

[2] Rupert B. Vance, *All These People: The Nation's Human Resources in the South*, Chapel Hill 1945, pp. 119–123; Gilbert Osofsky, *Harlem: The Making of a Ghetto: Negro New York 1890–1930*, New York 1965, pp. 105-158; McKelvey, *Metroplitan America*, pp. 38–40, 68–70.

politan vitality by diversifying their economic functions. They were impatient as a result to tackle some of the civic and social problems of the emerging metropolitan regions, but the rural-dominated legislatures blocked the way.

In every aspect of post-war reconstruction, leadership came from one metropolis or another. When President Wilson called a conference of governors and mayors at the White House in 1919 to consider the threat of widespread unemployment following the war, Pittsburgh alone was ready with a $13,870,000 budget for improvements. A main feature of its plan was smoke abatement, and the success it attained soon spurred Chicago and a half dozen other cities to launch similar efforts. By far the most troublesome problem confronting all cities in the post-war decade was the mounting flood of automobiles as their national production jumped from less than a million cars in 1918 to over four million five years later. Again it was the leading metropolises that supplied the innovations—the first system of traffic lights at Cleveland, the first parking courts at Chicago, the first shopping centres with facilities to park at Kansas City, and a network of divided highways at Detroit. Each successful innovation was quickly adopted in other metropolises and swelled their mounting outlays to unprecedented heights. In Detroit, where the city purchased the transit system in 1921 in order to assure its continued operation with 5 cent fares as a check on the excessive use of automobiles, concern lest the city's mounting debt would weaken its fiscal position prompted the local Bureau of Government Research to undertake a probing study, from which it concluded that the *per capita* debt and expenditures were in fact declining in the early twenties and justified large and rapid outlays on the city's proposed highway system.[3]

Highway improvements that stopped at the city line had a limited value, and the search for wider planning powers commenced in a dozen metropolises in the early twenties. Boston's metropolitan park developments and a few other metropolitan special-function authorities had previously pointed the way, but the first full scale regional planning effort was that sponsored by the Russell Sage Foundation for New York in 1922. The appointment of Thomas Adams, a regional planner from England, as director assured a wide interest, and the early progress reports of the New York Regional Plan spurred similar efforts within the next few years at Philadelphia, Chicago, Los Angeles and several other expanding metropolises. Landscape architects and planners collaborated with interested officials in drafting model plans for highway, park, and other public improvements extending throughout broad metropolitan regions. Unfortunately, as Professor Thomas H. Reed, a student of European practices, pointed

[3] McKelvey, pp. 45–55.

out, these volunteer bodies lacked not only the authority to make binding plans but also the power to launch improvements. At the request of a group of civic leaders in Pittsburgh, Reed drafted a charter for a federated city government for the Greater Pittsburgh area only to see it so mangled by the state legislature that a rural minority was able to defeat it at the polls. A similar bid by Cleveland for broader metropolitan government was likewise blocked by the rural-dominated legislature, prompting the leaders of several other expansive core cities to abandon the effort.[4]

Legislative restraints had little or no effect in the voluntary fields, and here the surging advance of metropolitan regions was most clearly evident. Most of the major central cities opened palatial new museums (forty-one in all during the 1920s) or expanded old ones; many erected new central libraries and established numerous branches in buildings donated by philanthropic citizens. Other residents, acting individually or as backers of cultural organizations, gave concert halls and in a score of cities supported symphony orchestras. In New York and a few other major metropolises, the officials of the central cities, recognizing the value of these cultural activities, began to make modest contributions to their maintenance. Practically all maintained public libraries and over a hundred established and supported junior colleges Most of these cultural institutions served and received support from the broader metropolitan area, and the pride and gratification that suburban as well as central-city residents shared in their activities was frequently demonstrated as inter-urban transit companies scheduled special trains to accommodate interested patrons. The same transit facilities often operated on a reverse route to carry central-city residents out to resort parks and other rustic retreats within the recreational province that surrounded each metropolis. The erection of radio sending stations in each major city and the pattern of distribution of its leading dailies bound the scattered residents of these broad districts more firmly into metropolitan communities.[5]

As the outward extension of metropolitan communities inncreased, the differences separating specific neighbourhoods were often accentuated. City planners and other officials, who had begun in the teens to recognize the need of every neighbourhood for park and playground facilities as well as schools, now discovered the more critical housing deficiencies of some neighbourhoods and began to debate the problems

---

[4] Roy Lubove, *Community Planning in the 1920's: The Contributions of the Regional Planning Association of America*, Pittsburgh 1964; Forbes B. Hays, *Community Leadership: The Regional Plan Association of New York*, New York 1965; McKelvey, pp. 45–46, 59–63. See also Document 28.

[5] Harold E. Stearns, ed., *Civilization in the United States*, New York 1922; McKelvey, pp. 63–68, 72–75.

of the slums. Pittsburgh, which in 1924 adopted a master plan calling for the provision of neighbourhood playgrounds within a fifteen-minute walk of every child, extended it five years later to include the entire metropolitan area; it was also one of the first cities to give public assistance to home construction. Milwaukee joined forces with its country to finance home construction for workers in the mid-twenties, yet several other cities that relied on philanthropic efforts in this field achieved larger results. Cincinnati and St Louis, as well as Boston, Philadelphia and New York, each saw the construction of projects of a hundred or more dwellings on vacant or cleared plots within the central core, and these, with several other cities, planned the development of new suburban communities for the more affluent families. Perhaps the most influential was the Country Club District laid out by J. C. Nichols at Kansas City in the mid-twenties with a golf course, shopping centres, and gas stations all properly provided for. But the most creative was the suburban subdivision of Radburn, New Jersey, designed by Clarence Stein and Henry Wright to supply each house a park setting and to eliminate the necessity for pedestrian street crossings.[6]

An older and more striking urban design, that of the steel-girdered skyscraper, had now become the charcteristic symbol of the great city. No aspiring metropolis was content without several of these towering structures to mark its business centre. Approximately half the 4,778 buildings of ten or more stories in 1929 were located in New York City, but thirty other places each boasted twenty or more such structures, and forty more had at least four, while Chicago, with 384 over ten and 65 over twenty stories, presented a skyline that appeared to rival that of Manhattan.

Yet the skyscraper was already proving as revolutionary in its impact as the automobile. The congestion created in the streets at its base could best be handled by rapid transit lines, but since only New York and three or four other metropolises supplied such facil-ities, other cities, which endeavoured to move the occupants of a dozen or more skyscrapers back and forth on trolleys, buses, and private cars, soon found their downtown streets jammed with traffic and the districts pockmarked with parking lots. Adjoining property owners, overshadowed and blighted by their towering neighbours, demolished many once handsome structures with the hope of finding backing for new towers of their own. By 1929, so many were tearing down and rebuilding that investors in one city after another felt over-committed, and, when the bankers became alarmed on this and other

[6] Lubove, pp. 31–44, 77–79; Clarence Stein, *Toward New Towns for America*, Liverpool 1951, pp. 12–69; McKelvey, pp. 44–48.

grounds, the bottom dropped out of the stock market and construction came to a grinding halt.

The stockmarket crash in October 1929 was only one of several insistent problems that demanded the attention of urban leaders that year. Many reformers were frustrated when the efforts of Pittsburgh, Cleveland, and a few other cities to federate with their suburbs were blocked (as we have seen) by their legislatures, and when similar bids for metropolitan planning authorities were sharply limited in scope in Chicago, Milwaukee, and elsewhere. State after state rejected the renewed pleas of their large cities for a reapportionment of the legislative seats to grant them an equitable representation.

The only course open to the distraught municipal leaders appeared to be a more persuasive approach to the court of public opinion, and to achieve it they redoubled their efforts to maintain effective national bodies. The government research bureaus and similar groups clubbed together in 1927 to maintain a Municipal Administrative Service in New York as a clearing house for information on cities. The National Municipal League, which collaborated in that effort and regularly gave a session or two at its annual conventions to the Government Research Conference, also cooperated with the International City Managers Association in promoting the spread of the council-manager form. The adoption of this plan by Cincinnati in 1924 and by Kansas City and Rochester a year later gave added prestige to the movement for the professionalization of urban government. In the great metropolises on the other hand, where reformers tended to rely on political action, the favoured plan was a strong mayor system, and Cleveland soon returned to this pattern. Some mayors such as Daniel W. Hoan of Milwaukee, Murray Seasongood of Cincinnati, and Frank Murphy of Detroit were able, despite weak charter provisions, to offer effective leadership.[7]

Though unrelated to their normal civic responsibilities, the stock market crash quickly involved all municipal leaders in grave new problems. Many cities had difficulty marketing bonds, and as investors withheld their funds public works and private enterprise were curtailed, abolishing thousands of jobs. As the number of unemployed increased, several of the more dynamic metropolises responded with self-confidence. Cincinnati, recently awakened to its civic responsibilities by a reform movement, had, that spring, adopted a plan to stabilize employment, and its citizen committees tackled the situation with vigour. Detroit, Boston, and several other cities also responded to the challenge by launching new public works projects, redoubling their charitable drives, and upgrading their job training

[7] McKelvey, pp. 56-60; Norman N. Gill, *Municipal Research Bureaus*, Washington 1944.

and placement facilities. But when, despite these efforts, unemployment continued to mount, Clarence A. Dykstra, city manager of Cincinnati, won support at the International City Manager's Convention in 1931 for a petition sent to Washington requesting federal funds for public works.[8]

The mayors of fity-eight cities attached their names to a similar plea that year for $1 billion for public works. President Hoover, conscious of the limited extent of federal responsibility in this field, persuaded the National Association of Community Chests to stage a unified drive by its affiliated and cooperating agencies, but the $85 million pledged that autumn soon proved hopelessly inadequate to meet the needs of the 385 cities and towns that participated. Forced by Detroit bankers to cut that city's outlays for improvements in 1932 from $18 million to $400,000, Mayor Murphy assembled the mayors of a score of cities at Detroit where they drafted an appeal to Washington for a $5 billion construction program. Hoover responded by approving the creation of the Reconstruction Finance Corporation and the Home Loan Banking Act, which promised a moderate flow of credit to self-liquidating projects but failed to relieve the crisis.

Overwhelmed by the size of their relief loads and frustrated by the retrenchments enforced by their bankers, twenty-three large cities voted Democratic for the first time in sixteen years and gave Roosevelt enough support to insure his election. This was not an idle switch, for the mayors of fifty cities gathered at Washington the next February to form the U.S. Conference of Mayors and to press their demands on the President and Congress. They had no official ties with the federal authorities, but their pleas speeded the passage of the National Industrial Recovery Act with its appropriation of $3.3 billion for public works and housing, and they hastened home to prepare applications for a share of these funds.[9]

The U.S. Conference of Mayors was only one of several pressure groups organized at Washington that year, but Paul V. Betters, its executive director, was soon so actively involved in pressing for new emergency relief funds, a new banking act to liberalize the flow of credit, and new subsidies of urban housing, that he could look back a few years later and declare that '1932 marked the beginning of a new era of federal-city relationships'. Several categories of urban social workers contributed to this development. Harry Hopkins and Frances Perkins from New York were influential within the administration, as Senator Robert F. Wagner was in Congress, but none played a more significant role than Fiorello H. LaGuardia who, as Mayor of

---

[8] McKelvey, pp. 77–82. See also Document 29.
[9] E. E. Robinson, *The Presidential Vote: 1896–1932*, Stanford 1934; McKelvey, pp. 82–89. See Document 30.

New York, was elected president of the Conference of Mayors in 1934 and for the rest of the decade led its delegations on frequent junkets to Washington where they helped in many ways to shape the course of the New Deal. Among the more significant innovations were the Resettlement Administration, which undertook the development of three Greenbelt towns, the Civil Aeronautics Authority, which promoted the improvement of municipal airports, and the various white-collar projects that supported unemployed artists and other representatives of urban culture.[10]

But the most significant new development was the federal housing program. Mrs Mary Simkhovitch, a New York social worker and friend of Mrs Roosevelt, had persuaded Senator Wagner in 1933 to include housing among the public works authorized under the NIRA. And two years later, backed by the petitions of numerous citizen housing associations as well as of the Conference of Mayors and supported by the evidence compiled by the real property inventories made in sixty-four cities under WPA grants, she again prodded Wagner to introduce a bill, which in 1937 became the first National Housing Act. The appropriation, cut in half at the last moment, provided $500 million to finance the construction of housing projects in cities equipped with the proper authorities and ready to meet federal standards. By August 1938 the U.S. Housing Authority had negotiated contracts with twenty-eight cities for the construction of over 30,000 dwelling units; in the next four months it approved similar projects in a hundred other cities, slightly exceeding its authorized expenditures. Again the Better Housing Associations and other bodies in a score of cities, backed by the National Association of Housing Officials, petitioned Congress for additional housing funds.[11]

The situation, however, had changed by the late thirties. Many who had been eager for federal intervention a few years before had become frustrated by the bureaucratic controls and delays, which that course involved, and some were turning with renewed hope to local and volunteer efforts. The establishment in 1938 of a joint headquarters at Chicago of a dozen national civic organizations increased their effectiveness and facilitated their collaboration in the publication of annual Municipal Year Books. Profiting by their improved knowledge of urban practices elsewhere, many cities introduced more efficient procedures and a few followed the lead of New York in adopting a sales tax to increase their revenues. The regional planning associations formed by several metropolises in the twenties

[10] Charles Garrett, *The LaGuardia Years*, New Brunswick, N.J., 1961, pp. 178–187; McKelvey, pp. 89–92.

[11] Edith E. Wood, *Slums and Blighted Areas in the United States*, Washington 1935; McKelvey, pp. 87–89, 95–98.

endeavoured to implement their reports, and the leaders in several expansive cities, notably Cleveland and Louisville, made renewed efforts to achieve a merger of their city and county governments, only to be rebuffed again by rural-dominated state legislatures. One course remained open, the reform of county government, particularly in metropolitan counties. Milwaukee's achievements in this respect prompted the National Municipal Association to devote several sessions to this subject during the mid-thirties and assured wide publicity for the successful 'streamlining' of metropolitan functions at Los Angeles County in 1938.[12]

Yet the resurgent metropolises, if somewhat more wary of federal control, were eager to secure a fuller share of its support. The federal subsidies for the airmail program had chiefly benefited the cities, but the exclusion of airports from its subsidies seemed unfortunate and was finally corrected as a result of united urban pressure in 1938. When the urban vote, particularly in states with large metropolises, increased the power of the New Dealers in 1936 and 1938, Congress finally directed that a portion of the federal highway funds should be spent to rebuild the streets that carried them through the cities. The cities had previously received some federal aid for street improvements under the Works Progress Administration, and many had erected new libraries, museums, concert halls, and sports arenas, as well as school buildings, with the aid of WPA funds. Some had extensively improved their parks and playgrounds and a few had built swimming pools and marinas and improved their beaches and golf courses. This federal assistance, given to provide jobs and restore the economy, had developed a new relationship between the cities and the federal government which the slow process of economic recovery helped to prolong.[13]

It was therefore not surprising that the first volume produced by the President's National Resources Committee in 1937 was a summary report on *Our Cities: Their Role in the National Economy*. Several of the contributors to that volume were enrolled from the University of Chicago where the most extensive study of the city was in progress. In contrast with the internal sociological analysis fostered under the leadership of Burgess and others in Chicago, several scholars in other centres were exploring the broader metropolitan character and the historic processes of America's urban development. A few men, notably Lewis Mumford, were debating the future course of city growth, and although many planners agreed with his plea for autonomous

[12] Hays, pp. 1–31; McKelvey, pp. 98–104.
[13] Roscoe C. Martin, *The Cities and the Federal System*, New York 1965, pp. 83–92; McKelvey, pp. 105–108.

regionalism, many urban officials were now convinced of their continued need for a wide variety of federal grants-in-aid.[14]

Thus the emergent metropolises, frustrated in their efforts to achieve regional polity, turned to Washington for leadership. Whether or not they would have been successful in combating a world-wide depression, if authorized to call upon the full energies of their metropolitan regions, the refusal of the states to grant such powers left the core cities in a desperate situation. When, as in the case of Detroit and a few other cities, forthright efforts to meet the challenge only deepened the crisis, a number of hard-pressed mayors assumed the lead in pressing for national relief. And since the novelty of the new relationship tended to moderate the federal appropriations and thus to prolong their application, the new federal-city alliance, bypassing the states, acquired a firm hold in practice and a solid basis in national politics, as the third-term election of President Roosevelt demonstrated.

[14] National Resources Committee, *Our Cities: Their Role in the National Economy*, Washington 1937, pp. 108–117.

9

The Metropolis in War and Peace: 1940-1960

In some respects World War II, like its predecessor, interrupted the metropolitan movement; in others it intensified these developments. Key urban leaders, such as New York's Mayor LaGuardia, were drawn into the war effort, in his case as Director of the Office of Civilian Defense where he coordinated federal and urban programs. Several long-stagnant cities, revitalized by war contracts, experienced new housing and labour shortages and received unexpected aid from the national authorities. Sanctioned by the surge of patriotism, planning acquired a new respectability, but the wide-spreading impact of the housing shortage and other urban problems soon revealed the limited power and scope of city planning and renewed the pressure for joint metropolitan and national action.

In contrast with the twenties, when the federal government had hastened to relinquish its war powers and to abandon its urban projects, the post-war problems of the middle and late forties drew the federal and municipal authorities into closer collaboration. Thus in 1947, when Congress authorized the funding of a national network of highways to be constructed by the states, it specifically designated a sizable portion of the huge appropriation for urban highways. Airports were even more clearly city institutions, and the Civil Aeronautics Act of 1946 authorized direct payments of grants-in-aid to municipal authorites that complied with federal standards in the maintenance of airports. President Truman assured his urban backers, that year, that Congress would also soon provide grants-in-aid for the proper equipment of hospitals and health centres, as well as to combat water pollution and slums. And while the funds actually appropriated were, in most cases, minimal, they at least broadened the scope of city-federal relations and prepared the way for the adoption of more generous funding measures in the early fifties.[1]

[1] Martin, *Cities and the Federal System*, pp. 83–121; McKelvey, *Metropolitan America*, pp. 127–131, 141–144, 156–157.

The crucial breakthrough occurred in housing, which ranked for at least two decades as the most critical urban problem. During the war the federal government allotted over $1 billion to defense housing projects in some 125 cities, and at its close, responding to the pleas of veterans' groups, citizen housing associations, and other local bodies, it provided additional subsidies for veterans' housing. In several hard pressed cities—Milwaukee and Pittsburgh as well as New York among others—non-profit corporations launched ambitious redevelopment projects to clear blighted districts for new housing and other uses. The huge costs involved quickly demonstrated the need for subsidies, and the U.S. Conference of Mayors, still headed by LaGuardia, earnestly requested federal assistance. Despite charges of socialism and fears that public housing would accelerate the migration of Negroes to the cities, so acute was the housing crisis that the conservative Republican Robert A. Taft joined the liberal Democrat Robert Wagner in sponsoring a housing act in the Senate which, when eventually passed in 1949, not only accepted the subsidy of low cost housing as a national responsibility but also extended the use of federal funds for slum clearance and urban redevelopment.[2]

The campaign for the housing act had, however, brought a new and troublesome issue to the fore. Some of the private redevelopment projects had deliberately sought to clear inner-city slums for downtown commercial and other profitable uses. Advocates of public housing rebutted the charge that slum clearance was Negro removal, but they were at the same time reluctant to approve the concentration of new public housing projects in traditional slum districts. Fortunately the U.S. Supreme Court, in three crucial decisions banning restrictive covenants that discriminated on the basis of colour, race, or creed, reversed in May 1948 the traditional stand of the lower courts and established the legal right of Negroes to move out of black ghettos and into neighbourhoods within their means. While that decision offered little hope to the poor, it gave encouragement to the bi-racial commissions of a dozen cities and spurred their campaigns for fair employment and open housing. In compliance with this trend the Solicitor General issued a directive, following the passage of the housing act, which denied federal aid to any project that practised racial discrimination.[3]

The passage of the housing act also raised the hopes of urban planners, but the difficulties it uncovered soon revealed the weak-

[2] Richard O. Davies, *Housing Reform During the Truman Administration,* Columbia, Mo. 1966; McKelvey, pp. 128–133.
[3] Paul F. Wendt, *Housing Policy, The Search for a Solution,* Berkeley 1962, pp. 163–165, 190–202; McKelvey, pp. 133–136; 68 *Supreme Court Decisions* May 1948, pp. 836–847.

nesses of the planning movement. Although in most cities the citizen planning councils and other volunteer groups had given way, by the late forties, to official planning staffs, the professional planners, who generally lacked either political weight or social influence, proved unable to pick firm sites for public housing projects or to make other crucial decisions. Moreover, the restricted scope of their jurisdiction, bounded by the city limits, compelled them, when faced with regional problems, to rely on volunteer agreements with the planners and other officials of the surrounding towns. In spite of the limited accomplishments of the Regional Plan Association of New York, similar efforts in other cities increased the number of regional planning councils to thirty-four by the end of the decade.[4]

Yet these informal councils could at best only clarify the issues that separated the core cities from their suburbs, and the leaders of several expanding metropolises made new attempts to consolidate their governments. Hostile state legislatures again rejected federal charters drafted for Boston, St Louis, and Pittsburgh, and suburban townsmen defeated similar plans at Miami and Seattle among other places. A few cities, most of them in the South, such as Louisville and Atlanta, achieved metropolitan proportions by annexing wide suburban tracts, a practice denied to most cities in the North by state laws protecting the home rule prerogatives even of rural towns. In several metropolises, following the example set by Los Angeles, the county government endeavoured to supply a number of urban services to suburban residents, but these makeshifts, like the special-function districts that multiplied in other growing metropolises, failed to provide the coordination and leadership many citizens craved.[5]

A major objective in the struggle for metropolitan government was the creation of the broader tax base needed to sustain more effective services. Obstructed in that quest by rural-dominated legislatures, several cities, such as Seattle and Denver, followed New York's lead in adopting a sales tax, while St Louis and a few others followed Philadelphia in experimenting with varied types of local income taxes. Of course, these measures, when applied within the confines of the central city, tended to spur the outward migration of its more mobile residents, but again the legislatures resisted a wider extension of these taxes. Renewed demands for the reapportionment of the state legislatures fell on deaf ears both at the state capitals and in the courts. Indeed one case, which involved an urban congressional district and reached the Supreme Court in 1946, prompted Justice Felix Frank-

[4] Forbes B. Hays, *Community Leadership*, pp. 1–94; McKelvey, pp. 136–139.
[5] Victor Jones, *Metropolitan Government*, Chicago 1942; John C. Bollens, *Special District Governments in the United States*, Berkeley 1957, pp. 54–64; McKelvey, pp. 138–141.

furter to declare that 'the Courts ought not to enter this political thicket'.[6]

Blocked in every effort to solve their own problems, metropolitan leaders turned with increased unanimity to the federal government for emergency assistance. To support their appeals they authorized surveys and engaged political scientists and other scholars to make elaborate studies of their municipal needs. An increasing number of sociologists, economic geographers, and even a few historians were engaging in urban research, and architects as well as social workers were acquiring a new awareness of the complexity of their urban problems.[7]

Despite the problems and uncertainties that surround them at the mid-century, most metropolitan leaders, responding to the dynamic growth of their communities, voiced confidence in their future. The census reports of 1940 and again in 1950 tabulated the stagnation or slow decline of many central cities, but revealed dramatic increases in practically all metropolitan districts. This circumstance, supported by the surging vitality displayed in the economic tables compiled by public and private bodies in each metropolis, renewed the pressure for metropolitan integration. Several ably-directed regional studies, at Cleveland, St Louis, and Seattle among other places, recommended the adoption of federal charters in order to bring the full energies of the broader community to bear on its problems. Recalcitrant proponents, however, of home rule for the towns blocked every effort, until, in 1953, the Province of Ontario in Canada directed the formation of a metropolitan legislature for Toronto and its twelve suburbs and gave it jurisdiction over such regional functions as roads, sewers, water supply, and land-use planning. Metropolitan Toronto, patterned roughly after the Greater London charter of a half century before, quickly attracted study groups from many troubled American cities.[8]

A shift in national politics brought additional support to the movement for metropolitan reorganization. Shortly after his election in 1952, President Eisenhower had appointed a Commission on Intergovernmental Relations to seek a proper balance between federal, state, and local governments. The President hoped to check and reduce the extensions of federal power, and the Commission report, when released in 1955, not only recommended a sharp reduction in federal grants-in-aid, but also strongly urged the states to promote a reorganization of local governments to enable urban communities to meet their responsibilities more effectively. This tacit endorsement of metropol-

[6] Larry M. Elison, *The Finances of Metropolitan Areas*, Ann Arbor 1964, pp. 81–98; McKelvey, pp. 139–140.
[7] Stein, *The Eclipse of Community;* McKelvey, pp. 144–151.
[8] McKelvey, pp. 158–161.

itan governments prompted a renewed effort in many cities to achieve that goal. Metropolitan studies multiplied in the late fifties and several submitted strong recommendations for action, but only one, in Dade County, Florida, produced favourable results.[9]

A major reason for the limited accomplishments of this campaign, despite the support given it by all the groups that comprised the dominant power structure, as defined by C. Wright Mills and other leading sociologists, was the rise of another issue that considerably complicated the reorganization question. Because of the restrictions on immigration from abroad, the continued growth of metropolitan populations in the 1940s and 1950s reflected a huge internal migration from rural to urban areas. Many of these newcomers hailed from the plantations of the South where new mechanical harvesters were displacing the field hands. More than a million Negroes moved to northern cities in the forties, and almost a million and a half in the fifties when many more headed for southern and western cities, raising the non-white residents of the 212 Standard Metropolitan Statistical Areas of 1960 to almost a fifth of their 112·8 million total. By far the great majority of the non-whites in the North were settling in the central cities and, partly because of their poverty, chiefly in the old blighted districts that had formerly served the most recent immigrants from abroad. Their mounting numbers there not only transformed these decaying districts into wretched slums, hastening the outward migration of the remaining whites, but also burdened the central cities with a host of problems that made their bids for metropolitan federation still more unwelcome in the suburbs. Dade County in Florida had taken action only when hard-pressed central Miami announced a plan to annex a few of its adjoining suburbs, and the suburban portions of the county retained control over the newly recognized metropolitan functions.[10]

Spurred in part by war contracts, and by President Roosevelt's ban against discrimination in employment, many southern cities enjoyed a surge of vitality. All but one of the nation's top ten in population growth in the forties, and all but two in the fifties, were located in the South or the Southwest. Some of this growth, which in most cases exceeded 100 per cent in these two decades, resulted from the annexation of adjoining suburbs, but these in any case were rapidly increasing in population. Among the newcomers in every city were thousands of

[9] John C. Bollens, ed., *Exploring the Metropolitan Community*, Berkeley 1961; Morris Janowitz. ed., *Community Political Systems*, Glencoe 1961; McKelvey, pp. 161–165.

[10] Karl E. and Alma F. Taeuber, *Negroes in Cities*, Chicago 1965, pp. 37–64; McKelvey, pp. 153–155, 162–165; Edward Sofen, *The Miami Metro Experiment*, Bloomington, Ind. 1963.

Negroes and, particularly in the Southwest, of other non-whites. San Diego and Phoenix, each of which experienced a growth of over 85 per cent in the forties, attracted an influx of poor Mexicans who occupied makeshift quarters on the outskirts that rivalled the shanty towns of the Negroes on the periphery of some of the other southern cities. In Birmingham, Memphis, and Montgomery, and in four other cities where they exceeded 35 per cent of the total, some Negroes developed attractive new suburban quarters, but the great majority crowded into the older districts abandoned by the whites. Because of the mild climate they escaped many of the hardships suffered by their fellows in Northern cities, but inadequate sanitary facilities and a general state of neglect combined to transform some of these districts into wretched slums.[11]

As the inner city problems in northern cities multiplied in the late fifties, many distraught mayors renewed their demands for federal assistance. A scholarly study, sponsored by the newly formed American Council to Improve Our Neighborhood (ACTION), questioned the assumption that metropolitan governments would be able to resolve controversial internal problems, and pointed to the need for an impartial arbiter who could perhaps effect a resolution with the aid of outside subsidies. Even a Presidential Commission, charged with the search for national functions that could properly be turned back to the states, found only two minor activities, which Congress however refused to surrender. Instead, responding to renewed pleas from the U.S. Conference of Mayors and other official and volunteer groups, the Congress in the late fifties extended its intervention in urban affairs in several new directions.[12]

As before, the housing program provided the chief instrument for federal action, but in the late fifties the needs of the cities transformed the old problem of a housing shortage into the much more difficult riddle of the slums. The non-controversial FHA funding of private home construction had brought a tremendous upsurge in home building, facilitating the migration of the middle classes to the suburbs, but as new housing starts soared to a record high by 1950, pressure mounted for a reduction in the public housing grants authorized the year before. The availability of federal funds for slum clearance under the 1949 Act brought numerous applications for

[11] Rupert B. Vance and N. J. Demerath, eds., *The Urban South*, Chapel Hill 1954, pp. 31–70, 124–133, 154–161; McKelvey, pp. 123, 148, 154–155, 180–181.

[12] Edward C. Banfield and Morton Grodzins, *Government and Housing in Metropolitan Areas*, New York 1958, pp. 7–152; Robert H. Connery and R. H. Leach, *The Federal Government and Metropolitan Areas*, Cambridge, Mass. 1960, pp. 102–115; McKelvey, pp. 164–168.

such projects, and many progressed to the demolition stage, uprooting thousands of poor slum dwellers, most of them Negroes, before adequate facilities were provided elsewhere. A clause in the housing act directing local redevelopment authorities to find homes for those displaced was so frequently disregarded that a new housing act of 1954 required the presentation of a Workable Program showing specific plans for resettlement before new redevelopment projects could be approved. Since the accelerated migration of Negroes to the cities had progressively inundated the worst inner city slums with non-whites, plans to clear them entailed the prior erection of public housing projects elsewhere in the city, and every selection of such sites brought an outburst of hostility from neighbourhood groups in the designated areas. The possibility that the creation of metropolitan authorities would open the suburbs to such an invasion presented still another block to that movement. The only alternative seemed to be the appropriation of additional federal funds to assist in the rehabilitation of old neighbourhoods, and at the earnest recommendation of the Conference of Mayors, ACTION and other concerned groups, Congress increased the urban renewal appropriation under the 1954 Act to $1,350 million within the next four years.[13]

Thus the housing problem was progressively overshadowed, complicated, and transformed by the eruption of the Negro revolution. The civil rights question was not exclusively an urban issue, but its dramatic rise in the 1950s was a direct consequence of the great migration of Negroes to the cities, where they could no longer be denied freedom. Groups of indignant Negro professionals in southern and border cities began in the early fifties to protest the separate-but-equal doctrine as applied to the public schools. Several cases reached the Supreme Court, which chose one from Topeka, Kansas, for the historic decision delivered by Chief Justice Earl Warren in May 1954. *Brown v. Board of Education,* reversing the old doctrine, held that 'Separate educational facilities are inherently unequal' and called for desegregation with 'all deliberate speed'. A number of borderland cities and a few in the South soon began to comply, but when the school board of Little Rock, Arkansas, announced plans to admit a few Negro children to its previously all-white high school, the state governor called out the militia to block their entrance. Affronted by the official defiance of the Supreme Court, President Eisenhower dispatched a contingent of paratroopers to Little Rock to enforce the court order.[14]

[13] Charles Abrams, *The City is the Frontier,* New York 1965, pp. 78–108; McKelvey, pp. 168–174.
[14] Benjamin Muse, *The Years of Prelude: The Story of Integration Since the Supreme Court's 1954 Decision,* New York 1964; McKelvey, pp. 174–182.

Despite widespread opposition by southern governors and legis-latures, other southern cities began slowly to accept token integration not only in the schools but at the public parks and beaches and, after a protracted strike led by the Rev Dr Martin Luther King of Mont-gomery, on the city-owned buses as well. The crucial arena, of course, was housing, and the national housing administrators, who in 1947 had dropped their earlier ban against the mixture of 'incompatible racial and social groups', began in 1954 to promote 'demonstration open occupancy projects in suitable key areas'. All of the sites chosen for these ventures were in northern cities and, even there, the effort to locate open housing projects in suburban areas met strong opposition. The courts repeatedly reaffirmed their 1948 ban on anti-Negro coven-ants in private land titles, but that negative approach scarcely dented the suburban resistance. To many urban leaders, Mayor Richard Lee of New Haven among them, the only solution lay in a forthright effort to rehabilitate the slums by a restoration and modernization of their housing and by an upgrading and retraining of their inhabitants. Aided by a Ford Foundation grant, Mayor Lee developed a promising program of neighbourhood redevelopment and demonstrated the need for larger federal appropriations for the social as well as the physical renewal of the central cities.[15]

Scholars, in increasing numbers, were studying not only the social problems of the slums, the suburbs, and other characteristic urban neighbourhoods, but also the relationships between neighbourhoods, classes, ethnic settlements, and other groups within specific cities and in cities in general. Some were seeking possible solutions of urban problems, others simply to understand and explain a baffling phen-omenon. But so rapid was the metropolitan development that the scholarly theories, like the reform efforts, were in constant flux. Thus as the conceptualization of a three-layered urban class structure, popular in the forties, gave way to a power structure thesis at the mid-century, which in turn began to prove inadequate as an explana-tion of the developments of the late fifties, so the municipal reformer's confidence shifted from home rule, to metropolitan reorganization, to federal grants-in-aid and back again as circumstances dictated. The sudden upsurge of the civil rights question, by complicating many urban trends and refuting several elaborately documented theories, supplied a reminder that the emerging metropolises were not scholarly abstractions but pulsating and complex human communities, which were playing a significant role in the nation's history.[16]

[15] McKelvey, pp. 181–183, 133–134; Davis McEntire, *Residence and Race*, Berkeley 1960, pp. 180–212, 299–339; Jean Lowe, *Cities in a Race with Time*, New York 1967, pp. 410–526.
[16] McKelvey, pp. 187–199.

And now, more clearly than in the past, the true nature of the urban role became apparent. Whether defined as in ancient symbols as a crossroads within a wall, or following Louis Wirth as 'a relatively large, dense and permanent settlement of socially heterogeneous individuals', a city was more than a market place within a circle of producers and consumers, more than a forum for the exchange of views and the formulation of policy, more even than a community of dissimilar but functionally interrelated residents. It was all of these and, in addition, a dynamic nucleus in a larger society with which it shared its material and cultural well being. The fortunes of the nation were not only linked with but increasingly comprised of those of its cities, and as the latter grew in number and size and clustered into metropolitan regions, new relationships evolved transforming the widely and sparsely settled United States into a closely knit though still unofficial union of metropolises.

10

The Metropolis and the Federal Government

The convergence of metropolitan and federal problems and trends reached an historic climax in the 1960s. Slum housing and blighted neighbourhoods, traffic-snarled streets and airways, budget-bound cities and school districts, polluted water and air, juvenile delinquency and crime, rebellious minorities and youths, overt and *de facto* segregation, disfranchised residents and under-represented districts, all commanded the attention not only of mayors, city councilmen and educators, but also of Congress, the Supreme Court and successive Presidents. Early in 1961, the newly elected President John F. Kennedy called for 'the energy and vision' needed to meet the problems of the cities, which he saw as the principal challenge to the 'New Frontier'. Three years later his successor Lyndon B. Johnson, accepting the urban problem as the basic task of the 'Great Society', produced an unmatched succession of legislative and administrative acts and court decisions that gave substance to a new form of creative federalism.

With clarity and decision, President Kennedy sounded a new federal attack on urban problems early in 1961. And while Congress was deliberating his calls for additional funds for housing, for the creation of a Department of Housing and Urban Affairs, and for authorization for federal grants-in-aid to urban cultural and planning programs, the President's Committee on Juvenile Delinquency boldly launched two experimental projects in New York—Mobilization for Youth on the Lower East Side and Haryou in Harlem—the pioneers of a new participatory technique for the rehabilitation of slum neighbourhoods.[1]

Kennedy moved most effectively in the administrative field. Robert C. Weaver, his appointee as head of the Housing and Home Finance Agency, made a forthright attempt to secure Workable Programs that

---

[1] Kenneth C. Clark, *Dark Ghetto: Dilemmas of Social Power*, New York 1965, pp. 35–45; McKelvey, *Metropolitan America*, pp. 205–207.

would assure a wholesome relocation of all residents, non-whites and others, displaced for slum clearance. Dismayed by the problems created by an extended bulldozing of blighted districts, he encouraged city officials to give increased attention to the rehabilitation of old neighbourhoods by enlisting the support of historical restoration societies and community associations. Grants by the Ford Foundation and other bodies, including the newly formed National Arts Foundation, helped to launch and maintain some of these renewal projects in cities such as New Haven where the progressive Mayor Richard C. Lee was ready and eager to supply vigorous local leadership.[2]

In some communities, however, the municipal officials felt stymied by the inadequate scope of their jurisdictions and the constricted weight of their representation. When, after repeated appeals, the state courts refused to enforce constitutional provisions calling for reapportionment, the Supreme Court, under Chief Justice Earl Warren, finally in *Baker v. Carr* ordered Tennessee to redraw its legislative districts to achieve a more equitable apportionment of urban and rural representatives. Forthright battles for reapportionment erupted in many states, but it soon became evident to the leaders of their major metropolises that the chief gains in representation would go to the expanding suburban districts, leaving the central cities weaker and more dependent than before on federal assistance.[3]

Fortunately one federal agency, the Advisory Commission on Intergovernmental Relations, established by Congress in 1959, was earnestly studying these problems. With a variety of urban viewpoints represented among the governors, legislators, and mayors who comprised its members, the commission's reports recommended the restructuring of some governmental responsibilities and the further development of metropolitan planning and administrative agencies. Scattered efforts at Richmond, Memphis, and San Antonio to achieve metropolitan federation again met defeat, however, though Nashville and Davidson County in Tennessee pressed successfully for a plan similar to that adopted by Miami and Dade County in the late fifties. Yet the federal charter granted to Nashville and its environs assured control to the suburban districts and, as at Miami, left the central city burdened with the care of most of its troublesome sores. As a result advocates of major urban redevelopment programs began to

[2] Jeanne R. Lowe, *Cities in a Race With Time,* pp. 341–351; McKelvey, pp. 201–205.

[3] Howard D. Hamilton, ed., *Legislative Apportionment: Key to Power,* New York 1964, pp. 32–55; McKelvey, pp. 202–203.

despair of the metropolitan approach and turned again to the federal government for responsible leadership and support.[4]

Part of the difficulty sprang, of course, from the competing economic aspirations of central city and suburban promoters. Ambitious projects for the redevelopment of old blighted areas near the business districts of expanding metropolises contributed to the rehabilitation of such central cities as Boston and Minneapolis as well as Pittsburgh. Rival plans for suburban plazas were seldom impeded by these inner-city developments, though the reverse was sometimes claimed, but at Boston, where the two programs progressed hand-in-hand, the dramatic success of the outer ring of technological industries and shopping plazas, straddling Route 128, called for the extension of the super-highway system into the heart of old Boston and spurred the erection there of towering new commercial buildings. Friction developed, however, as the bulldozers, opening broad channels for new highways and clearing blighted areas for new high-rise offices and luxury apartments, scattered the former residents to other parts of the city. Not all the displaced residents were Negroes and many even of the Negroes found better quarters in the process though generally at a higher price. But the forced removal shattered many old community ties and by dumping thousands of poor families into other modest neighbourhoods added to their local problems. As the development of some urban renewal projects fanned racial animosities, in Newark for example, city officials in many places gave increased emphasis to urban rehabilitation. By April 1963 more than ninety such projects had won approval, though their heavy reliance on code enforcement and on the reluctant cooperation of the absentee owners of the slum properties made progress slow and discouraging.[5]

In most cities, however, the desperate plight of the inner-city residents was due less to the demolition of old houses and the resultant loss of homes than to the rapid influx of poor newcomers eager to find shelter of any kind. Plans for the resettlement of the former residents of urban-renewal districts often broke down in practice as newcomers moved in before the emptied slum houses could be demolished. Northern cities, such as Rochester and Syracuse, which had attracted few Negroes in the past, now experienced a rapid influx that trebled their non-white populations within a period of fifteen years and inundated the old blighted areas abandoned by earlier ethnic minorities.

[4] Advisory Commission on Intergovernmental Relations, *Governmental Structure, Organization and Planning in Metropolitan Areas*, Washington 1961; Luther H. Gulick, *The Metropolitan Problem and American Ideas*, New York 1962; McKelvey, pp. 207–212.

[5] Herbert J. Gans, *The Urban Villagers, Group and Class in the Life of Italian-Americans*, Glencoe, Ill. 1962; James E. Wilson, ed., *Urban Renewal: The Record and the Controversy*, Cambridge, Mass. 1966; McKelvey, pp. 214–221.

Cities in the Far West and in the South also received large contingents, as mechanical cotton pickers and other technological devices displaced the farm hands. Four of the seven major metropolises that experienced annual increases of more than 3 per cent during the fifties and sixties were in the South, and the other three were in the West. And although none of the seven, except Washington, attracted as many Negroes as whites, in each of these rapidly growing cities and in many of more moderate growth the Negro was becoming a major factor in the central-city scene.[6]

And, in spite of the apparent progress of the civil rights movement in the 1950s, the ratio of segregation was generally increasing, particularly in the South. It was therefore not surprising that the Negro revolution should erupt first in that region and in cities that had previously enjoyed a tradition of peaceful relations between the races. Birmingham, the most intensively industrialized of all southern cities, had experienced a 4·1 per cent increase in segregation during the fifties, chiefly because the recent growth of its Negro population had concentrated in black neighbourhoods; it became as a result the logical choice of Dr Martin Luther King in April 1963 for the first city-wide non-violent demonstration against discrimination in employment and services. 'Sit-ins', 'freedom-rides' and other non-violent demonstrations spread from city to city throughout the South that summer and culminated in a great march on Washington on August 28th as the Negroes and their white sympathizers pressed for the adoption of a new civil rights act. As the movement gained momentum, boycotts against department stores and other establishments that discriminated against Negroes erupted in Philadelphia and other northern cities and in San Francisco and elsewhere in the West. Protests multiplied against the sham of token integration in southern schools and against *de facto* segregation in northern schools.[7]

The assassination of President Kennedy in hostile Dallas, in the midst of his battle for the Civil Rights Act, speeded its passage and committed his successor Lyndon Johnson to other Kennedy policies. Soon the new President was aggressively making the urban problem, which in his view included the dramatic confrontation there of affluence and destitution, the central concern of his War on Poverty and Great Society programs. The urgency of the urban projects was accentuated by the mounting clamour in the city streets. Every step forward seemed to arouse a greater clamour. The passage after a protracted

[6] Bernard J. Frieden, *The Future of Old Neighborhoods*, Cambridge, Mass. 1964; Charles Abrams, *The City is the Frontier*, New York 1965; McKelvey, pp. 221–223.

[7] Karl and Alma Taeuber, *Negroes in Cities*, Chicago 1965, pp. 39–41; McKelvey, pp. 221–223.

debate of the Civil Rights Act, including a fair-employment practices clause, prompted wide demands for its immediate application. Numerous marches and demonstrations, generally conducted with remarkable self-control, invited scattered acts of violence in response, chiefly for a time in rural southern areas, but led finally in the summer of 1964 to a series of street riots in Harlem, Brooklyn, and Rochester that marked a turn in the Negro revolution.[8]

The frustration and anger of Negro slum dwellers, released by incidents or rumours of police brutality, finally awakened the nation to the gravity of its urban problems. Not only was the anti-poverty bill hastily adopted, but other Presidential policies received increased support, extending grants-in-aid to the cities for studies of their rapid-transit and sanitary improvement needs, for water works extensions and open space acquisition, and for library and school development planning. President Johnson finally got the adoption of an act creating a Department of Housing and Urban Development and proceeded to appoint Dr Weaver as its head, the first Negro to be named to a President's Cabinet.[9]

Renewed and more violent rioting in succeeding summers demonstrated the complexity of the urban racial problems. Some of the most destructive riots erupted in such cities as Newark and Detroit where extensive renewal projects had been undertaken and a false confidence in their stability had developed. The extent of the remedial efforts, though overshadowed in every case by the magnitude of the problems, had added to the frustrations of many trapped in the vast pools of slum residents in these and other troubled cities, notably the Watts district of Los Angeles. To achieve a better coordination of remedial programs, President Johnson proposed a Demonstration Cities Act which Congress passed in 1966 as a Model Cities Program, under which the federal government supplied planning and development funds for a concerted attack on all aspects of a blighted neighbourhood's problems. Congress likewise increased its appropriations for public housing, for slum clearance and urban rehabilitation, and for metropolitan planning. But these appropriations appeared infinitesimal compared with the many billions required, as numerous witness before Senator Abraham Ribicoff's Subcommittee on the problems of the city testified.[10]

Unfortunately the riots, which dramatically proved the needs of

---

[8] Arthur I. Washow, *From Race Riot to Sit-In: 1919 and the 1960's*, Garden City, N.Y. 1966, pp. 232–244; Benjamin Muse, *Ten Years of Prelude*, New York 1964, pp. 301–240; McKelvey, pp. 223–226.

[9] Theodore H. White, *The Making of the President: 1964*, New York 1965, pp. 294–406; McKelvey, pp. 226–229.

[10] Martin, *The Cities and the Federal System;* McKelvey, pp. 233–236.

the inner cities, added to the hardships of the residents of the slums where most of the destruction occurred. Moreover the violence, which displaced the peaceful techniques of Dr King's demonstrations, called forth a show of force by the city police and the state militia that further aggravated the situation, resulted in numerous fatalities, and stirred expressions of a white back lash. Sober leaders, who saw that the Negro, like the Irishman, the German, the Jew and the Pole before him, was struggling to assert his identity and to achieve his place in the city, gradually succeeded in reestablishing order. Graphic views of the devastation in Detroit and elsewhere spurred a new determination on the part of industrialists and other business and civic leaders to undertake both corporate and public improvements designed to re-habilitate the slum neighbourhoods. Numerous philanthropic bodies joined the Ford Foundation in backing remedial programs in the city slums, and Urban America, successor to ACTION, collaborated with the U.S. Conference of Mayors in establishing the Urban Coalition linking business men and civic leaders in a nation wide attack, reaching into many cities, on the problems of the slums.[11]

A still more ambitious movement for the establishment of new cities developed in the early sixties. Following distantly the New Towns movement, which had made headway in England and on the Continent during the preceding half century, the promoters of Reston in Virginia, Columbia in Maryland, and numerous other new-city developments proposed a fresh start as the best method of correcting urban problems and relieving the population pressure on over-grown metropolises. Despite many setbacks and reorganizations, construction commenced and the first residents began to occupy several new cities by the mid-sixties.[12]

It was too early to judge the adequacy of the New Towns as residential communities, but the social deficiencies evident in many newly built suburbs suggested that housing was not the only serious urban problem. The mounting incidence of crime and the spread of serious forms of juvenile delinquency into affluent neighbourhoods demonstrated a need for nation-wide action on this urban problem. President Kennedy's Committee on Juvenile Delinquency had focused its attention on the problems of youths in blighted slum districts and on the particular needs of the Negro teenagers. No real solutions had been found, but many cities were endeavouring to tackle the school drop-out problem, to check the peddling of various kinds of drugs, and to provide summer jobs to reduce the number of idle youths in the streets. In spite of these efforts, the popularity of the image of the beatniks among teenagers on the campuses of urban universities as well as in the

[11] McKelvey, pp. 233–234; *Fortune*, August 1968, p. 91.
[12] McKelvey, pp. 234–236.

Greenwich Villages of the major metropolises and on the skid rows
of lesser cities created an atmosphere of youthful defiance of middle-
class standards that produced a number of spring-time riots at resort
areas and contributed to the student revolts on university campuses.
The anti-war movement had an international not an urban origin;
but its frequent demonstrations on the city streets, and the presence in
it of a Negro faction protesting at the use of black men to fight a
white man's war against another coloured race, drew the two protest
movements closer together and gave their frequent conflicts with the
police almost a revolutionary flavour—as the downtown riots in
Chicago at the time of the Democratic Convention in August 1968
demonstrated.[13]

Many urban leaders still looked to the public schools for a gradual
reduction and hopefully for a final elimination of racial prejudices.
Numerous southern cities had adopted a measure of token integration, following the Supreme Court's directives, but the slight progress
there was overshadowed by the conflict spreading through many
northern cities over the *busing* issue and other efforts to reduce the
de facto segregation that was progressively converting many inner-
city schools into Negro schools. Plans to *bus* inner-city pupils to outer
rim or suburban schools attracted support at such moderate sized
cities as Hartford, New Haven, and Rochester, but aroused opposition from defenders of the neighbourhood school. In the larger
metropolises, where the Negro pupils comprises a major portion of
the registration in all central-city schools, neither *busing* nor the creation of large campus schools, as proposed at Syracuse among other
places, offered a possible solution; a new movement developed in
New York for a decentralization of the system and the creation of
neighbourhood school boards with authority to manage their own
schools. Black power advocates quickly dominated some districts and
challenged the authority of the central board to appoint their teachers
and the power of the city-wide teachers union to protect the jobs of
its local members. Mayor Lindsay finally secured a compromise settlement of two successive strikes, but prospects for an early resolution of
these deep conflicts did not appear bright.[14]

As the problems of the cities increased, scholars in a half dozen
disciplines intensified their urban studies. Geographers charted the
boundaries and tabulated the resources of the growing number of
metropolitan regions; economists developed procedures for measuring
the input and output and other aspects of the urban economy in an

---

[13] Saul Bernstein, *Youths on the Streets*, New York 1964; Claude Brown,
Manchild in the Promised Land, New York 1965.
[14] Talcott Parsons and Kenneth Clark, eds., *The Negro American*, New
York 1966, pp. 472–489; McKelvey, pp. 222–224.

extended list of economic base studies; political scientists demonstrated that the power groups and decision makers in most
cities were plural rather than monolithic in structure; sociologists
turned finally from the study of power structures and class stratifica-
tion to an analysis of a great variety of social systems, which in turn
opened the way for social workers to explore the possibility of enlisting the participation of the disadvantaged in their own rehabilitation;
planners, discovering the limitations of model plans, faced the task of
developing planning as a process of urban growth responsive to the
needs and the tastes of each city.[15]

Historians, too, were studying the city and, as this review essay
discloses, they were discovering some astonishing continuities as well
as many dramatic shifts in the course of America's urban development. It was no surprise to see that the cities in the twentieth century,
as in the nineteenth, were nurseries of enterprise and popular if seldom
pleasant havens for newcomers. Yet a seldom noted corollary was the
service the American city performed to successive waves of newcomers that first discovered their ethnic identities in its polyglot
turmoil and eventually made their contribution to the urban community structure. More unexpected was the discovery that their function
as spearheads of the frontier in the early 1800s was resumed more
than a century later in Kennedy's 'New Frontier'. Perhaps the most
unexpected continuity, however, was the damper imposed on the
vitality and autonomy of certain cities by a sharply divided two-class
system, first in the colonial period when only the English ports on the
mainland that escaped it asserted their independence, and later in the
inert nineteenth century cities of the South, and more recently in the
many central cities of the last two decades where the black-white
confrontation poses a threat to the freedom of all.

These continuities have, however, been offset by some dramatic
shifts in urban developments. As the commercial and industrial growth
of the cities progressed, the early reliance on competition, nurtured
by many rival cities, proved ineffective first in the utility field but
gradually in the larger corporate area as well and created a new role
for urban leaders as champions of progressive regulations and civic
reforms. Perhaps the most significant historic shift occurred in the early
decades of the twentieth century as the diffusion of urban settlements
across the land gave way to a new gathering of urban energies into
metropolitan regions, each centreing in a core city that generally supplied its vitality and dominant function. When the states, controlled
by the rural-dominated legislatures, refused to grant the emerging
metropolises status and power adequate to perform their mounting

[15] Philip M. Hauser and Leo F. Schnore, eds., *The Study of Urbanization*,
New York 1965; McKelvey, pp. 187–199, 238–253.

functions, the hard-pressed central cities appealed in desperation to Washington, first for help in battling against the great depression, and, after the second World War, for assistance in meeting the housing, health, and educational needs of their teeming populations and for aid and leadership in the eradication of slums and the treatment of other inner-city ills. This new alliance between the cities and the national government has, under the pressure of a flooding migration of Negroes to the cities and of their mounting demands during the last two decades for civil and economic equality, given birth to a new federalism linking cities, states, and the national government in a potentially cooperative but tension-packed union, which is fostering a new participatory democracy on the local level. The proposed development of federated metropolises, joining the public and private energies of cities and suburbs in dynamic new communities, offers a regional alternative to the centralized and standardized nation so widely predicted and feared. The full impacts of the recent election on these trends remain to be seen.

DOCUMENTS

A. The Colonial Ports

Five documentary selections reveal significant relationships between the imperial objectives of the British mercantilists and the colonial ports they established in America. Few scholars have probed this era more diligently than George Louis Beer whose historical books, published more than a half century ago, have not only survived the test of time but have acquired a documentary flavour in the process. Although never focusing on the city, he clearly saw the basic role played by the British ports in the development of their American colonies, as a brief quotation (Doc. 1) from his comments on Boston in the 1660s will indicate. William Penn's description of his plans for Philadelphia in a letter of 1683 (Doc. 2) puts the intentions and aspirations of one of the leading colonial proprietors into clear focus. Later refinements in British colonial plans were incorporated in the Hat Act adopted by Parliament in 1732 (Doc. 3) and the Iron Act of 1750 (Doc. 4). Resentment against these and other restrictions contributed to the movement for independence, but the natural growth of the colonial ports nurtured a sense of self-reliance and freedom that would ultimately have produced the same effect. Few descriptions are more revealing of this development than that of Edumnd Burke (Doc. 5) and his cousin William Burke who together spent several months in the American colonies in the middle 1750s.

1. Boston in 1668

FROM *George Louis Beer, The Old Colonial System, 1660–1754, Part I—The Establishment of the System, 1660–1688,* New York 1912, II: 245–246, 326–327.

At this time it was said that Boston, a growing town of several thousand people, was "full of good Shopps well furnished with all kind of Merchandize and many Artificers and Trad'smen of all sorts." The basic industries of the colony were ship-building, fishing, and agriculture. A large number of boats were employed in the local fishery, and the best fish was sent to southern Europe and to the Spanish and Portuguese "Wine Islands," while that of poorer quality found a market in the English West Indies. In addition, they shipped pipe-staves, masts, lumber, some pitch and tar, beef, pork, horses, and corn to Virginia, Barbados, and the other West Indian islands. Part of these supplies came from the neighbouring colonies. In return, they brought back sugar and tobacco, which the Commissioners said "they after send for England." The exports to England consisted mainly of the large masts required by the ships of the line in the Royal Navy, which were scarce at all times in Europe, and were especially difficult to obtain during times of war, when the communications with the Baltic countries were precarious. During the Dutch war of 1665–1667, England drew freely upon the supply in New England. From England, Massachusetts imported wearing apparel, textiles, and utensils. The colony's comparatively extensive trade was carried well-nigh exclusively in its own shipping. In 1665, Massachusetts had about 132 ships, of which forty were from 40 to 100 tons, and twelve were even larger. Nearly all these ships were built in the colony, and unquestionably this development was in part due to the stimulus given by the English Navigation Act. But in addition Massachusetts, like Virginia, gave preferential treatment to its own shipping. By a law of 1667 all vessels of above twenty tons not belonging to Massachusetts had to pay tonnage dues in gunpowder for every voyage made there. . . .

New Plymouth's chief products were fish and provisions of all sorts—beef, pork, mutton, and some grain. The colony had no large vessels and no trade beyond the seas. A few small boats were employed in the fishery and in carrying the colony's surplus produce to Boston, whence it was transported to market. Boston was the colony's *entrepôt*. "Comodities Imported from beyond Sea wee haue none to us directly," wrote Governor Winslow in 1680, "but haue all our Supplies from our Neighbors of the Massachusetts." Similarly, the exports and imports of Rhode Island were inconsiderable. According to Governor Sanford's statement made in 1680, there were no merchants in Rhode Island "but the most of our Colloney live comfortably by improving the wildernesse." With the exception of a few sloops, the colony had no shipping, nor was there any trade with foreigners or Indians. Its chief exports were horses and provisions, and its main imports consisted of a small quantity of West Indian goods for local consumption. Connecticut was also essentially an agricultural community, raising wheat, corn and other grains, peas, pork, beef, horses, and lumber, which were for the most part transported to Boston and there exchanged for clothing. Some were also shipped to New York. This constituted the bulk of the colony's commerce, but, in addition, there was a small direct export trade to the West Indies and occasionally a ship took a cargo to the Madeiras.

The provisions thus obtained from the neighboring colonies constituted an important factor in Boston's trade.

2. The Plan for Philadelphia in 1683

FROM William Penn's Letter to the Society of Traders, 16 August,
1683, as quoted with notes by Albert Cook Myers, in his
Narratives of Early Pennsylvania West New Jersey and Delaware,
New York 1912, pp. 239–243.

Philadelphia, the Expectation of those that are concern'd in this
Province, is at last laid out to the great Content of those here, that
are any wayes Interested therein; The Scituation is a Neck of Land,
and lieth between two Navigable Rivers, Delaware and Skulkill,
whereby it hath two Fronts upon the Water, each a Mile, and two
from River to River. Delaware is a glorious River, but the Skulkill
being an hundred Miles Boatable above the Falls, and its Course
North-East toward the Fountain of Susquahannah (that tends to the
Heart of the Province, and both sides our own) it is like to be a great
part of the Settlement of this Age. I say little of the Town it self,
because a *Plat-form*[1] will be shewn you by my Agent, in which those
who are Purchasers of me, will find their Names and Interests: But
this I will say for the good Providence of God, that of all the many
Places I have seen in the World, I remember not one better seated;
so that it seems to me to have been appointed for a Town, whether
we regard the Rivers, or the conveniency of the Coves, Docks,
Springs, the loftiness and soundness of the Land and the Air, held by
the People of these parts to be very good. It is advanced within less
than a Year to about four Score Houses and Cottages, such as they
are, where Merchants and Handicrafts, are following their Vocations
as fast as they can, while the Country-men are close at their Farms;
Some of them got a little Winter-Corn in the Ground last Season, and
the generality have had a handsom Summer-Crop, and are preparing
for their Winter-Corn. They reaped their Barley this Year in the
Moneth called May; the Wheat in the Moneth following; so that there
is time in these parts for another Crop of divers Things before the
Winter-Season. We are daily in hopes of Shipping to add to our
Number; for blessed be God, here is both Room and Accommodation
for them; the Stories of our Necessity being either the Fear of our

[1] The map or plan of Philadelphia made by the surveyor general Thomas
Holme, in 1683, and first published the same year at the end of this pamphlet,
as *A Portraiture of the City of Philadelphia*.

Friends, or the Scare-Crows of our Enemies; for the greatest hardship we have suffered, hath been Salt-Meat, which by Fowl in Winter, and Fish in Summer, together with some Poultery, Lamb, Mutton, Veal, and Plenty of Venison the best part of the year, hath made very passable. . . .

For your particular Concern, I might entirely refer you to the Letters of the President of the Society;[2] but this I will venture to say, Your Provincial Settlements both within and without the Town, for Scituation and Soil, are without Exception; Your City-Lot is an whole Street, and one side of a Street, from River to River, containing near one hundred Acers, not easily valued, which is besides your four hundred Acers in the City Liberties, part of your twenty thousand Acers in the Countery. Your Tannery hath such plenty of Bark, the Saw-Mill for Timber, the place of the Glass-house so conveniently posted for Water-carriage, the City-Lot for a Dock, and the Whalery[3] for a sound and fruitful Bank, and the Town Lewis by it to help your People, that by Gods blessing the Affairs of the Society will naturally grow in their Reputation and Profit. I am sure I have not turned my back upon any Offer that tended to its Prosperity; and though I am

---

[2] The Free Society of Traders in Pennsylvania, a joint stock company, which had been planned and discussed in London throughout the year 1681, and of which great results were expected, received a liberal charter from Penn in March, 1682. Over two hundred persons in the British Isles, largely from among those most interested in the new colony, became subscribers to the stock, which had reached £10,000 in June 1682. A purchase of 20,000 acres of land in the province was made. The first officers were Dr Nicholas More, of London, president, at a salary of £150 per annum, John Simcock, of Cheshire, deputy, and James Claypool, of London treasurer, the latter two at £100 per annum. These officers removed to Pennsylvania, the president with about fifty servants of the society arriving at Philadelphia in the ship *Geoffrey* in October, 1682. The Principal trading house and offices were erected on the Society tract in the infant city, on the west side of Front Street—the main street—near the south side of Dock Creek, and at the foot of Society Hill, so named from the location of the company. Thence the society's city tract of about one hundred acres extended westerly in a tier of lots from Front Street on the Delaware to Schuylkill, flanked by Spruce Street on the south. This main station was the centre for the various activities of the society. From here whalers went fishing for whales to the entrance of the Delaware Bay, preparing their oil and whalebone on the shore near Lewes. At Frankford a grist-mill and a saw-mill on Tacony Creek, a tannery, brick kilns, and glass-works were conducted. Cargoes of English goods were brought in and sold at a profit, but collections being difficult, the officers tended to look after their private affairs to the detriment of those of the society, it suffered severe losses, and in a few years practically went out of business except as an owner of real estate.

[3] 'Advise what commodity whale oyl may be with you [in Barbados] for we [the Free Society of Traders] have 24 men fishing in the [Delaware] bay that are like to to make a good Voyage.' James Claypool's letter, dated Philadelphia, 10 Mo (December) 2, 1683.

ill at Projects, I have sometimes put in for a Share with her Officers, to countenance and advance her Interest. You are already informed what is fit for you further to do, whatsoever tends to the Promotion of Wine, and to the Manufacture of Linnen in these parts, I cannot but wish you to promote it; and the French People are most likely in both respects to answer that design: To that end, I would advise you to send some Thousands of Plants out of France, with some able Vinerons, and People of the other Vocation: But because I believe you have been entertained with this and some other profitable Subjects by your President, I shall add no more, but to assure you, that I am heartily inclined to advance your just Interest, and that you will always find me

Your Kind Cordial Friend,
WILLIAM PENN

Philadelphia, the 16th of the
  6th Moneth, call'd August,
  1683

3. An Act to Prevent the Exportation of Hats

FROM The Hat Act of 1 June, 1732, Danby Pickering, ed., *Statutes at Large*, Cambridge 1765, XVI: 304–305, 307–308.

Whereas the art and mystery of making hats in Great Britain hath arrived to great perfection, and considerable quantities of hats manufactured in this kingdom have heretofore been exported to his Majesty's plantations or colonies in America, you have been wholly supplied with hats from Great Britain; and whereas great quantities of hats have of late years been made, and the said manufacture is daily increasing in the British plantations in America, and is from thence exported to foreign markets, which were heretofore supplied from Great Britain, and the hatmakers in the said plantations take many apprentices for very small terms, to the discouragement of the said trade, and debasing the said manufacture: wherefore for preventing the said ill practices for the future, and for promoting and encouraging the trade of making hats in Great Britain, be it enacted by the King's most excellent majesty, by and with the advice and consent of the lords spiritual and temporal and commons in this present parliament assembled, and by the authority of the same, That from and after the twenty ninth day of September in the year of our Lord one thousand seven hundred and thirty two, no hats or felts whatsoever, dyed or undyed, finished or unfinished, shall be shipt, loaden or put on board any ship or vessel in any place or parts within any of the

British plantations, upon any pretence whatsoever, by any person or persons whatsoever, and also that no hats or felts, either dyed or undyed, finished or unfinished, shall be loaden upon any horse, cart or other carriage, to the intent or purpsoe to be exported, transported, shipped off, carried or conveyed out of any of the said British plantations to any other of the British plantations, or to any other place whatsoever, by any person or persons whatsoever. . . .

II. And be it further enacted by the authority aforesaid, That all and every the offender and offenders, offence and offences against this act, shall be subject and liable to the penalties and forfeitures herein after mentioned, that is to say, The said hats or felts dyed or undyed, finished or unfinished, so exported, transported, shipped off, carried, conveyed or loaden contrary to the true intent and meaning of this act, shall be forfeited, and that every of the offender and offenders therein shall likewise forfeit and pay the sum of five hundred pounds, for every such offence committed. . . .

VII. And it is hereby further enacted by the authority aforesaid, That no person residing in any of his Majesty's plantations in America shall, from and after the said twenty ninth day of September one thousand seven hundred and thirty two, make or cause to be made, any felt or hat of or with any wool or stuff whatsoever, unless he shall have first served as an apprentice in the trade or art of felt-making during the space of seven years at the least; neither shall any felt-maker or hat-maker in any of the said plantations imploy, retain or set to work, in the said art or trade, any person as journeyman or hired servant, other than such as shall have loyally served an apprenticeship in the said trade for the space of seven years. . . .

IX. Provided always, That nothing in this act contained shall extend to charge any person or persons lawfully exercising the said art, with any penalty or forfeiture for setting or using his or their own son or sons to the making or working hats or felts in his or their own house or houses, so as every such son or sons be bound by indenture of apprenticeship, for the term of seven years at the least, which term shall not be to expire before he shall be of the full age of twenty one years. . . .

X. Provided also, and be it enacted by the authority aforesaid, That every felt-maker residing in the said plantations, who at the beginning of this present session of parliament was a maker or worker of hats or felts, and being an householder, and likewise all such as were at the beginning of this present session apprentice, covenant servants, or journeymen in the same art or mystery of felt-making so as such apprentices serve or make up their respective apprenticeships, shall and may continue and exercise the trade or art of making hats and felts in the said plantations. . . .

4. *An act to encourage the importation of pig and bar iron from his Majesty's colonies in America*

FROM The Iron Act of 12 April, 1750, Ibid., XX: 97, 99–100.

Whereas the importation of bar iron from his Majesty's colonies in America, into the port of London, and the importation of pig iron from the said colonies, into any port of Great Britain, and the manufacture of such bar and pig iron in Great Britain, will be a great advantage not only to the said colonies, but also to his kingdom, by furnishing the manufacturers of iron with a supply of that useful and necessary commodity, and by means thereof large sums of money, now annually paid for iron to foreigners, will be saved to this kingdom, and a greater quantity of the woollen, and other manufactures of Great Britain, will be exported to America, in exchange for such iron so imported; be it therefore enacted by the King's most excellent Majesty, by and with the advice and consent of the lords spiritual and temporal, and commons, in this present parliament assembled, and by the authority of the same, That from and after the twenty fourth day of June, one thousand seven hundred and fifty, the several and respective subsidies, customs, impositions, rates, and duties, now payable on pig iron, made in and imported from his Majesty's colonies in America, into any port of Great Britain, shall cease, determine, and be no longer paid; and that from and after the said twenty fourth day of June, no subsidy, custom, imposition, rate, or duty, shall be payable upon bar iron made in and imported from the said colonies into the port of London; any law, statute, or usage to the contrary thereof in any wise notwithstanding. . . .

IX. And, that pig and bar iron made in his Majesty's colonies in America may be further manufactured in this kingdom, be it further enacted by the authority aforesaid, That from and after the twenty fourth day of June, one thousand seven hundred and fifty, no mill or other engine for slitting or rolling of iron, or any plateing-forge to work with a tilt hammer, or any furnace for making steel, shall be erected, or after such creation, continued, in any of his Majesty's colonies in America; and if any person or persons shall erect, or cause to be erected, or after such erection, continue or cause to be continued, in any of the said colonies, any such mill, engine, forge, or furnace, every person or persons so offending shall, for every such mill, engine, forge, or furnace, forfeit the sum of two hundred pounds of lawful money of Great Britain.

X. And it is hereby further enacted by the authority aforesaid, That every such mill, engine, forge, or furnace, so erected or continued, contrary to the directions of this act, shall be deemed a common nuisance; and that every governor, lieutenant governor, or commander in chief of any of his Majesty's colonies in America, where any such mill, engine, forge, or furnace, shall be erected or continued, shall, upon information to him made and given, upon the oath of any two or more credible witnesses, that any such mill, engine, forge, or furnace, hath been so erected or continued (which oath such governor, lieutenant governor, or commander in chief, is hereby authorized and required to administer) order and cause every such mill, engine, forge, or furnace, to be abated within the space of thirty days next after such information given and made as aforesaid. . . .

5. The Trade of Boston and New York

FROM Edmund Burke, *An Account of the European Settlements in America,* Fourth Edition, Dublin 1762, II: 166–170, 176–177, 184–186.

Boston, its Harbour and Trade

Though there are in all the provinces of New England large towns which drive a considerable trade, the only one which can deserve to be much insisted upon in a design like ours, is Boston; the capital of Massachusetts bay, the first city in New England, and of all North America. This city is situated on a peninsula, at the bottom of a fine capacious and safe harbour, which is defended from the outrages of the sea, by a number of islands, and rocks which appear above water. It is entered but by one safe passage; and that is narrow, and covered by the cannon of a regular and very strong fortress. The harbor is more than sufficient for the great number of vessels, which carry on the extensive trade of Boston. At the bottom of the bay is a noble pier, near two thousand feet in length, along which on the North side extends a row of warehouses. The head of this pier joins the principal street of the town, which is, like most of the others, spacious and well built. The town lies at the bottom of the harbour, and forms a very agreeable view. It has a town house, where the courts meet, and the exchange is kept, large, and of a very tolerable taste of architecture. Round the exchange, are a great number of well furnished booksellers shops, which find employment for five printing presses. There are ten churches within this town; and it contains at least twenty thousand inhabitants.

That we may be enabled to form some judgment of the wealth of this city, we must observe that from Christmas 1747, to Christmas 1748, five hundred vessels cleared out from this port only, for a foreign trade; and four hundred and thirty were entered inwards; to say nothing of coasting and fishing vessels, both of which are extremely numerous; and said to be equal in number to the others. Indeed the trade of New England is great, as it supplies a large quantity of goods from within itself; but it is yet greater, as the people of this country are in a manner the carriers of all the colonies of North America and the West-Indies, and even for some parts of Europe. They may be considered in this respect as the Dutch of America.

The commodities which the country yields are principally masts and yards, for which they contract largely with the royal navy; pitch, tar, and turpentine, staves, lumber, boards, all sorts of provisions, beef, pork, butter and cheese, in large quantities; horses and live cattle; Indian corn and pease; cyder, apples, hemp and flax. Their peltry trade is not very considerable. They have a very noble cod fishery upon their coast, which employs a vast number of their poeple; they are enabled by this to export annually above thirty two thousand quintals of choice cod fish, to Spain, Italy, and the Mediterranean, and about nineteen thousand quintals of the refuse sort to the West Indies, as food for the negroes. The quantity of spirits, which they distil in Boston from the molasses they bring in from all parts of the West-Indies, is as surprising as the cheap rate at which they vend it, which is under two shillings a gallon. With this they supply almost all the consumption of our colonies in North America, the Indian trade there, the vast demands of their own and the Newfoundland fishery, and in great measure those of the African trade; but they are more famous for the quantity and cheapness, than for the excellency of their rum.

They are almost the only one of our colonies which have much of the woollen and linen manufactures. Of the former they have nearly as much as suffices for their own clothing. It is close and strong, but a coarse stubborn sort of cloth. A number of presbyterians from the North of Ireland, driven thence, as it is said, by the severity of their landlords, from an affinity in religious sentiments chose New England as their place of refuge. Those people brought with them their skill in the linen manufactures, and meeting with very large encouragement, they exercised it to the great advantage of this colony. At present they make large quantities, and of very good kind; their principal settlement is in a town, which in compliment to them is called Londonderry. Hats are made in New England which in a clandestine way find a good vent in all the other colonies. The setting up these manufactures has been in a great measure a matter necessary to them; for as they have not been properly encouraged in some staple commodity, by which they might communicate with their mother country, while they were cut off from all other resources, they must either have abandoned the country, or have found means of employing their own skill and industry to draw out of it the necessaries of life. The same necessity, together with their convenience for building and manning ships, has made them the carriers for the other colonies.

The business of ship-building is one of the most considerable which Boston or the other sea-ports towns in New England carry on. Ships are sometimes built here upon commission; but frequently, the merchants of New England have them constructed upon their own account; and loading them with the produce of the colony, naval stores, fish, and fish-oil principally, they send them out upon a trading voyage to Spain, Portugal, or the Mediterranean, where having disposed of their cargo they make what advantage they can by freight, until such time as they can sell the vessel herself to advantage, which they seldom fail to do in a reasonable time. They receive the value of the vessel, as well as of the freight of the goods, which from time to time they carried, and of the cargo with which they sailed originally, in bills of exchange upon London; for as the people of New England have no commodity to return for the value of above a hundred thousand pounds, which they take in various sorts of goods from England, but some naval stores, and those in no great quantities, they are obliged to keep the balance somewhat even by this circuitous commerce, which though not carried on with Great Britain nor with the British vessels, yet centers in its profits, where all the money which the colonies can make in any manner, must center at last.

I know that complaints have been made of this trade, principally because the people of New England, not satisfied with carrying out their own produce, become carriers for the other colonies, particularly for Virginia and Maryland, from whom they take tobacco, which, in contempt of the act of navigation, they carry directly to the foreign market. Where, not having the duty and accumulated charges to which the British merchant is liable to pay, they in a manner wholly out him of the trade. . . .

The general plan of our management with regard to the trade of our colonies, methinks, ought to be, to encourage in every one of them some separate and distinct articles, such as not interfering, might enable them to trade with each other, and all to trade to advantage with their mother country. And then, where we have rivals in any branch of the trade carried on by our colonies, to enable them to send their goods to the foreign market directly; using at the same time the wise precaution which the French put in to practice, to make the ships so employed to take the English ports in their way home; for our great danger is, that they should in that case make their returns in foreign manufactures, against which we cannot guard too carefully. This, and that they should not go largely into manufactures interfering with ours, ought to be the only points at which our restrictions should aim. These purposes ought not to be compassed by absolute prohibitions and penalties, which would be unpolitical and unjust, but by the way of diversion, by encouraging them to fall into such things as find a demand with ourselves at home. By this means Great Britain and all its dependencies will have a common interest, they will mutually play into each other's hands, and the trade so dispersed, will be of infinitely more advantage to us, than if its several articles were produced and manufactured within ourselves. . . .

The City of New York

The city of New York contains upwards of two thousand houses, and above twelve thousand inhabitants, the descendants of Dutch and English. It is well and commodiously built, extending a mile in length, and about half that in breadth, and has a very good aspect from the sea, but it is by no means properly fortified. The houses are built of brick in the Dutch taste; the streets are not regular, but clean and well paved. There is one large church built for the church of England worship; and three others, a Dutch, a French, and a Lutheran. The town has a very flourishing trade, and in which great profits are made. The merchants are wealthy, and the people in general most comfortably provided for, and with a moderate labour. From the year 1749 to 1750 two hundred and thirty two vessels have entered in this port, and two hundred and eighty six cleared outwards. In these vessels were shipped six thousand seven hundred and thirty one tons of provisions, chiefly flour, and a vast quantity of grain; of which I have no particular account. In the year 1755 the export of flax seed to Ireland amounted to 12,528 hogsheads. The inhabitants (of the colony of New York) are between eighty and an hundred thousand; the lower class easy; the better rich, and hospitable; great freedom of society; and the entry to foreigners made easy by a general toleration of all religious persuasions. In a word, this province yields to no part of America in the healthfulness of its air, and the fertility of its soil. It is much superior in the great convenience of water carriage, which speedily and at the slightest expence carries the product of the remotest farms to a certain and profitable market.

Upon the river Hudson, about one hundred and fifty miles from New York, is Albany; a town of not so much note for its number of houses or inhabitants, as for the great trade which is carried on with the Indians, and indeed by connivance with the French for the use of the same people. This trade takes off a great quantity of coarse woollen goods, such as shrouds and duffils; and with these, guns, hatchets, knives, hoes, kettles, powder and shot; besides shirts and cloaths ready made, and several other articles. Here it is that the treaties and other transactions between us and the Iroquois Indiañs are negotiated.

B. Cities in the Early Federal Period

Two observant French visitors and one British traveller provide illuminating descriptions of life in the cities of the early federal period. The description of Boston in 1781 by the Abbé Robin, a chaplain attached to the 6,000 French troops brought to America by the Comte de Rochambeau to assist in the revolution, affords a clear view (Doc. 6) of a charming city that greatly impressed this cultured gentleman. Thomas Cooper, from Manchester England, who was interested in finding a place to settle himself, made a more factual description (Doc. 7) of the circumstances and prospects of the various cities he visited, comparing them with the provincial cities of Great Britain. The debt American cities owed to those of Europe is further suggested by a letter of Thomas Jefferson to Major L'Enfant (Doc. 8) in response to his request for assistance in the preparation of his plan for Washington. Few Europeans received a more enthusiastic welcome from all sections of the country than Lafayette on his tour of 1824 and 1825. The eagerness with which he was greeted by every active society in each of the many communities he visited enabled his companion, A. Levasseur to write a revealingly descriptive account (Doc. 9) of many aspects of America's urban life overlooked by most visitors.

6. Descriptive Account of Boston by the Abbe Robin in 1781

FROM Nathaniel B. Shurtleff, *A Topographical and Historical Description of Boston*, Boston 1871, pp. 67–71.

A happy change of wind and weather brought us safe into the harbour of Boston. From this road, which is interspersed with several agreeable little Islands, we discovered through the woods, on the side toward the west, a magnificent prospect of houses, built on a curved line, and extending afterwards in a semi-circle above half a league. This was Boston. These edifices which were lofty and regular, with spires and cupolas intermixt at proper distances, did not seem to us a modern settlement so much as the ancient city, enjoying all the embellishments and population, that never fail to attend on commerce and the arts.

I

The inside of the town does not at all lessen the idea that is formed by an exterior prospect: a superb wharf has been carried out above two thousand feet into the sea, and is broad enough for stores and workshops through the whole of its extent; it communicates at right angles with the principal street of the town, which is both large and spacious, and bends in a curve parallel to the harbour; this street is ornamented with elegant buildings, for the most part two or three stories high, and many other streets terminate in this, communicating with it on each side. The form and construction of the houses would surprise an European eye; they are built of brick, and wood, not in the clumsy and melancholy taste of our ancient European towns, but regularly and well provided with windows and doors. The wooden work or frame is light, covered on the outside with thin boards, well plained, and lapped over each other as we do tiles on our roofs in France; these buildings are generally painted with a pale white colour, which renders the prospect much more pleasing than it would otherwise be; the roofs are set off with balconies, doubtless for the more ready extinguishing of fire; the whole is supported by a wall of about a foot high; it is easy to see how great an advantage these houses have over ours, in point of neatness and salubrity. . . .

This city is supposed to contain about six thousand houses, and thirty thousand inhabitants; there are nineteen churches for the several sects here, all of them convenient, and several finished with taste and elegance, especially those of the Presbyterians and the Church of England; their form is generally a long square, ornamented with a pulpit, and furnished with pews of a similar fabrication throughout. The poor as well as the rich hear the word of God in these places in a convenient and decent posture of body.

Sunday is observed with the utmost strictness; all business, how important soever, is then totally at a stand, and the most innocent recreations and pleasures prohibited. Boston that populous town, where at other times there is such a hurry of business, is on this day a mere desert; you may walk the streets without meeting a single person, or if by chance you meet one, you scarcely dare to stop and talk with him. . . .

Nobody fails here of going to the place of worship appropriated to his sect. In these places there reigns a profound silence; an order and respect is also observable which has not been seen for a long time in our Catholic churches. Their psalmody is grave and majestic, and the harmony of the poetry, in their national tongue, adds a grace to the music, and contributes greatly towards keeping up the attention of the worshippers.

All these churches are destitute of ornaments. No addresses are made to the heart and the imagination; there is no visible object to suggest to the mind for what purpose a man comes into these places, who he is and what he will shortly be. Neither painting nor sculpture represent those great events which ought to recall him to his duty and awaken his gratitude, nor are those heroes in piety brought into view, whom it is his duty to admire and endeavour to imitate. The pomp of ceremony is here wanting to shadow out the greatness of the being he goes to worship; there are no processions to testify the homage we owe to him, that great Spirit of the Universe, by whose will Nature itself exists, through whom the fields are covered with harvests, and the trees are loaded with fruits. . . .

Piety is not the only motive that brings the American ladies in crowds to the various places of worship. Deprived of all shows and public diversions whatever, the church is the grand theatre where they attend, to display their extravagance and finery. There they come dressed off in their finest silks, and overshadowed with a profusion of the most superb plumes. The hair of the head is raised and supported upon cushions to an extravagant height, somewhat resembling the manner in which the French ladies wore their hair some years ago.

7. *American and British Cities Compared*

FROM Thomas Cooper, *Some Information Respecting America*, London 1794, pp. 48–50.

In Boston, New York, Philadelphia, and Baltimore, the state of society is much the same as in the large towns of Great Britain, such as Birmingham, Bristol, Liverpool, and Manchester. The American towns I have just enumerated, contain together about the same number of inhabitants as the English towns just mentioned; that is, about 200,000. Boston, in 1791, contained 18,038 inhabitants. New York, 33,131. Philadelphia, 42,520. Baltimore, 13,503: Richmond, 3,761. Alexandria, 2,748. Lexington, in Kentucky, 834. Since that year the increase has been equivalent to make up the aggregate that I state. New York, for instance, is a perfect counterpart of Liverpool: the situation of the docks, the form of streets, the state of the public buildings, the inside as well as the outside of the houses, the manners, the amusements, the mode of living among the expensive part of the inhabitants—all these circumstances are as nearly alike, in the towns last mentioned, as possible. In all the American towns above noticed, there are theatres and assemblies. They are, in short, precisely what the larger and more opulent provincial towns of Great Britain are. Hence also you may easily conceive, that European comforts and conveniences are not scarce. In fact, you may find in Philadelphia or

New York, every article of that description usually kept in the shops in the English towns I have referred to, in equal plenty, but not indeed equally cheap. To the price of all articles of luxurious furniture (pictures, pier glasses, carpets, &c.) add one-third to the English price, and you have the full American price. House-rent is also much the same as in the places hitherto compared: if any thing, somewhat dearer in America for houses of the same size and convenience. The houses in the one set of towns as in the other, are built of brick and stone. In the country, houses of equal convenience are as cheap as in the country of Great Britain.

Provisions (milk and butter excepted, at Philadelphia and southward) are a full third cheaper than in similar places of Great Britain. Butter, in Boston and New York, is cheaper than in Philadelphia, where it is from 15d to 20d per lb. Cheese about the same price as with you, but not so good. Firing in the great towns very dear, a chord of hiccory wood, 8 feet by 4 feet and 4 feet, selling in Philadelphia and New York, in winter, at 7 dollars. In the country it would be about 1 dollar and a half.

8. Jefferson to L'Enfant

FROM *The Writings of Thomas Jefferson*, H. A. Washington, ed., 1859 ed. III–236–7.

Philadelphia April 10. 1791

TO MAJOR L'ENFANT
Sir
        I am favored with your letter of the 4 instant, and in complyance with your request I have examined my papers and found the plans of Frankfort on the Mayne, Carlsruhe, Amsterdam, Strasburg, Paris, Orleans, Bordeaux, Lyons, Montpelier, Marseilles, Turin, and Milan, which I send in a roll by this Post. They are on large and accurate scales, having been procured by me while in those respective cities myself. And they are connected with the notes I made in my travels, and often necessary to explain them to myself, I will beg your care of them and to return them when no longer useful to you, leaving you absolutely free to keep them as long as useful. I am happy that the President has left the planning of the Town in such good hands, and have no doubt it will be done to general satisfaction. Considering that the grounds to be reserved for the public, are to be paid for by the acre, I think very liberal reservations should be made for them; and if this be about the Tyber and on the back of the town, it will be of no injury to the commerce of the place,

which will undoubtedly establish itself on the deep waters towards the Eastern branch and mouth of Rock Creek; the water about the mouth of the Tyber not being of any depth. Those connected with the Government will prefer fixing themselves near the public grounds, in the center, which will also be convenient to be resorted to as walks from the lower and upper town. Having communicated to the President, before he went away, such general ideas on the subject of the Town, as occurred to me, I make no doubt that, in explaining himself to you on the subject, he has interwoven with his own ideas, such of mine as he approved: for fear of repeating therefore, what he did not approve, and having more confidence in the unbiassed state of his mind, than in my own, I avoid interfering with what he may have expressed to you. Whenever it is proposed to prepare plans for the Capitol, I should prefer the adoption of some one of the models of antiquity, which have had the approbation of thousands of years, and for the President's House I should prefer the celebrated fronts of modern buildings, which have already received the approbation of all good judges. Such are the Galerie du Louvre, the Gardens meubles, and two fronts of the Hotel de Salm. But of this it is yet time enough to consider, in the mean time I am with great esteem Sir &c

TH: JEFFERSON

9. Philanthropy and Culture in American Cities

FROM A. Levasseur, *Lafayette in America in 1824 and 1825,* New York 1829, I: 89–91, 162–164. II:75.

Among all the public schools visited by General Lafayette, that which excited the most lively interest was the "Free School of Young Africans," founded and directed by the society for the emancipation of the blacks. The General was accompanied to the school, as he had been at the others, by a great number of ladies, who all bestowed assiduous care on those institutions. There it was announced to him, that he had been elected a member of the society at the same time with Mr. Grenville Sharp and Mr. Thomas Clarkson. The appointment too well corresponded with his character and known opinions relating to the slavery of the blacks, not to give him a deep feeling. Immediately afterwards, a young black child approached, and addressed him with spirit in the following manner: "You see, General, several hundreds of poor children of the African race, now before you. They participate here in the benefits of education with the whites, and they like them learn to cherish the memory of the services you have rendered to America. They also revere in you an ardent friend of the emancipation of our race, and a worthy member of the society to which we owe so much gratitude."

It would require much time, and would be very difficult for me, to give precise details concerning the benevolent establishments of New York. They are very numerous; and as every one of them is the production of a society or of a private exertion, it would be necessary, if one wished to make them well known, to give the history of each. It may be said, in general terms, of them all, that they are under the protection, and not under the influence of the government. The greater part of the administration employments are performed without appointments or honours, by men who regard their nomination to these employments as honourable testimonies of public esteem, and who fill them with corresponding zeal and probity. There is generally no salary paid, unless to persons in an inferior employment, or in details which require the sacrifice of the whole time of the person employed. The greater part of these establishments are founded either by societies or by legacies; they are supported by public subscriptions, or by assistance from the government. Thus, for example, in looking through the register of the House or Asylum for orphans, which was founded in 1806, we perceive that this establishment received, in the course of the year 1822, five hundred dollars from the Legislature of the state; two hundred and eighty seven dollars as its part of the funds allowed to public schools throughout the state, and 1430 dollars from private subscriptions: five hundred dollars in interest on a legacy from Mr. Jacob Sherred; twenty five dollars in interest on a legacy made by Mrs. Maria Williams: three hundred and ninety dollars in anonymous subscriptions: one hundred and seventeen dollars given by the Magdalen Society; nineteen dollars in work done by the children, &c., &c., besides a great number of individual presents, such as books, cloths, buttons, fruit, combs, &c. Whatever be the nature or value of the gifts, they are received by the directors, who scrupulously register them, with the names of the donors. By the aid of these contributions, wisely employed, this Asylum, between 1806 and 1822, received and educated four hundred and forty children, two hundred and forty three of them are now placed in situations, useful both to themselves and to society.

In the Poor House there are more than 1000 individuals of both sexes and all ages.

The Great Hospital of New York may contain nearly 2000 sick. Foreigners, although under the same treatment, are placed in a separate wing of the building.

In all those establishments we were struck with the cleanliness of the wards, the whiteness of the linen, the good quality of the food, and above all, with the mild and affectionate conduct of those employed in them, towards the persons intrusted to their care. It was easily to be seen, that the directors were animated by something more valuable than salaries; the esteem of the public.

The persons who accompanied us, and who seemed well informed assured us that there are in the city of New York more than forty charitable and philanthropic societies, whose common zeal greatly contributes to the support of the institutions we have visited, and the assistance of private sufferers.

After having visited the Academy of Arts, where among a great number of casts, engravings, and paintings, there is hardly any thing remarkable except the collection of pictures by Trumbull, and the collection of engravings sent to the Academy by Napoleon. We went to the Public Library; it contains more than 20,000 volumes, the choice of which has been directed by taste; and every thing appeared to us in very good order. The public are admitted every day except Sundays; but no one is allowed to take books home, except the subscribers, who are five hundred in number.

During the second visit to New York, we also went several times to the two theatres: but it would be very difficult for me to express an opinion of them, as every time that General Lafayette appeared, he became the object of attention to such a degree, and the tumult raised by the expressions of joy by the spectators was so great, that it was impossible for the actors to continue their performance. . . .

In the succeeding days we visited almost every thing in the city of Baltimore, which appeared to me one of the most beautiful cities in the Union. Although the streets are all very wide and regular, it has not the monotony of Philadelphia. The ground has so varied a surface, that every part of the city presents a different aspect from various parts.

From several elevated points in the city, the eye embraces, not only the mass of buildings, but also a part of the harbour, the bright waters of the Chesapeake, and the dark forests which extend afar, and seem placed to increase, by their relief, the effect of the magical picture of a city containing 60,000 souls, created within a period of less than half a century. The inhabitants of Baltimore, appear in general to possess a decided taste for the fine arts. I have already remarked that they owe to a Frenchman their evident superiority in music, above all the other cities in the union: it is also to a Frenchman that they are indebted for the beauty of their architecture. Most of the public monuments were built after the plans of M. Godfrey who has long resided among them. The Unitarian church is a masterpiece for simplicity and elegance. The monument erected to the memory of the citizens who died in defence of Baltimore during the last war, is in a severe style, and of beautiful execution. That raised in honour of Washington, also resembles, both in height and figure, our column in the Place Vendôme, in Paris. It is built of beautiful white marble; and its situation, on a small eminence, makes it conspicuous from all parts of the city, and even from a great distance on the bay.

The harbour is safe and convenient. It however sometimes happens, that in severe winters, it is obstructed with ice. Although situated nearly two hundred miles from the sea, it is much frequented. The great number of rivers which fall into the Chesapeake, render Baltimore a place of active internal trade; yet a very sensible reduction is remarked in the commerce of the port within a few years, the first causes of which are differently accounted for. It is thought that the difficulties will soon be removed, or at least, that they will partially cease to operate, when the noble plan of a railway shall be executed, which will open and facilitate new communications with the Ohio.

Baltimore appeared to me one of the cities most agreeable for a residence. The inhabitants, although ardently devoted to all sorts of business, are not ignorant of those studies which form the taste, and extend the resources of the mind. There are several learned societies: one of which, the Newtonian Society of Maryland, founded in 1818, affords much encouragement to the study of Natural History. The Economical Society was founded in 1819, for the encouragement of manufactures and domestic economy. The Agricultural Society is no less remarkable than the others, for the services it renders, and the merits of its members. Before our departure, we all had the honour of becoming honourary members of this society. The Anatomical Cabinets of Messrs. Chiappi and Gibson, the museum of Natural History, and Gallery of Pictures of Mr. Peale, and the Minerological Cabinet of Mr. Gilmore, are beautiful amateur collections. The City Library contains about 14,000 volumes, and is entirely free to the public. What adds a great charm to the advantages which Baltimore possesses within itself, is the vicinity of Washington, the seat of the central government, which, during the sessions of Congress, presents great attractions to persons who wish to attend the political debates. However, at Baltimore, as in all New England, Sunday is rather dull, and the religious practices austere: yet the tolerance enjoyed is absolute. Twelve sects, at least, are found in the city; the most numerous of which is the Catholic. Yet, although they have the numerical force, they are as gentle, tolerant, and charitable as the others; because they know that they could find no support from the laws, if they were disposed to intrigue and govern, as in some parts of Europe.

This city, so fine, and so interesting, only fifty years since, was but an assemblage of a few ill-constructed houses. In 1790 its population suddenly rose to 13,503 inhabitants: and later census show 26,514 in 1800; 35,583 in 1810; 65,738 in 1820. At the present time (1824) it is estimated at more than 65,000, of whom, at least 50,000 belong to the white population, and 11,000 to the free coloured. The remaining 4,000 have still the misfortune to be slaves. Happily the number of the last is daily diminishing. The progress of philanthropy, and the true interest of the city, well understood, although slow, is, however constant; and the friends of humanity have a right to hope, that the inhabitants of Baltimore, before many years, will finish by ridding themselves of the scourge of slavery, which may be called a shameful one, if it were not known what obstacles they had to surmount up to the present time, to renounce the abominable inheritance which England bequeathed to the United States, as if to punish them for breaking the colonial chain.

Luxury and the arts, in being introduced among the population of Baltimore, have not brought with them the effeminacy and corruption which some pretend are their inseparable companions. The defence of Baltimore in the last war, is enough to prove that its inhabitants are still, as in the days of their glorious revolution, passionately attached to liberty, and the courageous defenders of their independence. . . .

Savannah is the largest town in the state of Georgia, and is situated on the right bank of the river of the same name, about seventeen miles from its mouth. Its streets, wide and straight, all cross at right angles, and are planted on each side with rows of very handsome trees, called the pride of India, for which the inhabitants of the southern states have a strong predilection. Although situated forty feet above the level of the river, the situation of Savannah is unhealthy; the yellow fever rarely fails to visit it every autumn, with fatal effects. The trade, however, is very active, and its port, which admits vessels drawing fourteen feet water, annually exports cotton to the value of sixteen millions of dollars. The population amounts to 7,523 inhabitants, thus divided: 3,557 whites, 582 free blacks, and 3,075 slaves. The number of persons employed in manufactures, is almost equal to those devoted to commerce, who are about six hundred.

C. The First Urban Frontier

Two rival western journalists, both of whom published a descriptive volume on the West in 1828, supply revealing comments on the character of the early towns, their economic rivalries, and their social and cultural aspirations. James Hall, a writer and banker from Philadelphia, spent several months on a tour of the western settlements in 1821–22 and wrote a series of 'Letters from the West' first published in the *Port Folio* and issued in book form in 1828. His description of Pittsburgh (Doc. 10) has the romantic flavour characteristic of the young republic and the practical interest in economic detail that increasingly animated American cities. Timothy Flint from Massachusetts, a graduate of Harvard and a sometimes missionary as well as journalist, also spent several years touring the western settlements before settling for a time at Cincinnati where he published the *Western Monthly Review* from 1827 to 1830. Here he also brought out a two volume compendium of his writings from which I have quoted illuminating descriptions of Lexington, Louisville, and Cincinnati Doc. 11).

10. *Pittsburgh and Its Vicinity*

FROM James Hall, *Letters from the West*, London 1828, pp. 21–23, 32–38.

Pittsburgh was first laid out in the year 1765; it was afterwards laid out, surveyed, and completed on its present plan, in 1784, by Colonel George Woods, by order of Tench Francis, Esq., attorney for John Penn, and John Penn, junior. The increase of the town was not rapid until the year 1793, in consequence of the inroads of the savage tribes, which impeded the growth of the neighboring settlements. The western insurrection, more generally known as the "Whisky War," once more made this the scene of commotion, and is said to have given Pittsburgh a new and thriving impulse, by throwing a considerable sum of money into circulation. Since that time it has increased rapidly, and a few years ago was erected into a city.

Pittsburgh and its vicinity may proudly challenge comparison in beauty of scenery and healthfulness of situation. Surrounded by hills and vallies which, in the seasons of verdure, are clothed in the richest vegetation, commanding points may be found in every direction, from which the eye is delighted with the most romantic scenes. Three noble streams contribute to diversify the prospect, embellishing and enlivening an endless variety of Nature's loveliest pictures.

Grant's-hill, an abrupt eminence which projects into the rear of the city, affords one of the most delightful prospects with which I am acquainted; presenting a singular combination of the bustle of the town, with the solitude and sweetness of the country. How many hours have I spent here, in the enjoyment of those exquisite sensations which are awakened by pleasing associations and picturesque scenes! The city lay beneath me, enveloped in smoke—the clang of hammers resounded from its numerous manufactories—the rattling of carriages and the hum of men were heard from the streets—churches, courts, hotels, and markets, and all the "pomp and circumstances" of busy life, were presented in one panoramic view. Behind me were all the silent soft attractions of rural sweetness—the ground rising gradually for a considerable distance, and exhibiting country seats, surrounded with cultivated fields, gardens, and orchards. On either hand were the rivers, one dashing over beds of rock, the other sluggishly meandering among the hills;—while the lofty eminences beyond them, covered with timber, displayed a rich foliage, decked and shadowed with every tint of the rainbow. Below the town, the Ohio is seen, receiving her tributary streams, and bearing off to the West, burthened with rich freights. The towns of Allegheny on the right hand, and Birmingham on the left—the noble bridges that lead to the city in opposite directions—the arsenal, and the little village of Laurenceville, in the rear, added variety to the scene. . . .

It would require more room than I can afford, and more patience than I possess, to give you a detailed account of all the branches of commerce and manufactures which contribute to the prosperity of Pittsburgh. The latter have flourished here extensively, in consequence of the variety of raw materials indigenous to the country, the abundance of fuel, the salubrity of the climate, the cheapness of provisions, the convenience of the markets, and the enterprising spirit of the people. The most important branch includes articles manufactured of iron, a metal which is found in great abundance in the neighbouring mountains, whence it is brought in *pigs* and *bars* to this place, at a small expence, and here wrought for exportation. Most of the machinery for this and other purposes is propelled by steam, the management of which has been brought to great perfection; but the neighbourhood also affords many fine water-courses, some of which are occupied; cannon, of a very superior quality, have been cast here for the United States Service. The manufacture of glass, which was introduced by the late General O'Hara, about the year 1798, has been carried on with great success; there are now a number of establishments in operation, which produce large quantities of window-glass, and other ware of the coarser sort, and one, at which flint glass is made and ornamented with great elegance. Messrs. Bakewell, Page, and Bakewell, have the credit of having introduced the latter branch of this manufacture; and their warehouse presents an endless variety of beautiful ware, designed and executed in a style which is highly creditable to their taste and perseverance. Manufactories of wool and cotton have been supported with some spirit, but, as yet, with little success. We have a foolish pride about us, which makes our gentlemen ashamed of wearing a coat which has not crossed the Atlantic; I hope we shall grow wiser as we grow older. Articles of tin and leather are fabricated at Pittsburgh to an astonishing amount. So long ago as 1809, boots and shoes were manufactured to the amount of seventy thousand dollars; saddlery to the amount of forty thousand, and tin ware to the amount of twenty-five thousand dollars, in one year. In the same year, hats were made to the amount of twenty-five thousand dollars, and cabinet ware to the amount of seventeen thousand. In addition to these, there have been tan-yards, rope-walks, manufactories of white lead and paper, and extensive ship-yards.[1] You will perceive that I have made this enumeration from data collected several years ago; the increase of population and business has been great, since that time; and when I add, that in addition to the branches already mentioned, all the other mechanic arts receive a proportionable share of attention; it will be seen, that as a manufacturing town, Pittsburgh stands in the first rank, and her rapid rise and progress may be adduced as a proud testimony of American enterprise.

The commerce and trade of Pittsburgh arise partly from her manufactories, and partly from having long been the place of deposit for goods destined for the western country; all of which, until very recently, passed from the Atlantic cities, through this place, to their respective points of destination. They are brought in waggons, carrying from thirty-five to fifty hundred pounds each, and embarked at this place in boats. Upwards of four thousand waggon loads of merchandize have been known to enter Pittsburgh in the course of one year, by the main road from Philadelphia alone, in which is not included the baggage and furniture of travellers and emigrants, nor is notice taken of arrivals by other routes. This business has brought an immense quantity of money into circulation at Pittsburgh; but it has lately been much injured by the competition of Wheeling, and the introduction of steam-boats upon the Ohio. The wealth of this

[1] Nor should I forget some half dozen printing offices and several book stores, which have been instrumental in consuming a vast deal of ink and paper.

place, however, and its local advantages, must long sustain it against all opposition; and if the capital of her citizens should eventually be drawn from any branch of commerce, it will probably be thrown into the manufactories, where the profits will be as great, and much more permanent. Some of the finest steam-boats which navigate the Ohio, the James Ross, the General Neville, and many others, were built here.

This is also a *port of entry,* and here—even here, at the source of the Ohio—have ships been built, laden, and cleared out, for the distant ports of Europe. A curious incident connected with this subject was mentioned by Mr. Clay on the floor of Congress. "To illustrate the commercial habits and enterprise of the American people, (he said) he would relate an anecdote of a vessel, built, and cleared out at Pittsburgh for Leghorn. When she arrived at her place of destination, the master presented his papers to the custom-house officer, who would not credit them, and said to him, "Sir, your papers are forged: there is no such port as Pittsburgh in the world; your vessel must be confiscated.' The trembling captain laid before the officer the map of the United States—directed him to the gulf of Mexico—pointed out the mouth of the Mississippi—led him a thousand miles up it to the mouth of the Ohio, and thence another thousand up to Pittsburgh. 'There, Sir, is the port whence my vessel cleared out.' The astonished officer, before he had seen the map, would as readily have believed that this vessel had been navigated from the moon."

Of the society I have but little to say, for that is entirely a matter of taste. Strangers are generally pleased with it, for if they do not find, among the male inhabitants, that polished urbanity which distinguishes many of the small towns of the south and west, they are amply repaid for the absence of it by the sweetness and affability of its female denizens, among whom there is a sufficiency of beauty and grace to decorate a ball-room to great advantage. Indeed, I have seldom beheld finer displays of female loveliness than I have witnessed here. There is a small theatre, occasionally occupied by strollers, but often destined to exhibit the histrionic genius of the young gentlemen of the place, among whom the enacting of plays was formerly a fashionable amusement. On such occasions the *dramatis personae* were represented by a select company, regularly organized, among whom were some beardless youths who personated the females. In this manner some fine displays of genius have been elicited; the ladies smiled graciously on the enterprise, and the whole was conducted with great decorum.

A seminary of learning has been founded at the town of Allegheny, called the "Western University," and liberally endowed with land by the State Legislature; but it is not yet organized. An academy in

Pittsburgh has heretofore presented the means of classical education, and a number of minor schools have been supported, among which may be mentioned the Sabbath schools, conducted with great spirit and benevolence, by a society composed of the religious of different denominations. There has been also an admirable school for young ladies, and a library company has been established here.

11. Lexington, Louisville and Cincinnati

FROM Timothy Flint, *A Condensed Geography and History of the Western States, or the Mississippi Valley*, Cincinnati 1828, II: 185–190, 321, 323–328.

Lexington, and Louisville in Kentucky

Lexington is the commercial metropolis of the state; and until very lately, was the largest town on the south side of the Ohio, above New Orleans. Nashville, probably, vies with it, at present, in size. Few towns in the western country, or the world, are more delightfully situated. It has an air of neatness, opulence and repose, that render it a pleasant town to the eye of a stranger. It is situated in the heart of the richest country in Kentucky. Nothing can be more beautiful than the scenery and the farms in the neighborhood. The frequency of handsome villas, and fine and ornamented rural mansions, might lead to the impression, that we were near a large commercial metropolis. A beautiful branch of the Elkhorn runs through the town, and waters it plentifully. The main street is a mile and a quarter in length, eighty feet wide, handsomely paved, and in the sumptuousness of the buildings, holds a respectable competition with the towns of the Atlantic country. In the center of the town is the public square, surrounded by large and handsome buildings. In this square is the market house, which is amply supplied with all the products of the state. It contains over 1,000 houses, and about 7,000 inhabitants. The presbyterians have three churches, and the methodists, baptists, seceders, episcopalians, and Roman catholics, one each. The court house is a spacious and respectable building. The masonic hall and bank make a handsome appearance. The university buildings are situated in a beautiful square, and are large and handsome. The hotels and taverns are noted for their size and convenience. The appearance of show and splendor, and the display of merchandize are sure to strike Atlantic strangers, who see the town for the first time, with surprise. There are the customary numbers of all kinds of stores, and of all kinds of pursuits and employments. The woollen manufactory, built by Mr. Prentiss, about a mile from the town, is a noble establishment. In addition to an adequate number of all the common manufactures of large towns, the staple manufactures of the place are cordage and bagging. It is supposed, that the amount of manufactures of this article is nearly a million of dollars. The woollen establishment manufactures broad clothes, cassimeres, blankets and flannels. The manufacture of paper is extensive, as is also that of cotton. The number of beautiful mansions, visible on all the ways of approach to the city, prepare the stranger to be pleased with it. The inhabitants are a cheerful, gay and conversable people, most of them capable of conversing upon literary subjects. The professional men are more than commonly intelligent; and many distinguished men have had their origins here. The University with its professors and students, and the numerous distinguished strangers that are visiting here, during the summer months, add to the attractions of the city. The people are addicted to hospitality and parties; and the tone of society is fashionable and pleasant. Strangers generally are found to be delighted with a visit here, and are introduced with ease to all, that is respectable and interesting in the place. There are large towns in the West; but none, that convey higher ideas of the luxury, refinement and polish of the country.

Louisville, at the falls of the Ohio, is about the size of Lexington, or perhaps, at this time, more populous. In a commercial point of view, it is by far the most important town in the state. The main street is nearly a mile in length, and is as noble, as compact, and has as much the air of a maritime town, as any street in the western country. It is situated on an extensive sloping plain, below the mouth of Beargrass, about a quarter of a mile above the principal declivity of the falls. The three principal streets run parallel with the river, and command fine views of the villages, and the beautiful country on the opposite shore. It has several churches, among them, churches for the presbyterians, baptists, and Roman catholics. The mouth of Beargrass affords an admirable harbor for the steam boats, and river craft. The public buildings are not numerous, but respectable; and the people are more noted for commercial enterprise, than for works of public utility. It has a proportion of all the mechanic establishments, common in the western country; and very considerable manufactories of cordage and bagging. There is naturally a connection between this town and Portland, two miles below the mouth of Beargrass. The large steam boats, that run between this town and New Orleans, seldom are able to pass over these falls; and perhaps, on an average, not more than two months in the year. Of course they lie by in the fine harbor, made by the eddy of the falls. There are always great numbers of steam boats lying there, either for repair there, or on the opposite side of the river; or advertised as up for a trip. It is the greatest port for steam boats between Pittsburgh and Natchez. The cargoes of the steam boats, that are intended for the country above are obliged to be discharged here, and drayed around the falls to the mouth of Beargrass. Lines of steam boats from above and below meet here, and ordinarily have an understanding. One cause of the commercial prosperity of Louisville has been this necessity of its merchants being employed not only, as factors for the important business, that terminates at this town, but for all that, which passes up the Ohio. The falls have a romantic appearance from the town. The river is divided by a fine island, which renders the scenery more impressive and picturesque. Except in very high stages of water the whole width of the river, which is here a full mile, has the appearance of a great many broken rivers of foam, making their way over the falls.

A canal is now in successful progress, which is intended to remove this obstacle to the navigation of the Ohio. Mr. L. Baldwin, an intelligent and practical engineer, surveyed the ground, and directed the plan of the canal. It will be two miles in length, and the excavation is required to be forty feet in depth in some places. A part of this depth is cut from solid lime stone. It is on a scale to admit steam boats and vessels of the largest size. From the nature of the country, and from the great difference between the highest and lowest stages of the water, amounting to nearly sixty feet, it is necessarily a work of great magnitude. It will soon be completed, and in operation. There are various opinions, in reference to the bearing of this work upon the future prosperity of Louisville. Great part of the important and lucrative business of factorage will pass away from this place of course; and as boats can ascend from Louisville to Cincinnati, with at least as great a draft of water, as is required by the depth of the water from Louisville to the mouth of the Ohio, most of the boats from the Mississippi, that used to be arrested at the falls, will of course pass on to the country above. But other bearings of utility to this place, not yet contemplated, will, probably grow, out of the increased activity, given by the canal to business, and to commerce. No axiom is better established in these days, than that every part of a country, so connected as the whole coast of Ohio, flourishes, and increases with the growth of every other part. If the country, above and below, be flourishing, so also will be Louisville. Besides, this important town has intrinsic resources, which will not fail to make it a great place. More steam boats are up in New Orleans for this place, than for any other; and except during the season of ice, or of extremely low water, there seldom elapses a week, without an arrival from New Orleans. The gun of the arriving or departing steam boats is heard at every hour of the day and the night; and no person has an adequate idea of the business and bustle of Louisville, until he has arrived at the town. The country, of which this town is the county seat, is one of the most fertile, and best settled in the state. . . .

Cincinnati, in Ohio
Cincinnati is the chief town of this state, the emporium of the western country; and far larger than any other town in the Mississippi valley, except New Orleans. The next town to it, in point of numbers is Pittsburgh. Pittsburgh and Louisville, in commercial importance, rank next to this place; but each with a considerable interval. . . . The first laying out of the town was in 1789. In 1808, the land around Fort Washington, which belonged to the government, was sold in lots.

The town is built partly on the bottom, and partly on the hill. The ascent from the bottom to the hill was originally rough and precipitous. But wherever the plan of the corporation had been carried into effect, this ascent has been smoothed, and graduated, so as to be easy and pleasant, with a gentle angle of ascent. The upper part of the city is elevated from fifty to sixty feet above the lower part. Seven of the streets are sixty-six feet wide, and 396 feet apart. The cross streets, of the same width and distance, intersect them at right angles. The lots reserved for public buildings, are a fraction of a square between Main and Broadway streets, and an entire square between Fourth and Fifth streets.

The buildings stretch over an irregular extent of ground, occupying a very large space, that is not yet filled up; though the numerous buildings are rising upon it, in every direction. The central part of the town is very compact; and Main street would not discredit any town in the United States. Its public buildings are a court house, fifty-six feet by sixty feet, and 120 in height to the top of the dome; a public jail near the court house; three market houses, the one 300 feet in length, the other 200, and the third 150; the United States' bank, which has a front, including the wings, of sixty feet, two stories high, built of free stone in front, and presenting a very respectable appearance; the Medical college, fifty-four feet by thirty-six, and two stories high above the pediment. Besides its windows it has an octagonal sky light. The Hospital, or Lunatic Asylum is fifty-three feet in front, by forty-three in depth; three stories in height. It stands in a fine roomy lot, containing four acres. The Cincinnati college, formerly the Lancastrian seminary, has two projecting wings, and is eighty-eight feet in depth. The first presbyterian church is sixty-eight by eighty-five feet, surmounted with two cupolas. The Roman catholic cathedral is a very handsome church, 110 feet by fifty. The episcopal church is a respectable brick building. Besides these, there is a second presbyterian church, the methodist stone church, the Wesleyan methodist church, the first baptist church, the Enon baptist church, the German Lutheran

K

church, the New Jerusalem church, the Friends' church, the African church; and two or three other religious denominations occupy buildings, temporarily, as churches. The Cincinnati theatre is an indifferent looking building externally. It is 100 by forty feet; and has an Ionic portico. Beside these there are a number of splendid private mansions in this city.

This city is amply supplied with water from the Ohio by steam power. A chartered company has the management of this water; and they convey it to every family that chooses to have it, for a stipulated sum. The greater part of the families in the compact part of the city are already supplied with it.

There are four substantial fire engines, and as many fire companies under fine order and discipline. Five large brick cisterns are required to be kept constantly full of water. In cases of fire, these companies manoeuvre with great promptitude, skill and decision.

Every day in the week is a market day. The meats, fowls, vegetables, flour, meal, and fruits are admirable, both for quality and abundance. Lines of market wagons a half a mile in length are seen in the streets. The fruits and vegetables are improving every year. It seems to be the general impression of strangers, that for abundance, cheapness and excellence of the articles supplied, no town of the size in the United States is superior to Cincinnati.

The following are among the prominent charitable societies of the city. The humane society for recovering drowned persons. It has a fine apparatus and consists of 300 members. The Miami bible society. The female auxiliary society. The female charitable missionary society. The female association for the benefit of Africans. The western navigation bible and tract society. The Union Sabbath school society. The colonization society. Three masonic lodges. The commercial hospital and lunatic asylum. The state has made liberal appropriations for this institution; and it is already an efficient charity for those objects of wretchedness, for whose comfort it was provided. The Kidd fund appropriated 100 dollars a year forever for the education of the poor children and youth of Cincinnati. At present the possession of the ground, from which this fund was raised, is in litigation. The Woodward free grammar school of Cincinnati is a munificent charity; and promises to be an efficient one. It is hoped, that in 1828, the avails of this fund will be sufficient for the gratuitous education of sixty of the poor children of the city.

The medical college received a charter in 1820. In 1825, the number of medical students was eighty-two. The Cincinnati college was chartered in 1819. The Lancastrian school in the same building, which was suspended for some years, is now resumed under its former instructor. The Cincinnati female academy, under the care of Dr. Locke, is a school of the first class of its kind. The Cincinnati female school under the care of Messrs. Pickets, has also a high reputation. The classical academy under the care of Rev. C. B. M'Kee and Dr. Slack's school, have extensive reputation. There are a great number of respectable boarding and town schools, in which a number of children, far beyond the ordinary porportion for such a population are instructed. The Cincinnati reading room, is a respectable establishment of the kind. The Western museum is a noble institution, when the age of the city is taken into consideration. It is rich in the organic remains of the western country; in birds, fishes, reptiles and insects; in fossils and minerals; in botanical specimens, medals, coins, and tokens, in foreign and American antiquities; in panoramic views, wax figures and miscellaneous curiosities. The whole number of curiosities exceeds 10,000. Letton's museum is, also respectable, containing articles similar to the former, and is managed with great industry and enterprize by the properietor. Mr. Letton. The number of curiosities is between two and three thousand. The Cincinnati library contains 1,300 volumes, and is becoming of great utility to the general literature of the city. The apprentices library contains 1,200 volumes, and is intended for the benefit of apprentices and mechanics; and is one of the most beneficient and noble institutions in the city. There are twelve newspapers and periodical works published in the city. Efforts are now making to establish an academy of the fine arts, under the care of Mr. Eckstein. It is to be hoped, the citizens of the city will patronize this honorable enterprize.

The government of the city is vested in a mayor and aldermen; and its municipal judicature is in the city court. The city tax, in 1826, was nearly 30,000 dollars. The appropriations in the same year were 20,000; and the net revenue of the city 23,000. Much of the expenditure has been for the construction of quays, and wharfs, paving, and graduating the streets, paving gutters, and setting up curbstones. These works of public utility are pursued with great energy, economy and skill. It is believed, that no place in the United States carries into effect, works of this sort with more spirit and success. Cincinnati began to be settled in 1788. It began to be a village, in 1805. In 1810, the population was 2,300. In 1813, 4,000. In 1819, 10,283. In 1824, 12,016. In 1826, 16,230. Among these, there are twenty-eight clergymen, thirty-four attorneys, thirty-five physicians, 800 persons employed in mercantile pursuits, 500 in navigation, and 3,000 in manufactures. There are between thirty and forty considerable manufacturing establishments. Among which, the most important are the Cincinnati steam mill, the mill for sawing stone, which also contains four or five other manufacturing establishments under the same roof, and moved by the same power; the Phoenix foundry, the Franklin foundry, the Eagle foundry, Tift's steam engine establishment, Green's steam engine establishment, Shield's engine finishing establishment, Goodloe's and Harkness' establishment, which is a cotton factory; the AEtna foundry, Kirk's steam engine and finishing establishment; Allen & Co's. chemical laboratory, powder mill, Phoenix paper mill, the Cincinnati steam paper mill, the woollen factory, the sugar refinery, the white lead factory, Wells' type foundry, and printer's warehouse, three large boat yards for building steam boats, extensive hat manufactories, and cabinet furniture manufactories, ten printing establishments, from which issued, in 1826, nearly 200,000 books and pamphlets, besides newspapers and periodicals. The whole value of the manufactures, in all the departments of industry in this city, is estimated at 1,850,000 dollars.

Cincinnati is a place of extensive importation, for the supply of the extensive country, that depends upon it. There are a number of respectable mercantile firms, two of which import directly from Europe. It is expected, that it will soon become a port of entry. At present its commerce is as extensive, as the courses of steam and keel boats; and it is increasing every year. Sixty steam boats have already been built here; burthen 11,225 tons. Some of the largest and most beautiful boats, that have appeared on the western waters, have recently been built here. Between the 5th and 12th of February, 1827, arrived in this port and departed from it twenty-one steam boats, tonnage 4,117.

D. Cities as Nurseries of Enterprise

Among the articulate visitors to America in the pre-Civil War decades were several experts in the field of industry and trade. Michael Chevalier a French economist was the first in 1834 to arrive on an official inspection tour of public works in the States. His observations (Doc. 12) on the transport arteries of the leading cities clearly delineated the urban strategy of the period. Sir Joseph Whitworth, an ingenious mechanic who had perfected the planing machine, improved other machine tools, and won honour and knighthood at home, visited America as a member of the royal commission to the New York Industrial Exhibition in 1853 and observed and described improvements in industrial methods. His report (Doc. 13) is a revealing document on early American technology. The self-made Scottish journalist, William Chambers, described other aspects of urban enterprise, as his comments on the schools and libraries of Boston and the working conditions in the factories at Lowell, will demonstrate (Doc. 14). Another Scottish journalist and poet, who visited and lectured in most American cities in 1857-58, described St. Louis at the height of its most dramatic boom (Doc. 15).

12. Lines Extending Across the Alleghanies

FROM Michael Chevalier, *Society, Manners, and Politics in the United States: Being a Series of Letters on North America,* Boston 1839, pp. 230–232, 234–235, 237–240, 261–262.

The works which have hitherto almost wholly occupied, and still chiefly occupy, the attention of statesmen and business men in the United States, are those designed to form communications between the East and the West. There are on the Atlantic coast four principal towns, which long strove with each other for the supremacy; namely, Boston, New York, Philadelphia, and Baltimore. All four aimed to secure the command of the commerce of the new States which are springing up in the fertile regions of the West; and they have sustained the struggle with different degrees of success, but always with a rare spirit of intelligence. They have not, however, been equally favoured in respect to natural advantages. Boston is too far north; she has no river which permits her to stretch her arms far towards the West, and she is surrounded by a hilly country, which throws great obstacles in the way of rapid communication, and makes all works designed to promote it expensive. Philadelphia and Baltimore are shut up by ice almost every winter, and this obstruction is, on the part of the latter,[1] a drawback from the other advantages of her position, her greater nearness to the Ohio, her more central latitude, and the beauty of her bay, which is above 250 miles in length, and receives numberless streams, as the Susquehanna, Potomac, Patuxent, Rappahannock, &c. Philadelphia is badly placed; Penn was led astray by the beauty of the Schuylkill and the Delaware; he thought that the broad plain spread out between their waters to the width of nearly three miles, would afford an admirable site for a city, whose streets should be run with regularity, and whose warehouses, easy of access, would permit thousands of vessels to load and unload at once. He forgot to secure for his city a great hydrographical basin, capable of consuming the merchandise which it should import, and of sending it in return the products of its own labour, and he neglected to make an examination of the Delaware, which he took for a great river, but which, unluckily is not so. . . .

New York is, then, the queen of the Atlantic coast. This city stands on a long, narrow, island, between two rivers (the North [Hudson] River and the East River); ships of any burden and in any numbers may lie at the wharves; the harbour is very rarely closed by ice; it can be entered by small vessels with all winds, and by the largest ships at all times except when the wind is from the northwest. New York has beside the invaluable advantage of standing upon a river for which some great flood has dug out a bed through the primitive mountains, uniformly deep, without rocks, without rapids, almost without a slope, and cutting through the most solid mass of the Alleghanies at right angles. The tide, slight as it is on this coast, flows up the Hudson to Troy, 160 miles from its mouth; and such is the nature of its bed, that whale-ships are fitted out at Poughkeepsie and Hudson, of which the former is 75 and the latter 116 miles above New York, and that, except in the lowest stage of water, vessels of 9 feet draft can go up to Albany and Troy, in any tide. . . .

The project of a canal between New York and Lake Erie, which had already been discussed before the war, was eagerly taken up again after the peace. . . . Notwithstanding all opposition, this State, which did not then contain a population of 1,300,000 inhabitants, began a canal 428 miles in length, and in eight years it had completed it at a cost of 8,400,000 dollars. Since that time it has continued to add numerous branches, covering almost every part of the State, as with net-work. In 1836, the State had completed 656 miles of canal includ-

[1] This difficulty is almost wholly, if not quite, remedied by ice-boats.

ing slack-water navigation, at the expense of 11,962,712 dollars, or 18,235 dollars per mile.[2]

The results of this work have surpassed all expectations; it opened an outlet for the fertile districts of the western part of the State, which had been before cut off from a communication with the sea and the rest of the world. The shores of Lake Erie and Ontario were at once covered with fine farms and flourishing towns. The stillness of the old forest was broken by the axe of New York and New England settlers, to the head of Lake Michigan. The State of Ohio, which is washed by Lake Erie, and which had hitherto had no connection with the sea except by the long southern route down the Mississippi, had now a short and easy communication with the Atlantic by way of New York. The territory of Michigan was peopled, and it now contains 100,000 inhabitants, and will soon take rank among the States.[3] The transportation on the Erie Canal exceeded 400,000 tons in 1834, and it must nearly reach 500,000 tons in 1835. The annual amount of tolls from the canals, and at moderate rates, is about one million and a half dollars. The population of the city of New York increased in the ten years, from 1820 to 1830, 80,000 souls[4] New York is become the third, if not the second port in the world, and the most populous city of the western hemisphere. . . .

When there could no longer be a doubt of the speedy completion of the Erie Canal, Philadelphia and Baltimore felt that New York was going to become the capital of the Union. The spirit of competition aroused in them a spirit of enterprise. They wished also to have their routes to the West; but both had great natural obstacles to overcome. . . . It became necessary for them, therefore, to climb the loftiest heights, and thence to descend to the level of the Ohio with their works.

What is called the Pennsylvania canal is a long line of 400 miles, starting from Philadelphia, and ending at Pittsburgh on the Ohio. It was begun simultaneously with several other works, at the expense of the state of Pennsylvania, in 1826. It is not entirely a canal; from Philadelphia a railroad 81 miles in length, extends to the Susquehanna at Columbia. To the Columbia railroad, succeeds a canal, 172 miles

[2] The official statements of the Canal Board, Feb. 23, 1837, are here given instead of those of M. Chevalier. The statement in the text does not include the Black River Canal and the Genesee Valley Canal, begun in 1837, with a total length of 168 miles, exclusive of 40 miles of improved navigation in the Black River; estimated cost, 3,000,000 dollars.—TRANSL.

[3] Michigan became a State in 1837, at which time it had a population of 175,000 souls.—TRANSL.

[4] The increase of the population has since been at a still more rapid rate; from 1830 to 1835, the number of inhabitants increased from 203,000 to 270,000, or including Brooklyn, from 218,000 to 294,000.—TRANSL.

in length, which ascends the Susquehanna and the Juniata to the foot of the mountains at Holidaysburg. Thence the Portage railroad passes over the mountain to Johnstown, a distance of 37 miles, by means of several inclined planes constructed on a grand scale, with an inclination sometimes exceeding one tenth, which does not, how-ever, deter travellers from going over them.[5] From Johnstown a second canal goes to Pittsburgh, 104 miles. . . .

The Pennsylvania canal, begun in 1826, was finished in 1834. . . .

Still less than Philadelphia, could Baltimore think of a continuous canal to the Ohio. Wishing to avoid the transhipments which are neces-sary on the Pennsylvania line, the Baltimoreans decided on the con-struction of a railroad extending from their city to Pittsburgh or Wheeling, the whole length of which would be about 360 miles. It is now finished as far as Harper's Ferry on the Potomac, a distance of 80 miles, and the company seem to have given up the design of carrying it further. It will here be connected with the Chesapeake and Ohio Canal, of which I shall speak below, as the Columbia railroad is connected with the Pennsylvania canal. It is probable, that, on approaching the crest of the Alleghanies, the canal will in turn give away to a railroad across the mountains, and thus the Maryland works will be similar to the Pennsylvania line.[6]. . .

Three railroads extend from Boston in different directions; the first, 26 miles in length, to the manufacturing city of Lowell, which is thus become a suburb of Boston, and the second, 44 miles in length, to Worcester, the centre of an important agricultural district. The former cost 60,000 dollars a mile, the latter 32,000. The third road is the Providence railroad, already mentioned above as one of the links in the great chain from north to south. The Lowell railroad enters into competition with the Middlesex canal; the Worcester road is to be continued to the River Hudson, where it will terminate oppo-site Albany. It will also be connected with the city of Hudson, 30 miles below Albany, by a railroad extending from West Stockbridge. It will thus become to Boston a Western Railroad, which name it has in fact

[5] The maximum of inclination allowed by our *Administration des Ponts-et Chaussees* (board of public works) is 1/200; in the great lines executed at the expense of the government, the inclination has generally been kept below 1/333 which is the maximum adopted in the fine railroad from London to Birmingham.

[6] In 1836 the Maryland legislature voted the sum of 8,000,000 dollars in aid of public works, of which 3,000,000 were appropriated to the Baltimore and Ohio railroad, and 3,000,000 to the Chesapeake and Ohio Canal, and rest is divided between several works, one of which is intended to connect Annapolis, the capital, with the Potomac. Baltimore has also subscribed 3,000,000 dollars towards aiding the completion of the railroad. (Virginia and Wheeling have also subscribed 1,000,000 each for the same object, and so far from being come to a stand, the Baltimore and Ohio railroad is now pushed on with great vigor towards Cumberland.—TRANSL.)

received. A company has been authorized to execute the portion between Worcester and Springfield, a distance of 54 miles, the whole distance from Boston to Albany being 160 miles.[7] The Eastern railroad, a fourth work is about to be undertaken, passing through Lynn, famous for its boots and shoes, Salem, a little city which carries on an extensive trade with China, Ipswich, Beverley, and Newburyport towards Portland, the principal town in the northern extremity of the Union.

13. Technology and Enterprise in American Cities

FROM Sir Joseph Whitworth and George Wallis, *The Industry of the United States in Machinery, Manufactures and Useful and Ornamental Arts,* London 1854, pp. 9–14.

The energetic character of the American people is nowhere more strikingly displayed than in the young manufacturing settlements that are so rapidly springing up in the Northern States.

A retired valley and its stream of water become in a few months the seat of manufactures; and the dam and water-wheel are the means of giving employment to busy thousands, where before nothing more than a solitary farm-house was to be found. Such, in a few words, is the history of Waterbury, and all the Naugatuck settlements of Holyoke, Chicopee, Lowell, and Laurence.

Waterbury is situated in the Naugatuck valley, about 24 miles north of New Haven. It contains many manufacturing establishments, carried on principally by joint-stock companies. Besides other firms, there are 28 companies of which the greater number are employed in the manufacture of rolled and sheet brass, copper wire, buttons, German silver, pins, cutlery, hooks-and-eyes. The others are employed in manufacturing hosiery, felt, cloth, webbing, covered buttons, umbrella trimmings, leather, &c.

Great facilities are afforded in many of the States for the formation of manufacturing companies. The liabilities of partners not actively

[7] During the session of 1836 the Legislature of Massachusetts subscribed 1,000,000 in aid of the Western Railroad; this measure was the first step taken by the State in the promotion of public works, and indicates a complete revolution in its policy on this point. (This act was immediately followed by similar acts in aid of the several other railroads now in progress in the State, and in 1838, by a further grant of the credit of the state to the Western Railroads to the amount of 1,200,000 dollars. That work will be completed to Springfield in October (1839), and the section between Springfield and West Stockbridge is already far advanced towards its completion. The Lowell railroad has been extended to Nashua, and an eastern branch is now completed to Haverhill, of which a continuation towards Exeter is now in progress.—TRANSL.)

engaged in the management are limited to the proportion of the capital subscribed by each, and its amount is published in the official statements of the company. In the case of the introduction of a new invention, or a new manufacture, the principle of limited liability produces most beneficial results. Persons who, from their connections or occupations, are likely to be interested in, or profit by, the new invention or manufacture, readily associate together and subscribe capital to give the new proposal a fair trial, when they are assured that their risk will not extend beyond the amount which they may choose to contribute.

The cost of obtaining an act of incorporation is very trifling; in one case where the capital of the company amounted to $600,000 (£120,000), the total cost of obtaining an incorporation was 50 cents (2s. 1d.).

Upwards of 200 men are employed by one of the companies in the manufacture of buttons, hinges, daguerrotype plates and frames.

The round-shaped button is formed by two punches, one working inside the other, each being driven by a separate eccentric, and the inside punch having the longer stroke. By this arrangement the disc is forced through the die, and drops into box, thus saving the labour of picking out, which is necessary where a single punch and solid die are used. The spindle of the polishing lathe in which the button is fixed whilst being burnished, makes 10,000 revolutions per minute.

The lathe in which the oval frames, used as settings for daguerreotypes, are turned, has an oval chuck, and a stationary cutting-tool fixed to the slide rest, for "truing out" the previously punched oval. Two milling-tools are used, one for forming the bevilled edge, the other for ornamenting the face of the oval frame. The milling-tool, as it revolves, is allowed to swivel so as to accommodate itself to the oval. When the bevilled edge has been formed, the first milling-tool is removed and another substituted while the work revolves. One workman is able to turn, and ornament by milling, two gross of frames per day.

No description of the machinery used in pin-making can be given, as the process of "papering" is all that is permitted to be seen.

The pins are all papered by machinery; they are placed in a shallow feeding-dish in an inclined position, so as to allow them to descend gradually as they are shaken by a quick vibratory motion. They fall from the spout of the feeding-dish upon the centre of an inclined shallow trough, about 18 inches long, through which runs lengthwise a slit sufficiently wide to admit a shank of a pin, and yet suspend it by its head. It being a matter of chance when a pin falls from the spout, whether it will drop into the slit or slide down the trough, a sufficient number are allowed to descend to insure the filling of the slit by those which happen to fall favourably.

The superfluous pins slide down into a box, from which they are again lifted from time to time to the upper feeding-dish. The descending line of suspended pins is conducted by the slit (which is curved at its lower end) to a sliding frame, which is worked by the woman who attends the machine.

The frame carries a dozen grooves, and in each of these a pin is deposited as it passes under the slit; the pins are thus arranged in a row, with their points all turned the same way. The sheet of paper for receiving them is placed by the attendant on a grooved table, and deep folds are pressed into it at equal distances, and into the cross ridges thus formed a row of pins is pushed by the carrying-frame at every thrust forward.

Under no circumstance whatever are strangers allowed to enter the rooms in which the pin-making machines are at work. The workmen employed are obliged to enter into a bond, and find two sureties, that they will not disclose anything relative to the machinery. The company prefer keeping their mode of operation a secret in this way to taking out a patent.

Three different descriptions of machines are employed in making hooks-and-eyes,—the wire being let in on one side of the machine, and a completed hook or eye dropped out on the other. The machines appear to make them at the rate of about 100 per minute. About 80 hands are employed, who are said to make 1,200 packs of pins, each containing 3,360 pins, and 2,500 gross of hooks-and-eyes, per day.

The cutlery and file works are conducted on a limited scale. Many beautifully finished knives were exhibited in the New York Exhibition, and were said to command a higher price than those of a similar class imported from this country.

The artisans are employed principally on piece-work. In the cutlery department one workman will earn $70 (about £14) per month, while the earnings of others occupied on precisely the same kind of work only amounted to $30 (£6) per month.

Thus it will be seen that each workman does the best he can for himself, irrespective of others, and reaps the reward due to his superior skill and industry.

The manufacture of locks appears to be rapidly extending. In an establishment at Pittsburgh employing 350 men in making locks, coffee-mills, coping presses, &c., good work is turned out.

Another at New Haven, Connecticut, employs about 200 men in making locks and lock-handles. The latter are made of coloured clays, so mixed as to present a grained appearance. They are first moulded by hand, then turned in a self-acting lathe with great rapidity, and afterwards baked in a furnace. Padlocks are made at New Haven of a superior quality to those of the same class ordinarily imported from this country, and are not more expensive.

The celebrity attained by New England in the manufacture of clocks gives a peculiar interest to a visit to these manufactories. At one in Connecticut 250 men are employed, and the clocks are made at the rate of 600 per day, and at a price varying from $1 to $10, the average price being $3.

The frames of the clocks are stamped out of sheet brass, and all the holes are punched simultaneously by a series of punches fixed at the required distances. The wheels also are stamped out of brass sheet, and a round beading is raised by a press round their rims, for the purpose of giving them lateral strength. They are cut by a machine having three horizontal axes, carrying each a cutter placed about 4 inches apart. The first cutter is simply a saw, and the second rounds off the teeth. In cutting an escapement wheel, the first cutter is made to cut each tooth entirely round, and then either the second or third axis with its cutter is used for finishing. The pulleys on the three axes are driven by one driving pulley with three straps working over and in contact with each other.

The plates forming the clock faces, and other discs, are cut out by circular shears. The beaded rims intended to go round the clock faces, varying in size from 15 inches downwards, are stamped in concentric rings out of a disc, and then made of the required form by means of dies and a stamping-press.

The ogee-form given to the wooden framing of the common clock is formed by a revolving cutter of the required shape, making 7,000 revolutions per minute, over which the piece of wood is passed by hand, — the requisite pressure downwards being given at the same time.

A circular cutter fixed on a horizontal axis is also used for roughly planing the back parts of the wooden clock. Its diameter is about 18 inches, and it has four lateral projections, carrying four cutters, two gouges, and two chisels. These revolve round a fixed circular centre plate, of about a foot in diameter, against which the work is pressed as it is passed along. Each clock passes through about 60 different hands: more than half the clocks manufactured are exported to England, and of these a large portion are re-exported to other markets.

It is worthy of remark, that the superiority obtained in this particular manufacture is not owing to any local advantages; on the contrary, labour and material are more expensive than in the countries to which the exportations are made; it is to be ascribed solely to the enterprise and energy of the manufacturer, and his judicious employment of machinery.

In a large manufactory at Hartford, from 400 to 500 men are employed in making revolving pistols at the rate of from 1,200 to 1,500 per week.

Self-acting machinery and revolving cutters are used for making all
the separate parts, and the tools are made and repaired in a machine-
shop which is attached to the works. In another establishment at
Worcester, Connecticut, 175 men are employed in manufacturing
guns, rifles, and pistols. Revolvers are made in large numbers with
barrels on the old principle, and proved by hydraulic pressure.

14. Schools, Libraries and Factories

FROM W[illiam] Chambers, *Things as they are in America,*
Philadelphia 1854, pp. 219–222.

Although only a few days in the city and its neighbourhood, I had an
opportunity of making some satisfactory inquiries respecting the prevalent system of elementary education, and of visiting some of the excellent literary institutions with which the intelligent inhabitants of
Boston have had the good taste to provide themselves. The Athenaeum,
consisting of a library and reading-room, was the finest thing of the
kind I had seen in America; for, besides a collection of 50,000
volumes, there was a gallery of paintings and sculpture of a high class.
Among institutions of a more popular character, may be noticed the
Mercantile Library Association, at whose rooms I was shewn a collection of about 13,000 volumes; also, the Lowell Institute, established
by a bequest of 250,000 dollars, for the purpose of providing free
lectures on science, art, and natural and revealed religion. Some
movements were on foot to widen the sphere of intellectual improvement by means of a free library and otherwise: and from the great
number of publishing establishments, it was evident that the demand
for literature was considerable. 'Everybody reads and everybody buys
books,' said a publisher to me one day; and he added: 'every mechanic,
worth anything at all, in Massachusetts, must have a small library
which he calls his own; besides, the taste for high-class books is perceptibly improving. A few years ago, we sold great quantities of
trashy Annuals; now, our opulent classes prefer works of a superior
quality.' At the same time, I learned that a number of copies of instructive popular works which I had been concerned in publishing, had
been imported for the use of school-libraries; and as there are about
18,000 such libraries in the United States, the amount of books of
various kinds required for this purpose alone may be supposed to be
very considerable.

Like most visitors of Massachusetts, I made an excursion to Lowell
—a manufacturing city of 37,000 inhabitants, at the distance of
twenty-five miles northwest of Boston. A railway-train occupied an

hour in the journey, which was by way of Lexington—a small town at which the first shots were fired (April 19, 1775) at the beginning of the revolutionary struggle. The country traversed was level, enclosed, and here and there dotted over with pretty villages and detached dwellings, in the usual New England style. Lowell may be described as a village of larger growth, composed of houses of brick or wood, disposed in straight lines forming spacious and airy streets. Several railways centre at the spot, but there is little noise or bustle in the thoroughfares. All the children are at school, and most of the adult inhabitants are in the several manufactories. The day is sunshiny and pleasant, and a few infants are playing about the doors of neat dwellings in the short streets which lead to the mills. These mills are of the ordinary cotton-factory shape—great brick-buildings, with rows of windows with small panes, and all are enclosed within courtyards, or otherwise secluded from intrusion.

The whole of the Lowell mills being moved by water-power, we agreeably miss the smoky atmosphere which surrounds the Lancashire factories. The power is derived from the Merrimack, a river of considerable size, which is led by an artificial canal from a point above a natural fall in its course, to the various works. In 1853, there were twelve incorporated manufacturing concerns in Lowell and its neighbourhood; principally engaged in cotton spinning and weaving, carpet-manufacturing, calico-printing, and machine-making. The chief and oldest of the various corporations is the Merrimack Manufacturing Company, established in 1822, and possessing a capital of 2,500,000 dollars. Its operations are carried on in six large buildings; it has at work 71,072 spindles, 2,114 power-looms, employs 1,650 females and 650 males, and makes 377,000 yards of cloth per week. The goods it produces are prints and sheetings. Besides going over the extensive works of this establishment, I visited the mills of the Lowell Manufacturing Company, where I found 800 females and 500 males employed principally in the spinning of wool and weaving of carpets—the designs of these articles being good, with bright and decided colours.

Cotton-spinning and weaving factories are pretty much the same all the world over, and I do not feel entitled to say that there was any remarkable exception in the establishments which here fell under my notice. In each there prevailed the greatest neatness and regularity. The females employed were tidy in dress, yet not very different in this respect from what I had seen in factories at home; for the nature of the work does not admit of finery, and it is only at leisure hours and on Sundays that silks and parasols make their appearance. In the windows of one of the large factories, I saw that flowers in pots were a favourite subject of culture, which I accepted as a token of the good taste of these young lady-artisans. Boarding-houses, generally the property, and under the supervision of the mill-owners, are situated at a short distance from the factories. These houses are of brick, three stories in height, and have exteriorly the aspect of what we should call dwellings of the middle class. Of the orderliness of these establishments, their neatly furnished rooms, pianos, and accommodations of various kinds, it is unnecessary for me to go into particulars; neither need I call to remembrance the literary exercitations of the female inmates, demonstrated by the *Lowell Offering*, and *Mind among the Spindles*. Among American girls, the general objection to domestic service is not attended with any dislike to working in factories. Many young women, the daughters of farmers, do not therefore disdain to employ themselves three or four years at Lowell, in order to realise a sum which will form a suitable dowry at marriage, to which, of course, all look forward as a natural termination of their career at the mills; and as no taint of immorality is attachable to their conduct while under the roof of any of the respectable boarding-houses, they may be said to be objects of attraction to young farmers looking out for wives. I was informed that, latterly, a number have come from Lower Canada, and return with quite a fortune to the parental home.

15. St Louis and its Steamboats

FROM Charles Mackay, *Life and Liberty in America: Sketches of a Tour in the United States and Canada in 1857–1858*, New York 1859, pp. 141–145.

St. Louis remains, next to Cincinnati, the greatest city of the West; but, as its growth has been more rapid than that of its sister on the Ohio, and as it contains within itself far greater elements of prosperity and increase, it is likely, within a few years, to surpass it in trade, population, and extent. It is already the largest and most flourishing place between Cincinnati and San Francisco, and will, in all probability, within a quarter of a century contain and employ half a million of people. It is situated on the Mississippi, about twenty miles below the point at which that river, pure and lucent in all its upper course, receives the dark and muddy waters of the Missouri. . . .

It was not until 1820, when the population of St Louis was under 5,000, that the place became of any importance. Twenty years afterward the population reached 17,000. In 1852 it exceeded 100,000, and in 1857 it was variously estimated at from 150,000 to 180,000. It is still rapidly increasing. English, Irish, German, and the surplus population of such old states and communities as Massachusetts, Connecticut and others in New England, continually flock into it, and beyond it, to add to its wealth, and to develop the resources of the great and fertile regions lying between the Mississippi and the Rocky Mountains, and the remote sources of the Missouri. . . .

The levee of St Louis extended along the right bank of the Mississippi for nearly six miles, about half of which length is densely built upon. No city in the world offers to the gaze of the spectators such a vast assemblage of river steam-boats. As many as one hundred and seventy, loading and unloading, have been counted along the levee at one time. These vessels which, like all those that ply on the Mississippi and the Ohio, are of peculiar construction, painted white, and with two tall black funnels, are built for internal traffic, and would play but a sorry part in the salt water if the wind blew ever so little. But for riverine purposes they are admirable, and, were it not for the occasional mischance of a collision in the fog, or the still more frequent casualty of a blow-up from the bursting of a boiler, would afford the traveler the safest, as they do the pleasantest, mode of conveyance in America. The people of St Louis are as proud of their steam-boats as of their city. . . .

For steam tonnage it is estimated that St Louis is the third city in the Union. New York ranks first, with a tonnage in the year 1854 of 101,478; New Orleans second, with a tonnage of 57,147; and St Louis third, with a tonnage little inferior to that of New Orleans itself, amounting to 48,557. The manufactures of St Louis are numerous and important, and comprise twenty flour-mills, about the same number of saw-mills, twenty-five founderies, engine and boiler manufactories and machine-shops, eight or ten establishments engaged in the manufacture of railroad cars and locomotives, besides several chemical, soap, and candle works, and a celebrated type foundry, which supplies the whole of the Far West with the types that are absolutely necessary to the creation of all new cities in the wilderness. A church, a forge, a hotel, and a daily newspaper—with these four, aided by a doctor or two, and as many lawyers and bankers, a newly-named city will take its place on the map, and speculators who have bought land at a dollar and a quarter per acre will look to make their fortunes by simply holding on to their purchase until streets run over their grounds, and they become in America such men as the Duke of Bedford, Lord Portman, and the Marquis of Westminster are in London, and Lord Derby in his town of Preston.

St Louis contains two theatres, and the two finest lecture-rooms in the United States. The upper and lower rooms of the Mercantile Library Association are unrivaled for this purpose; and neither New York nor Boston contains any lecture-rooms at all compared to them for elegance of construction and decoration, or adaptability to the end proposed.

E. Urban Reconstruction and Diffusion

The urbanization of America entered a new stage in the 1860s, one in which the reorganization and reconstruction of old cities overshadowed the continued development of new towns. A number of penetrating studies by native and foreign observers document the mounting concern over the internal structure of the cities. The problems of the slums, first dramatically revealed at New York in the draft riots in the Civil War, and the civic response to the housing problem are ably set forth by Lawrence Veiller in a carefully documented chapter published in 1903 (Doc. 16). The relation of the successive immigrant invasions of the poorer districts to the development of the slums is vividly described by Jacob A. Riis, a police reporter for the New York *Tribune*. Commencing in the late 1870s, his articles provided abundant material for a moving account of *How the Other Half Lives* first published in 1890. An immigrant himself from Denmark, Riis described the ethnic settlements springing up in many cities, but most abundantly in New York, with compassion and understanding (Doc. 17). The crucial character of these problems was again demonstrated when on the publication of Lord Bryce's two weighty volumes on *The American Commonwealth*, the chapters on the weaknesses and imperfections of city governments attracted major attention. His description of Tammany in New York (Doc. 18) was especially revealing and provided an incentive to later civic reform.

16. Tenement House Reform in New York City

FROM Lawrence Veiller, 'Tenement House Reform in New York City, 1834–1900' in Robert De Forest and L. Veiller, eds., *The Tenement House Problem*, New York 1903, I: 92–97, 100–104.

The Council of Hygiene in New York City
Not, however, till the first-fruits of thirty years of municipal neglect had been gathered in the terrible "draft riots" of 1863, did the community become aroused to the dangers of the evils which surrounded them. When in those troublous times, during our Civil

War, the tenements poured forth the mobs that held fearful sway in the city, during the outbreak of violence in the month of July, then, for the first time, did the general public realize what it meant to permit human beings to be reared under the conditions which had so long prevailed in the tenement houses in New York City.

Mr. N. P. Willis, a leading journalist, writing at that time, thus describes the impression made upon him by the sight of these persons: "The high brick blocks of closely packed houses where the mobs originated seemed to be literally hives of sickness and vice. It was wonderful to see and difficult to believe that so much misery, disease, and wretchedness could be huddled together and hidden by high walls, unvisited and unthought of so near our own abodes. Lewd but pale and sickly young women, scarcely decent in their ragged attire, were impudent, and scattered everywhere in the courts. What numbers of these poorer classes are deformed, what numbers are made hideous by self-neglect and infirmity! Alas, human faces look so hideous with hope and self-respect all gone, and familiar forms and features are made so frightful by sin, squalor, and debasement! To walk the streets as we walked them in those hours of conflagration and riot were like witnessing the day of judgment, with every wicked thing revealed, every sin and sorrow blazingly glared upon, every hidden abomination laid before hell's expectant fire."

Heeding this warning, some few months later, in the spring of 1864, the leading citizens of New York formed themselves into what was known as the "Citizens' Association" for the purpose of taking steps to improve the sanitary condition of the city. The alarmingly high death-rate of New York at that time (there being one death in every thirty-five of the inhabitants) became a subject of the most careful thought and investigation. Accordingly, the Citizens' Association formed a subcommittee known as the Council of Hygiene and Public Health, which included the leading physicians of the city. The Council of Hygiene organized in the month of April in the year 1864, and at once determined to undertake a complete and thorough sanitary investigation of the entire city. The city, which at that time was coincident with Manhattan Island, was divided into twenty-nine districts; an experienced physician was appointed as sanitary inspector in each ward, and during a period of nine months the most thorough, complete and scientific sanitary inspection ever made of any city was made of the city of New York. This investigation embraced a description of the character of the soil throughout each district, the number of buildings, the purposes for which they were used, whether business buildings, churches, schools, dwellings, or tenement houses; whether built of brick, stone, iron, or wood; the character of the streets, how paved, and whether provided with sewers. The "tenant houses" were a subject of special investigation in every district; the most notorious ones were fully described, not only as to their construction, but as to the character of the people living in them, the sickness prevailing, the death-rate in each, including nearly every conceivable detail. In addition to these investigations there were recorded the number of vacant lots, the number of liquor stores, brothels, stores for the sale of food, the number of stables, the influence of stables upon disease, the prevalence of preventable disease in the districts, infantile diseases and mortality, and the excessive crowding of houses upon the lots. Seldom has a piece of social or sanitary work been better done. . . .

As a result of the disclosures made by the Council of Hygiene in 1865 came the first legislative action in regard to tenement houses in this country. The first step was the establishment of the Metropolitan Board of Health in 1866, and one year later, in 1867, the enactment of the tenement house law. This act, after defining a tenement house as "Any house, building, or portion thereof which is rented, leased, or hired out to be occupied, or is occupied, as the home or residence of more than three families living independently of one another, and doing their own cooking upon the premises, or by more than two families upon a floor, so living and cooking and having common right in the halls, stairways, yards, water-closets, or privies, or some of them," provided that no building should be used as a tenement house unless every sleeping room had a ventilator or transom window of an area of 3 square feet over the door connecting with the adjoining room or with the outer air; that every such house should be provided with a proper fire-escape to be approved by the Building Inspector; that the roof over the main hall should be provided with a proper ventilator; and that it should be kept in good repair and not allowed to leak, and that all stairs should be provided with proper banisters; also that every house should be provided with good and sufficient water-closets or privies, and that there should not be less than 1 to every 20 occupants, and that where there was a sewer in the street in front of such a house, the privies or closets should be connected with the sewer; that no cesspool should be allowed in connection with a tenement house unless where it was unavoidable; that the yards of all new tenement houses should be graded and drained, and connected with the sewer; that no basement or cellar rooms should be occupied without a permit from the Board of Health, and that, even then, such rooms should not be occupied unless 7 feet in height from the floor to the ceiling, and also 1 foot of the height above the surface of the ground adjoining the same, nor unless there was an open area properly drained, 2 feet 6 inches wide, extending along the front of the room, nor unless the room had an external window opening of at least 9 square feet. It was further provided that no underground room should be occupied for sleeping purposes without a written permit from the Board of Health. All tenement houses were also required to be provided with proper receptacles for garbage and other refuse, and the storage of combustible material was prohibited, as was the keeping of animals, except dogs and cats. All tenements were further required to be kept free from accumulation of dirt and filth and garbage at all times. The name and address of the owner of every tenement house was also required to be posted in a conspicuous place in each building. The health officers were to have free access to such buildings at all times, and the Board of Health was authorized to have vacated buildings that were unfit for habitation by reason of being infected with disease or likely to cause sickness among the occupants, or dangerous from want of repair. The law further provided that where there was a front and rear building to be erected on the same lot, there should be a clear, open space, between the buildings if they were one story high, of 10 feet; 15 feet, if they were two stories high; 20 feet, if they were three stories high; and 25 feet, if they were more than three stories high; also that at the rear of every new tenement house there should be a clear open space of 10 feet between it and any other building, but, unfortunately, discretion was given to the Board of Health to modify these requirements as to the amount of space when they saw fit. The law also provided that every habitable room should be at least 8 feet high, except rooms in attics, and that every habitable room should have at least one window connected with the external air, or, over the door, a ventilator leading into the hall, or into another room having connection with the external air; also that the total area of windows in every room communicating with the external air should be at least one-tenth of the superficial area of the room; also that every habitable room of less area than 100 square feet which did not communicate directly with the external air and did not have an open fireplace should be provided with a separate ventilating flue. Every new tenement house was required also to have a chimney or open fire-place running through every floor of the building, and for each set of rooms. New tenements were also required to have proper recept-acles for ashes and rubbish, and running water was to be furnished at one or more places in the house or in the yard. Cellars were required to be cemented so as to be water-tight, and the halls on each floor were required to be so arranged as to open directly to the outer air. A violation of the act was made a misdemeanor, punishable by a fine of not less than $10 or more than $100, or by imprisonment for not more than ten days for each day that the violation continued, or by both such fine and imprisonment, in the discretion of the court. . . .

When one considers that there were, in 1867, 15,000 tenement houses erected before the passage of any tenement house law, without regard to the safety or health of the occupants, one begins to realize the magnitude of the task which confronted the newly organized Board of Health. The reports of the Association for Improving the Condition of the Poor for the following five years show a decided improvement in the tenement houses of the city, especially in regard to cellar dwellings and to the general sanitary condition of buildings, the Sanitary Police being able to enforce greater cleanliness than had heretofore existed. While the new law has remedied certain defects, . . . yet it soon became evident that it did not meet the conditions in such a way as to secure good types of buildings among those newly erected. . . .

In 1877 Mr. Alfred T. White of Brooklyn, having seen the model tenements of Sir Sidney Waterlow's Industrial Dwellings Company in London, became imbued with the idea that the best way in which he could benefit the working people of New York City, or of his own city of Brooklyn, was by providing them with decent, comfortable homes. He accordingly built his well-known "Home Buildings" in Brooklyn, upon plans similar to those of the Improved Industrial Dwellings Company of London, and one year later, directly opposite, built an entire block of similar model tenements, with a large park or courtyard in the centre. From the time they were built these tenements have been a success, both socially and financially. Wide publicity was given to this extraordinarily successful experiment of Mr. White's, the result being that great interest was stimulated in the tenement house problem. . . .

The Tenement House Competition, 1879

In December of 1878, Mr. Henry C. Meyer, at that time the proprietor of the newspaper known as the *Sanitary Engineer,* and who was much interested in this movement, in connection with Messrs. D. Willis James, F. B. Thurber, Henry E. Pellew, and Robert Gordon, offered prizes of $500 for the best architectural designs for a tenement house on an ordinary city lot, 25 feet wide by 100 feet deep. A special programme setting forth the conditions of this architectural competition was printed in the *Sanitary Engineer,* and the following gentlemen were appointed a jury of award to determine the merits of the different plans: Mr. R. S. Hatfield, architect; Professor Charles F. Chandler, President of the Board of Health; Rev. John Hall, Rev. Henry C. Potter, and Robert Hoe.

No less than 190 architects from all parts of the United States, and even from Canada and Great Britain, sent in plans in competition. These plans, numbering 206, were placed on free exhibition and attracted widespread interest. Many of the plans were reproduced in the papers at that time, and the *Sanitary Engineer,* the journal which had inaugurated the competition and had authorized the prizes, printed an elaborate series of articles, reproducing the ten leading plans and describing the merits of each in detail. The first prize was awarded to Mr. James E. Ware, and from this time dates the introduction into the tenement house system of New York City of what was known as the "double-decker dumb-bell tenement," so called because of the shape of the outline of the building, which in the middle tapers in, very much like the handle of a dumb-bell.

This is the type of tenement house which today is the curse of our city. Many people have pointed out that what was considered a model tenement in 1879 is in 1900 considered one of the worst types of tenement houses ever constructed. Had these people studied more thoroughly the movement for tenement house reform, they would have found that in 1879 there was almost universal condemnation of the award of the prize to this type of building. In this connection, it is not inappropriate to quote part of an editorial from the *New York Times,* dated March 16, 1879. "The prizes offered by a committee of gentlemen appointed by the proprietor of the *Sanitary Engineer* have been conferred upon the designers of tenement house plans. The limitations of the designs by the architects were the shape of the lots, and cheapness of construction; they were required to plan a cheap house or houses with air and light in the rooms, on a lot 25 feet broad, enclosed between other houses, and 100 feet deep. If the prize plans are the best offered, which we hardly believe, they merely demonstrate that the problem is insoluble. The three which have received the highest prizes offer a very slightly better arrangement than hundreds of tenements now do. . . . But it may be fairly said that if one of our crowded wards were built up after any one of these prize designs, the evils of our present tenement house system would be increased tenfold."

How true this prophecy of 1879 was, we today fully realize, for we are reaping the evils of that system of the prize plan of 1879, built all over the crowded wards of this city; and, in truth, the evils that threatened the city in 1879 *have* been increased tenfold. It is this plan which has produced a system of tenement houses unknown to any other city, which has produced the evil of the air shaft,—a product solely of New York, and one which makes our housing conditions the worst in the world. . . .

In 1884 Professor Felix Adler, of the Society for Ethical Culture, delivered a series of lectures upon the terrible conditions of the tenement houses at that time; his own work and the work of members of his society among the poor in the city having given him an insight into the wretched condition of their dwellings. This series of lectures created great interest in the public press, and the community became thoroughly roused to the necessity for reform in this direction. Accordingly, a bill was introduced in the Legislature and passed on June 2, 1884, appointing a commission "to examine and to investigate and inquire into the character and condition of tenement houses, lodging houses, and cellars in the city of New York. . . ."

The recommendations made by the Tenement House Commission of 1884 to the Legislature did not, however, result in legislation until 1887, when the Tenement House Law was amended in several important particulars, the main change being the increasing of the number of sanitary police from thirty to forty-five, fifteen of these to spend their time in the inspection of tenement houses exclusively.

17. The Ethnic Settlements

FROM Jacob A. Riis, *How the Other Half Lives,* New York 1890, 1906 ed., pp. 22–27.

The once unwelcome Irishman has been followed in his turn by the Italian, the Russian Jew, and the Chinaman, and has himself taken a hand at opposition, quite as bitter and quite as ineffectual, against these later hordes. Wherever these have gone they have crowded him out, possessing the block, the street, the ward with their denser swarms. But the Irishman's revenge is complete. Victorious in defeat over his recent as over his more ancient foe, the one who opposed his coming no less than the one who drove him out, he dictates to both their politics, and, secure in possession of the offices, returns the native his greeting with interest, while collecting the rents of the Italian whose house he has bought with the profits of his saloon. . . .

New York's wage-earners have no other place to live, more is the pity. They are truly poor for having no better homes; waxing poorer in purse as the exorbitant rents to which they are tied, as ever was serf to soil, keep rising. The wonder is that they are not all corrupted, and speedily, by their surroundings. . . .

The Italian scavenger of our time is fast graduating into exclusive control of the corner fruit-stands, while his black-eyed boy monopolizes the boot-blacking industry in which a few years ago he was an intruder. The Irish hod-carrier in the second generation has become a bricklayer, if not the Alderman of his ward, while the Chinese coolie is in almost exclusive possession of the laundry business. The reason is obvious. The poorest immigrant comes here with the purpose and ambition to better himself and, given half a chance, might be reasonably expected to make the most of it. To the false plea that he prefers the squalid homes in which his kind are housed there could be no better answer. The truth is, his half chance has been too long wanting, and for the bad result he has been unjustly blamed.

As emigration from east to west follows the latitude, so does the foreign influx in New York distribute itself along certain well-defined lines that waver and break only under the stronger pressure of a more gregarious race or the encroachments of inexorable business. A feeling of dependence upon mutual effort, natural to strangers in a strange land, unacquainted with its language and customs, sufficiently accounts for this.

The Irishman is the true cosmopolitant immigrant. All-pervading, he shares his lodging with perfect impartiality with the Italian, the Greek, and the "Dutchman," yielding only to sheer force of numbers, and objects equally to them all. A map of the city, colored to designate nationalities, would show more stripes than the skin of a zebra, and more colors than any rainbow. The city on such a map would fall into two great halves, green for the Irish prevailing in the West Side tenement districts, and blue for the Germans on the East Side. But intermingled with these ground colors would be an odd variety of tints that would give the whole the appearance of an extraordinary crazy-quilt. From down in the Sixth Ward, upon the site of the old Collect Pond that in the days of the fathers drained the hills which are no more, the red of the Italian would be seen forcing its way northward along the line of Mulberry Street to the quarter of the French purple on Bleecker Street and South Fifth Avenue, to lose itself and reappear, after a lapse of miles, in the "Little Italy" of Harlem, east of Second Avenue. Dashes of red, sharply defined, would be seen strung through the Annexed District, northward to the city line. On the West Side the red would be seen overrunning the old Africa of Thompson Street, pushing the black of the negro rapidly uptown, against querulous but unavailing protests, occupying his home, his church, his trade and all, with merciless impartiality. There is a church in Mulberry Street that has stood for two generations as a sort of milestone of these migrations. Built originally for the worship of staid New Yorkers of the "old stock," it was engulfed by the colored tide, when the draft-riots drove the negroes out of reach of Cherry Street and the Five Points. Within the past decade the advance wave of the Italian onset reached it, and to-day the arms of United Italy adorn its front. The negroes have made a stand at several points along Seventh and Eight Avenues; but their main body, still pursued by the Italian foe, is on the march yet, and the black mark will be found overshadowing to-day many blocks on the East Side, with One Hundredth Street as the centre, where colonies of them have settled recently.

Hardly less aggressive than the Italian, the Russian and Polish Jew, having overrun the district between Rivington and Division Streets, east of the Bowery, to the point of suffocation, is filling the tenements of the old Seventh Ward to the river front, and disputing with the Italian every foot of available space in the back alleys of Mulberry Street. The two races, differing hopelessly in much, have this in common: they carry their slums with them wherever they go, if allowed to do it. Little Italy already rivals its parent, the "Bend," in foulness. Other nationalities that begin at the bottom make a fresh start when crowded up the ladder. Happily both are manageable, the one by rabbinical, the other by the civil law. Between the dull gray of the Jew, his favorite color, and the Italian red, would be seen squeezed in on the map a sharp streak of yellow, marking the narrow boundaries of Chinatown. Dovetailed in with the German population, the poor but thrifty Bohemian might be picked out by the sombre hue of his life as of his philosophy, struggling against heavy odds in the big human bee-hives of the East Side. Colonies of his people extend northward, with long lapses of space, from below the Cooper Institute more than three miles. The Bohemian is the only foreigner with any considerable representation in the city who counts no wealthy man of his race, none who has not to work hard for a living, or has got beyond the reach of the tenement.

Down near the Battery the West Side emerald would be soiled by a dirty stain, spreading rapidly like a splash of ink on a sheet of blotting paper, headquarters of the Arab tribe, that in a single year has swelled from the original dozen to twelve hundred, intent, every mother's son, on trade and barter. Dots and dashes of color here and there would show where the Finnish sailors worship their djumala (God), the Greek peddlars the ancient name of their race, and the Swiss the goddess of thrift. And so on to the end of the long register, all toiling together in the galling fetters of the tenement. Were the questions raised who makes the most of life thus mortgaged, who resists most stubbornly its levelling tendency—knows how to drag even the barracks upwards a part of the way at least toward the ideal plane of the home—the palm must be unhesitatingly awarded the Teuton. The Italian and the poor Jew rise only by compulsion. The Chinaman does not rise at all, as at home, he simply remains stationary. The Irishman's genius runs to public affairs rather than domestic life; wherever he is mustered in force the saloon is the gorgeous centre of political activity. The German struggles vainly to learn his trick; his Teutonic wit is too heavy, and the political ladder he raises from his saloon usually too short or too clumsy to reach the desired goal. The best part of his life is lived at home, and he makes himself a home independent of the surroundings, giving the lie to the saying, unhappily become a maxim of social truth, that pauperism and drunkenness naturally grow in the tenements. He makes the most of his tenement, and it should be added that whenever and as soon as he can save up money enough, he gets out and never crosses the threshold of one again.

18. The Tammany Ring in New York City

FROM James Bryce, *The American Commonwealth*, New York 1910 edition, (original, 1893), II: 379–382, 387–395.

Although I have described in previous chapters the causes which have induced the perversion and corruption of demoratic government in the great American cities, it seems desirable to illustrate more fully, from passages in the history of two such cities, the conditions under which those causes work and the forms that perversion takes. . . . I take New York and Philadelphia as examples because they are older than Chicago, Pittsburgh, and St. Louis, larger than Boston and Baltimore. And I begin with New York, because she displayed on the grandest scale phenomena common to American cities, and because the plunder and misgovernment from which she has suffered have become specially notorious over the world.

From the end of the eighteenth century the State and (somewhat later) the city of New York were, more perhaps than any other State or city, the seat of intrigues and the battle-ground of factions. Party organizations early became powerful in them, and it was by a New York leader—Marcy, the friend of President Jackson—that the famous doctrine of "the Spoils to the Victors" was first formulated as already the practice of New York politicians. These factions were for a long time led, and these intrigues worked, by men belonging to the upper or middle class, to whom the emoluments of office were desirable but not essential. In the middle of the century, however, there came a change. The old native population of the city was more and more swollen by the immigration of foreigners: first of the Irish, especially from 1846 onwards; then also of the Germans from 1849 onwards; finally of the Polish and Russian Jews, as well as of Italians and of Slavs from about 1883 onwards. Already in 1870 the foreign population, including not only the foreign born but a large part of their children who, though born in America, were still virtually Europeans, constituted a half or perhaps even a majority of the inhabitants; and the proportion of foreigners has since then grown still larger.[1] These

[1] In 1870, 44 per cent of the population of New York were of foreign birth; in 1880, 39 per cent; in 1890, 42 per cent; in 1900, 37 per cent. The percentage of persons who were practically foreigners was and is of course much greater,

newcomers were as a rule poor and ignorant. They knew little of the institutions of the country, and had not acquired any patriotic interest in it. But they received votes. Their numbers soon made them a power in city and State politics, and all the more so because they were cohesive, influenced by leaders of their own race, and not, like the native voters, either disposed to exercise, or capable of exercising, an independent judgment upon current issues. From among them there soon emerged men whose want of book-learning was overcome by their natural force and shrewdness, and who became apt pupils of those arts of party management which the native professional politicians had already brought to perfection.

While these causes were transferring power to the rougher and more ignorant element in the population, the swift developments of trade which followed the making of the Erie Canal and opening up of railway routes to the West, with the consequent expansion of New York as a commercial and financial centre, had more and more distracted the thoughts of the wealthier people from local politics, which required more time than busy men could give, and seemed tame when compared with that struggle over slavery, whereon, from 1850 to 1865, all patriotic minds were bent. The leading men, who fifty years earlier would have watched municipal affairs and perhaps borne a part in them, were now so much occupied with their commercial enterprises or their legal practice as to neglect their local civic affairs, and saw with unconcern the chief municipal offices appropriated by persons belonging to the lower strata of society.

Even had these men of social position and culture desired to retain a hold in city politics, the task would not have been easy, for the rapid growth of New York, which from a population of 108,000 in 1820 had risen to 209,000 in 1830, to 813,000 in 1860, and to 942,000 in 1870, brought in swarms of strangers who knew nothing of the old residents, and it was only by laboriously organizing these newcomers that they could be secured as adherents. However laborious the work might be, it was sure to be done, because the keenness of party strife made every vote precious. But it was work not attractive to men of education, nor suited to them. It fell naturally to those who themselves belonged to the lower strata, and it became the source of the power they acquired.

Among the political organizations of New York the oldest and most powerful was the Tammany Society. It is as old as the Federal government, having been established under the name of the Columbian Society in 1789, just a fortnight after Washington's inauguration, by

because it includes many of the sons born in the United States of persons still imperfectly Americanized. It is true that some of the recent immigrants do not for a time obtain votes, but against this must be set the fact that the proportion of adults is much larger among the immigrants than in the whole population.

an Irish American called William Mooney, and its purposes were at first social and charitable rather than political. In 1805 it entitled itself the Tammany Society, adopting, as is said, the name of an Indian chief called Tammanend, or Tammany, and clothing itself with a sort of mock Indian character. . . . Till 1822 it had been governed by a general meeting of its members but with its increased size there came a representative system; and though the Society proper continued to be governed and its propety held by the "sachems," the control of the political organization became vested in a general committee consisting of delegates at primary meetings throughout the city, which that organization was now beginning to overspread. This committee, originally of thirty-three members, numbered seventy-five in 1836, by which time Tammany Hall had won its way to a predominant influence on city politics. Of the present organization I shall speak later.

The first sachems had been men of some social standing, and almost entirely native Americans. . . . After 1850, however, the influx from Europe transformed its membership while adding to its strength. The Irish immigrants were, both as Roman Catholics and in respect of such political sympathies as they brought with them, disposed to enter the Democratic party. Tammany laid hold of them, enrolled them as members of its district organizations, and rewarded their zeal by admitting a constantly increasing number to posts of importance as district leaders, committeemen, and holders of city offices. When the Germans arrived, similar efforts were made to capture them, though with a less complete success. Thus from 1850 onwards Tammany came more and more to lean upon and find its chief strength in the foreign vote. Of the foreigners who have led it, most have been Irish. Yet it would be wrong to represent it, as some of its censors have done, as being predominately Irish in its composition. There have always been and are now vast numbers of native Americans among the rank and file, as well as a few conspicuous among its chiefs. It contains many Germans, possibly one-half of the German voters who can be reckoned as belonging to any party. And to-day the large majority of the Russian and Polish Jews (very numerous in some parts of the city), of the Czechs and other Austro-Hungarian Slavs, and possibly also of the Italians, obey its behests, even if not regularly enrolled as members. . . .

Thus at the beginning of 1869 the group already mentioned found itself in control of the chief offices of the city, and indeed of the State also.[2] Hall was mayor; Sweeny was city chamberlain, that is to say, treasurer of the city and county; Tweed was street commissioner and

[2] 'On the 1st of January, 1869,' said Mr. Tilden, 'when Mr. A. Oakley Hall became mayor, the Ring became completely organized and matured.' Pamphlet entitled *The New York City Ring: Its Origin, Maturity, and Fall*, New York 1873.

president of the Board of Supervisors; Connolly, comptroller, and thus in charge of the city finances. Meanwhile their nominee, Hoffman, was State Governor, able to veto any legislation they disliked, while on the city bench they had three apt and supple tools in Cardozo, Barnard, and McCunn. Other less conspicuous men held minor offices, or were leagued with them in managing Tammany Hall, and through it, the city. But the four who have been first named stood out as the four ruling spirits of the faction. . . .

In the reign of the Ring there is little to record beyond the use made by some of them of the opportunities for plunder, which this control of the municipal funds conferred. Plunder of the city treasury, especially in the form of jobbing contracts, was no new thing in New York, but it had never before reached such colossal dimensions. Two or three illustrations may suffice.

Large schemes of street-opening were projected, and for this purpose it became necessary to take and pay compensation for private property, and also, under the State laws, to assess betterment upon owners whose propety was to be benefited. . . . Under the auspices of some members of the Ring, Commissioners for the carrying out of each improvement were appointed by the Ring judges,—in the famous case of the widening of Broadway by Cardozo in a perfectly novel manner. Those members and their friends then began quietly to purchase property in the spots which were eventually taken by the Commissioners, and extravagent compensation was thereupon awarded them, while other owners, who enjoyed no secret means of predicting the action of the Commissioners, received for similar pieces of land far smaller sums, the burden of betterment also being no less unequally distributed as between the ringsters and other proprietors. In this way great sums passed from the city to those whom the Ring favoured, in certain cases with commissions to some of its members. . . .[3]

In the autumn of 1870 the Ring seemed securely seated. Tweed, the master spirit, was content to scoop in money, and enjoy the licentious luxury which it procured him; though some declared that he had fixed his eyes upon the American legation in London. Sweeny preferred the substance to the ostentation of power; and Connolly's tastes were as vulgar as Tweed's, without the touch of open-handedness which seemed to palliate the latter's greed. Cardozo, however, had his ambitions, and hungered for a place on the Supreme Federal Bench; while Hall, to whom no share in the booty was ever traced, and who may not have received any, was believed to desire to succeed Hoffman as Governor of the State, when that official should be raised

[3] Details may be read in *North American Review*, Vol. CCXLVI, pp. 131–135.

by the growing influence of Tammany to the Presidency of the United States. No wonder the Ring was intoxicated by the success it had already won. It had achieved a fresh triumph in re-electing Hall as Mayor at the end of 1870; and New York seemed to lie at its feet.

Its fall came suddenly; and the occasion sprang from a petty personal quarrel. A certain O'Brien, conspicuous as a leader in a discontented section of the Democratic party, was also personally sore because he had received an office below his hopes, and cherished resentment against Sweeny, to whom he attributed his disappointment. A hench-man of his named Copeland, employed in the auditor's office, happened to find there some accounts headed "County Liabilities" which struck him as suspicious. He copied them, and showed them to O'Brien, who perceived their value, and made him copy more of them, in fact a large part of the fraudulent accounts relating to the furnishing of the Court House. Threatening the Ring, with the publication of these compromising documents, O'Brien tried to extort payment of an old claim he had against the city; but after some haggling the negotiations were interrupted by the accidental death of Watson, the Auditor. Ultimately O'Brien carried his copies to the New York *Times*, a paper which had already for some months past been attacking Tammany with unwonted boldness. On the 8th of July, 1871, it exposed the operations of the Ring; and denounced its members, in large capitals, as thieves and swindlers, defying them to sue it for libel. Subsequent issues contained extracts from the accounts copied by Copeland; and all were summed up in a supplement, published on July 29th and printed in German as well as English, which showed that a sum of nearly $10,000,000 in all had been expended upon the Court House, whose condition everybody could see, and for armoury repairs and furnishings. Much credit is due to the proprietor of the *Times,* who resisted threats and bribes offered him on behalf of the Ring to desist from his onslaught and perhaps even more to the then editor, the late Mr. Louis J. Jennings, whose conduct of the campaign was full of fire and courage. The better classes of the city were now fully aroused, for the denials or defences of the mayor and Tweed found little credence. On September 4th a meeting of citizens was held, and a committee of seventy persons, many of them eminent by ability, experience, or position, formed to investigate the frauds charged, which by this time had drawn the eyes of the whole State and country. It is needless to recount the steps by which Connolly, the person most directly implicated, and the one whom his colleagues sought to make a scapegoat of, was forced to appoint as deputy an active and upright man (Mr. A. H. Green), whose possession and examination of the records in the comptroller's office proved invaluable. The leading part in the campaign was played by Mr. Samuel J. Tilden, chairman of the Democratic party in the State, afterwards Governor of the State, and in 1876 candidate for the Federal Presidency against Mr. Hayes. Feeling acutely the disgrace which the Ring had brought upon the Democratic party, he was resolved by pursuit and exposure to rid the party of them and their coterie once for all; and in this he was now seconded by all the better Democrats. But much was also due to the brilliant cartoons of Mr. Thomas Nast, whose rich invention and striking drawing presented the four leading members of the Ring in every attitude and with every circumstance of ignominy.[4] The election for State offices held in November was attended by unusual excitement. The remaining members of the Ring, for Connolly was now extinct and some of the minor figures had taken to flight, faced it boldly, and Tweed in particular, cheered by his renomination in the Democratic State Convention held shortly beforehand, and by his re-election to the chairmanship of the General Committee of Tammany, now neither explained nor denied anything, but asked defiantly in words which in New York have passed into a proverb, "What are you going to do about it?" His reliance on his own district of the city, and on the Tammany masses as a whole, was justified, for he was re-elected to the State Senate and the organization gave his creatures its solid support. But the respectable citizens, who had for once been roused from their lethargy, and who added their votes to those of the better sort of Democrats and of the Republican party, overwhelmed the Machine, notwithstanding the usual election frauds undertaken on its behalf. Few of the Ring candidates survived, and the Ring itself was irretrievably ruined.

[4] Tweed felt the sharpness of the weapon. He said once. 'I don't care a straw for your newspaper articles: my constituents don't know how to read, but they can't help seeing them damned pictures'; and indeed there was always a crowd round the windows in which *Harper's Weekly* (then admirably edited by the late Mr George William Curtis) was displayed.

F. Cities in the Progressive Movement: 1890-1910

As the cities grew in size and complexity their residents formed new institutions and reorganized old ones to meet their needs. Some, such as the commercial exchanges, were designed to promote the interest of a special group and these sometimes attracted criticism as monopolistic in practice, but the Kansas City Live Stock Exchange successfully defended its activities in court, as its president testified before the U.S. Industrial Commission (Doc. 19). Efforts to maintain competition in the utility field soon proved impractical in most cities and gave way to a variety of regulatory practices culminating at Boston in the sliding scale system perfected in 1906 for the regulation of gas rates (Doc. 20). Few institutions proved more effective in the attack on urban problems than the settlement houses, as Jane Addams in her account of *Twenty Years at Hull House* demonstrates (Doc. 21). A favorite technique of the reformers was to make a detailed survey of the problem area, and the comprehensive Pittsburgh Survey (Doc. 22) provided a model for community surveys in many cities during the next decade. By one route or another most urban reformers in the progressive era sought political action, as Frederic C. Howe records it in *The Confessions of a Reformer* (Doc. 23).

19. Commercial Exchanges—History and Purpose

FROM U.S. Industrial Commission, *Report of the Relations and Conditions of Capital and Labor Employed in Manufactures and General Business,* Washington 1901, VII: 16–17, 994.

Mr. McCoy, ex-president of the Kansas City Live Stock Exchange, presents a discussion of the history and value of commercial exchanges. In illustration of their importance he gives a list of 31 American exchanges which had in 1897 a total membership of 19,715, and the aggregate value of whose membership was $111,915,000. He declares that these institutions are as indispensable to our present material development as the railroad or the telegraph, and that they regulate practically all the commercial and financial transactions of the civilized world. He says that their purposes are, first, to establish, protect, and build up the market in the particular line of trade which they concern, and so to increase the commercial importance of the cities in which they are established; and, second, to provide just and equitable rules for the transaction of business between members and with the public, and to insure the operation of commercial machinery with the least possible friction. By means of the exchanges the public stands assured that every authorized dealer will perform his functions under the most exacting standard of moral honesty, and that a departure from this standard involves a correction more speedy and effectual than can be devised by legislature or courts. Mr. McCoy quotes a declaration of a British royal commission, appointed in 1877 to examine into the history, operation, and rules of the London Stock Exchange, to the effect that by means of the Exchange those who bought and sold in its markets were "bound in their dealings by rules for the enforcement of fair dealing and the repression of fraud, capable of affording relief and exercising restraint far more prompt and often more satisfactory than any within the reach of the courts of law."

It is a prominent feature of exchanges to provide a method for the arbitration of disputes. In some instances the provision is merely permissive; in others a member is bound to arbitrate at the request of the other party; in others all disputes must be arbitrated whether the parties wish it or not; in others a member must arbitrate a controversy even with a nonmember at the latter's request. The policy of the exchanges is to enforce contracts whether they are legally binding or not.

The exchanges have been attacked on the ground that they are monopolies, and also on the ground of the alleged arbitrariness of their rules. The Kansas City Live Stock Exchange was attacked under the antitrust law of 1890. It gained a complete victory. Judge Peckham declared, in delivering the opinion of the United States Supreme Court in this case, that the agreement lacked every ingredient of monopoly. "Any person of good character and credit whose interests are centered at the Kansas City stock yards" can be admitted to the Kansas City Live Stock Exchange. Membership is unlimited in the great majority of commercial exchanges. In a few, such as the New York Stock Exchange and the New York Produce Exchange, which impose a limit, the reason is that it is considered impracticable to operate with larger numbers. As to the rules of the exchanges, they constitute a codification of the usages and customs which have been established in the particular markets. The rules are designed to secure a free and open market, where dealings shall be matter of record and public knowledge. The courts are unanimous in saying that no person has a right to be admitted to such an organization, and that admission

M

is a matter wholly within the discretion of the organization itself. It
follows that when admission is granted, it is upon the condition that
all the rules and regulations of the body shall be observed.

Kansas City stock market

Mr. McCoy says that Kansas City is the second live-stock market in
the world, Chicago being the first. The sales of live stock in Kansas
City in 1898 amounted to $112,650,000, or an average of about
$360,000 a day. The live stock comes from the North, South, West, and
some from the East. During 1898 Kansas City received live stock from
about 33 States and Territories. About 95 per cent of all the cattle
received there are either slaughtered there or sold to go back into
the country as feeders; of the rest, some are bought by the exporters,
some are shipped to such cities as Buffalo, Philadelphia, and
Cincinnati, and a very small proportion are bought by speculators
and forwarded to Chicago in the hope of making an advance.

In his testimony (p. 994) Mr. McCoy submitted a list of 31 exchanges which show in 1897 a total membership of 19,715, the aggregate value of whose membership is $111,915,090.

Name of exchange	Number of members.	Value.	Membership, aggregate value.
New York Stock Exchange	1,100	$35,000	$38,500,000
Boston Stock Exchange	150	12,500	1,875,000
Philadelphia Stock Exchange	230	8,000	1,810,000
Chicago Stock Exchange	445	1,500	667,500
San Francisco Stock Exchange	200	6,000	1,200,000
Chicago Board of Trade	1,900	10,000	19,000,000
New York Produce Exchange	3,000	10,000	30,00,0000
St. Louis Merchants' Exchange	3,000	2,500	7,500,000
Boston Board of Trade	975	350	334,000
Philadelphia Commercial Exchange	490	1,000	490,000
Baltimore Corn and Flour Exchange	550	250	137,500
Buffalo Grain Exchange	478	100	47,800
Detroit Board of Trade	125	50	6,250
Toledo Produce Exchange	100	250	25,000
Milwaukee Chamber of Commerce	600	1,000	600,000
Kansas City Board of Trade	200	1,000	200,000
Peoria Board of Trade	105	500	52,500
Minneapolis Chamber of Commerce	538	1,000	538,000
Duluth Board of Trade	185	500	92,500
New York Coffee Exchange	312	1,000	312,000
New Orleans Cotton Exchange	377	1,000	377,000
New York Cotton Exchange	450	10,000	4,500,000
Memphis Cotton Exchange	165	500	82,500
New York Estate Exchange	500	1,000	500,000
New York Consolidated Exchange	2,050	125	256,250

Chicago Live Stock Exchange	698	1,500	1,017,000
St. Louis Live Stock Exchange	128	1,250	160,000
Kansas City Live Stock Exchange	300	2,500	750,000
Indianapolis Live Stock Exchange	60	500	30,000
Omaha Live Stock Exchange	204	1,000	201,000
Buffalo Live Stock Exchange	100	500	50,000
Total	19,715	....	111,915,000

20. The Sliding Scale in Franchise Rates at Boston

FROM Delos F. Wilcox, *Municipal Franchises, A Description of the Terms and Conditions upon which Private Corporations enjoy Special Privileges in the Streets of American Cities,* New York 1910, pp. 560–563.

The first gas franchise in Boston was granted by the board of aldermen August 27, 1822, to certain individuals who later received a corporate charter from the Massachusetts legislature under the name of the Boston Gas Light Company. By their original franchise from the city they were authorized to lay iron gas pipes underneath the sidewalks subject to the direction of the commissioner of highways. A little later they were given the right to cross the street with their pipes. Under the company's state charter it was required to get the consent of the mayor and board of aldermen before opening the ground in any part of the public streets. As a matter of fact, gas was not supplied until towards the close of 1828. The price from that date to 1844 was $5 per 1000 cubic feet and has since been gradually reduced till on July 1, 1907, it was fixed at 80 cents.

The experience of Boston with gas franchises has been in many respects similar to that of other cities. In Massachusetts, however, gas companies are authorized under general law to "dig up and open the ground in any of the streets, avenues and highways" of the city "so far as is necessary to accomplish the objects of the corporation," but this may be done only "with the consent in writing of the mayor and aldermen." Cities are authorized to construct, purchase, lease and maintain within their corporate limits one or more plants for the manufacture or distribution of gas. They are not permitted, however, during the pendency of proceedings to bring about municipal ownership, arbitrarily to revoke any rights granted to a person or corporation engaged in the gas business. It also provided by the statutes that in any city where a gas company is in active operation no other gas company shall dig up and open the streets for the purpose of laying gas pipes without the consent of the local authorities "granted after notice by publication or otherwise to all parties interested and a public hearing." While the local authorities unquestionably have the right, subject to the approval of the State Board of Railroad Commissioners to revoke street railway locations, there seems to be no provision of law upon which to base a claim of similar authority in regard to the locations of gas mains. Moreover, it is believed that a duly organized gas company could not be prevented from laying its main by arbitrary action of the city authorities and could not be compelled to accept onerous conditions other than reasonable regulations for the opening and care of the streets and the protection of life and propety.

A considerable number of gas companies were incorporated from time to time by special acts of the state legislature to supply gas in different portions of Boston and its environs. Finally, in 1903 an act was passed to bring about the consolidation of eight existing companies to form the Boston Consolidated Gas Company, which was to be organized "for the purpose of making, selling and distributing gas for light or other heating, cooking, chemical and mechanical purposes." This new company was authorized to take over from the eight constitutent companies all their "property, locations, rights, licenses, powers, privileges and franchises," except as otherwise expressly provided. The special charter of one of these companies, the Massachusetts Pipe Line Gas Company, was amended so that it should no longer be compulsory for the local authorities to grant the company locations for its pipe lines. This particular charter already provided that the company should be subject to the regulations and restrictions made by the local authorities in regard to their street work, that it should restore all streets opened by it to as good a state as they were in when opened "and to the satisfaction of the local authorities of the city." Locations granted by the local authorities were made expressly subject to revocation with the consent of the State Board of Gas and Electric Light Commissioners. This company's charter was also amended so as to require the approval of the local authorities for the leasing, purchase or operation of the works or distributing system of any other gas company. The Boston Consolidated Gas Company was by express provision of its charter endowed with the privileges conferred by the law authorizing the purchase of gas works by cities. The privilege of most importance in this connection was the right to have the company's plant purchased by the city at its fair market value as a preliminary to the establishment of municipal gas works.

By another special act of the State Legislature approved May 26, 1906, the sliding scale was established to determine the rate which this company might charge for its product. The standard rate fixed by this statute for gas supplied to the company's patrons was to be 90 cents per 1000 cubic feet, and the standard rate of dividends to be paid by the company to its stockholders was fixed at 7% on the par value of the capital stock. It was then provided that if during any year the maximum net rates charged by the company had been less than the standard rate of 90 cents, during the following year the company should be authorized to declare dividends exceeding the standard rate of 7% to the amount of 1/5 of 1% additional for every one cent of reduction in the maximum net price of gas below the standard price. The company was required to publish annually in the month of September in one or more newspapers of Boston a report of the preceding fiscal year showing the cost per 1000 cubic feet of gas in the holders. This cost was to be itemized so that wages at the works and the main items of materials would be shown separately. This report was also to show the cost per 1000 feet of distribution and the amount per 1000 feet charged for depreciation or maintenance repairs, together with any other items of account that might be prescribed from time to time by the State Board of Gas and Electric Light Commissioners. This board was given authority upon petition of the mayor of board of aldermen to revise, after a hearing, the company's method of determining the cost of gas and "to determine finally and conclusively the actual cost of gas furnished, and the clear profits made by the said company applicable to payment of dividends."

21. *Settlement House Activities*

FROM Jane Addams, *Twenty Years at Hull House,* New York 1939 ed., pp. 302–305, 311–312.[1]

We find increasingly, however, that the best results are to be obtained in investigations as in other undertakings, by combining our researches with those of other public bodies or with the State itself. When all the Chicago Settlements found themselves distressed over the condition of the newsboys who, because they are merchants and not employees, do not come under the provisions of the Illinois child labor law, they united in the investigation of a thousand young newsboys, who were all interviewed on the streets during the same twenty-four hours. Their school and domestic status was easily determined later, for many of the boys lived in the immediate neighborhoods of the ten Settlements which had undertaken the investigation. The report embodying the results of the investigation recommended a city ordinance containing features from the Boston and Buffalo regulations,

[1] Reprinted by permission of the Macmillan Co., New York, N.Y.

and although an ordinance was drawn up and a strenuous effort was made to bring it to the attention of the the the aldermen, none of them would introduce it into the city council without newspaper backing. We were able to agitate for it again at the annual meeting of the National Child Labor Committee which was held in Chicago in 1908, and which was of course reported in the papers throughout the entire country. This meeting also demonstrated that local measures can sometimes be urged more effectively when joined to the efforts of a national body. Undoubtedly the best discussions ever held upon the operation and status of the Illinois law, were those which took place then. The needs of the Illinois children were regarded in connection with the children of the nation and advanced health measures for Illinois were compared with those of other states.

The investigations of Hull-House thus tend to be merged with those of larger organizations, from the investigation of the social value of saloons made for the Committee of Fifty in 1896, to the one on infant mortality in relation to nationality, made for the American Academy of Science in 1909. This is also true of Hull-House activities in regard to public movements, some of which are inaugurated by the residents of other Settlements, as the Chicago School of Civics and Philanthropy, founded by the splendid efforts of Dr. Graham Taylor for many years head of Chicago Commons. All of our recent investigations into housing have been under the department of investigation of this school with which several of the Hull-House residents are identified, quite as our active measures to secure better housing conditions have been carried on with the City Homes Association and through the cooperation of one of our residents who several years ago was appointed a sanitary inspector on the city staff.

Perhaps Dr. Taylor himself offers the best possible example of the value of Settlement experience to public undertakings, in his manifold public activities of which one might instance his work at the moment upon a commission recently appointed by the governor of Illinois to report upon the best method of Industrial Insurance or Employer's Liability Acts, and his influence in securing another [commission] to study into the subject of Industrial Diseases. The actual factory investigation under the latter is in charge of Dr. Hamilton, of Hull-House, whose long residence in an industrial neighborhood as well as her scientific attainment, give her peculiar qualifications for the undertaking. . . .

It was as early as our second winter on Halsted Street that one of the Hull-House residents received an appointment from the Cook County agent as a county visitor. She reported at the agency each morning, and all the cases within a radius of ten blocks from Hull-House were given to her for investigation. This gave her a legitimate opportunity for knowing the poorest people in the neighborhood and also for understanding the county method of outdoor relief. The commissioners were at first dubious of the value of such a visitor and predicted that a woman would be a perfect "coal shute" for giving away county supplies, but they came gradually to depend upon her suggestion and advice.

In 1893 this same resident, Miss Julia C. Lathrop, was appointed by the governor a member of the Illinois State Board of Charities. She served in this capacity for two consecutive terms and was later reappointed to a third term. Perhaps her most valuable contribution towards the enlargement and reorganization of the charitable institutions of the State came through her intimate knowledge of the beneficiaries, and her experience demonstrated that it is only through long residence among the poor that an official could have learned to view public institutions as she did, from the standpoint of the inmates rather than from that of the managers. Since that early day, residents of Hull-House have spent much time in working for the civil service methods of appointment for employees in the county and State institutions; for the establishment of State colonies for the care of epileptics; and for a dozen other enterprises which occupy that borderland between charitable effort and legislation. In this borderland we co-operate in many civic enterprises for I think we may claim that Hull-House has always held its activities lightly, ready to hand them over to whosoever would carry them on properly.

22. The Pittsburgh Survey

FROM Russell Sage Foundation, *The Pittsburgh District, Civic Frontage*, New York 1914, pp. 3–6.

At the close of the field work in 1908 we summed up under eight heads the results of the Pittsburgh Survey as to the conditions of life and labour among the wage-earners of the American district. We found:

I. An altogether incredible amount of overwork by everybody, reaching its extreme in the twelve hour shift for seven days in the week in the steel mills and the railway switchyards.

II. Low wages for the great majority of the laborers employed by the mills, not lower than in other large cities, but low compared with prices,—so low as to be inadequate to the maintenance of a normal American standard of living; wages adjusted to the single man in the lodging house, not to the responsible head of a family.

III. Still lower wages for women, who receive for example in one of the metal trades, in which the proportion of women is great enough to be menacing, one half as much as unorganized men in the same shops and one-third as much as the men in the union.

IV. An absentee capitalism, with bad effects strikingly analogous to those of absentee landlordism, of which also Pittsburgh furnishes noteworthy examples.

V. A continuous inflow of immigrants with low standards, attracted by a wage which is high by the standards of southeastern Europe, and which yields a net pecuniary advantage because of abnormally low expenditure for food and shelter and inadequate provision for the contingencies of sickness, accident, and health.

VI. The destruction of family life, not in any imaginary or mystical sense, but by the demands of the day's work, and by the very demonstrable and material method of typhoid fever and industrial accidents; both preventable, but costing in single years in Pittsburgh considerably more than a thousand lives, and irretrievably shattering nearly as many homes.

VII. Archaic social institutions such as the aldermanic court, the ward school district, the family garbage disposal, and the unregenerate charitable institution, still surviving after the conditions to which they were adapted have disappeared.

VII. The contrast,—which does not become blurred by familiarity with detail, but on the contrary becomes more vivid as the outlines are filled in,—the contrast between the prosperity on the one hand of the most prosperous of all the communities of our western civilization, with its vast natural resources, the generous fostering of government, the human energy, the technical development, the gigantic tonnage of the mines and mills, the enormous capital of which the bank balances afford an indication; and, on the other hand, the neglect of life, of health, of physical vigor, even of the industrial efficiency of the individual. Certainly no community before in America or Europe has ever had such a surplus, and never before has a great community applied what it has so meagerly to the rational purposes of human life. Not by gifts of libraries, galleries, technical schools, and parks, but by the cessation of toil one day in seven and sixteen hours in the twenty-four, by the increase of wages, by the sparing of lives, by the prevention of accidents, and by raising the standards of domestic life, should the surplus come back to the people of the community in which it is created. . . .

The adverse social conditions brought out by the reports were such as not infrequently accompany progress. They are incidents of the production of wealth on a vast scale. They are, however, remediable whenever a community thinks it worth while to remedy them. If hardships and misery such as we found in Pittsburgh were due to poverty of resources, to the unproductivity of toil, then the process of overcoming them might indeed be tedious and discouraging. Since they are due to haste in acquiring wealth, to inequity in distribution, to the inadequacy of the mechanism of municipal government, they can be overcome rapidly if a community so desires.

There were many indications that at the time of the Pittsburgh Survey the community was awakening to these adverse conditions, and that it was even then ready to deal with some of them. In the five years that have intervened it has dealt with others. More important, an increasing number of citizens, city officials, officers of corporations, business men, and social workers, are entirely ready to enter with others and with one another on the dispassionate search for causes and remedies, recognizing the body of adverse conditions that remain, recognizing that distinction lies not in ostrich-like refusal to see them, but in statesmanlike willingness to gauge them and to understand them, and so far as it is possible to remove them.

23. A Civic Club

FROM Frederic C. Howe, *The Confessions of a Reformer,* New York 1925, pp. 80–82.[1]

My next experience was to be a happier one. One night at a dance I met a fledgling lawyer like myself, a young Harvard graduate named Morris Black, of a prosperous and respected Hungarian family. We drifted into talk, told one another what we thought of our dirt-begrimed law-books, how we hated the petty things we were doing in the justice of the peace courts, laughed over the stupidities of our practice. We felt alike about life. He was emotional, moody, full of vital energy, a musician. I was reserved and undemonstrative. From our first meeting we were inseparable. We dined and drank and tramped together. His home became my own.

Out of memories of the comradeship of college *kneipes* we organized the Beer and Skittles Club, which rather by accident took on a serious purpose. Cleveland at that time was about to erect a city hall, the county was planning a new court-house, a public library and a new federal building were to be put up, the old disgraceful Union passenger-station was to be replaced by a new, imposing one. Both Black and I had lived in Germany and we saw the possibility of combining these structures into a splendid group, as is done in many of the capitals of Europe. We invited the editorial writers of each

[1] Reprinted by permission of Charles Seribner & Sons, New York, N.Y.

of the Cleveland papers to join the club, and unfolded to them a plan of developing a great civic centre. We prepared illustrated stories of the grouping of public buildings in Vienna, Paris, Budapest, Dresden, and Munich, and printed them in the Sunday papers. We induced the local chapter of the Institute of Architects to hold a competition for plans. Finally, when the subject had gotten well into people's minds, we went to Harry Garfield, who was then the president of the Chamber of Commerce, and asked him to appoint a committee to further the idea. From this time on the chamber made the plan one of its chief objectives. Yet nobody knew from what source the continued agitation was directed or that any particular group was keeping the subject alive. . . .

Later, when I was in the city council, I introduced the legislation that committed the city to the project, and Cleveland has since carried through a monumental planning enterprise. It purchased a great stretch of land, running from the business centre to the lake front. The land was planned by an expert commission with sunken gardens and parking, with a wide mall running down the centre. Flanking the mall a city hall, county court-house, federal building, public library, and convention auditorium have been erected, with a Federal Reserve Bank Building not far distant. A uniform style of architecture and a uniform skyline insured harmony and unity of effect in this splendid attempt at city-building.

G. The Emergence of Metropolitan Regionalism

Arthur Feiler, a visitor from Germany in 1920, vividly described the astonishing upsurge of skyscrapers in New York, Chicago, and a few other great cities, as well as the dynamic life in their exchanges and the tumult in their streets. He concluded, however, that 'the real America lies farther inland' and proceeded to describe Cleveland and Milwaukee, which he found to be characteristic of many other metropolitan cities (Doc. 24). Two of the most important functions of the emerging metropolitan core cities were regional leadership in banking and industry. Thus the establishment of the Federal Reserve System in 1914 and the selection of twelve Federal Reserve cities effected a reorganization of the nation's banking structure and provided a basic new regionalism (Doc. 25). In similar fashion the creation of ordinance districts during the first World War provided a regional organization of the nation's industrial activities around twenty-one industrial metropolises (Doc. 26).

24. Skyscrapers and Ethnic Settlements

FROM Arthur Feiler, *America Seen Through German Eyes,* Translated by Margaret L. Goldsmith, New York 1923, pp. 27–28, 29–31.

Skyscrapers are the first thing which a foreigner sees when he comes to America. The dizzy loftiness of the Manhattan skyline seems to loom above the arriving ship like a citadel raised on high by the cyclops. At first no details can be distinguished. The picture is seen as a whole, an amazing agglomeration of iron and cement. A spire, a tower, or a dome, are conspicuous here or there, and one building is seen to be twice as high as its neighbor. The whole fantastic picture seems to have been jumbled together promiscuously with no fixed plan, and this very irregularity of the scene makes it all the more impressive. Wilhelm Schafer has called early German romanesque cathedrals "Castles of the Saviour" and, with libelous cynicism, American skyscrapers have been called "Cathedrals of Commerce." It is indeed appropriate that often their lack of a definite style is hidden behind gothic scrolls which are pasted onto their walls. Occasionally, on Broadway, one may see a pathetic little church, which has remained standing. By comparison its steeple no longer points to heaven. In Chicago a church has even been built on top of a skyscraper: on the ground floor of this same building neckties and straw hats can be bought, higher up there are twelve stories filled with offices of various kinds, and on the fourteenth floor, there is the church. Capitalism turned into stone—these buildings are the embodiment of capital's unrestrained power. . . .

But New York, with its enormous population (in 1920 it was larger than London), is not America. New York is only the narrow gateway leading to the great American Continent. A quarter of New York's population (1,991,547) was born in Europe. If the suburbs are excluded, the proportion is even higher. These immigrants landed in America and stuck to the port of entry. There are 480,000 Russians, chiefly Russian Jews. Their ghetto in New York looks just like the Jewish quarter in Vilna or in Whitechapel. There are 390,000 Italians and their washing, dangling between the houses, waves in the breezes just as it does in Naples. There are 200,000 Irish, 200,000 Germans, 150,000 Poles and 125,000 Austrians. These foreigners, as well as swarms of others of all nationalities, all colors, races and faiths, live in New York, closely crowded together and separated from the rest of the population. They are exposed to exploitation in every form; they are still faced with the problem of fighting their way into the real America. Often it is only their children who succeed in winnning this fight.

The real America lies farther inland, in the cities having a million population, more or less, and in the smaller towns. Evil slums can be seen in cities, to which some industrial enterprise has brought foreign workers by carloads so as to exploit them systematically. In these slums, like the ones in Cleveland, the little houses swarm with all kinds of foreigners. New shacks are crowded even into the narrow spaces which originally separated these houses. Sheds are turned into dwellings, sometimes a second or even third story is built on top of them. The result is a maze of narrow alleys crowded in the evening with children and with untidy women, wearing the wide jackets and the large shawls typical of their homes somewhere in eastern Europe. It is indeed a dreary picture of exploited poverty. In places, however, where this first stage of misery has been overcome, the situation is entirely different. Take for instance a city like Milwaukee, "German" Milwaukee in the "German" State of Wisconsin. The river valley is a tremendous industrial district. For a long distance there is one plant after another, but on the hills rising from this valley and extending to the beautiful shores of the lake, is a residential district with broad streets. The people who live here do not remember the cramped meagerness of Europe. The houses, except in the congested center of the town, usually have five rooms, kitchen and bath, electric light, gas for cooking and a garage on the premises. Similarly favorable conditions also prevail in the older, less prosperous districts, which are inhabited largely by wage-earners, except that here duplex houses are more general. The Poles live in such a district and I wonder whether Mr. Klabustensky, who is perhaps employed in a large tannery, ever dreamed of such luxuries when he lived in old Europe? Adjoining this part of town are Milwaukee's newer districts where the wealthy upper stratum, the middle class and more prosperous workers live. This part of Milwaukee is like a real garden city, with trim single houses. The people in them are living in light and freedom.

25. Designation of the Federal Reserve Districts and Banks

FROM *U.S. Senate Documents*, 63rd Congress 2nd Session, 1914, XVI: 361–363.

The federal reserve act directs the Reserve Bank Organization Committee to "designate not less than 8 nor more than 12 cities, to be known as Federal reserve cities"; to "divide the continental United States, including Alaska, into districts, each district to contain only one of such Federal reserve cities"; and to apportion the districts "with due regard to the convenience and customary course of business." The act provides that the districts may not necessarily be coterminous with any State or States.

In determining the reserve districts and in designating the cities within such districts where Federal reserve banks shall be severally located, the organization committee has given full consideration to the important factors bearing upon the subject. The committee held public hearings in 18 of the leading cities from the Atlantic to the Pacific and from the Great Lakes to the Gulf, and was materially assisted thereby in determining the districts and the reserve cities.

Every reasonable opportunity has been afforded applicant cities to furnish evidence to support their claim as locations for Federal reserve banks.

More than 200 cities, through their clearing-house associations, chambers of commerce, and other representatives, were heard. Of these, 37 cities asked to be designated as the headquarters of a Federal reserve bank.

The majority of the organization committee, including its chairman and the Secretary of Agriculture, were present at all hearings and stenographic reports of the proceedings were made for more deliberate consideration. Independent investigations were, in addition, made through the Treasury Department, and the preference of each bank as to the locations of the Federal reserve bank with which it desired to be connected was ascertained by an independent card ballot addressed to each of the 7,471 national banks throughout the country which had formally assented to the provisions of the Federal reserve act.

Among the many factors which governed the committee in determining the respective districts and the selection of the cities which have been chosen were:

First. The ability of the member banks within the district to provide the minimum capital of $4,000,000 required for the Federal reserve bank, on the basis of 6 per cent of the capital stock and surplus of member banks within the district.

Second. The mercantile, industrial, and financial connections existing in each district and the relations between the various portions of the district and the city selected for the location of the Federal reserve bank.

Third. The probable ability of the Federal reserve bank in each district, after organization and after the provisions of the Federal reserve act shall have gone into effect, to meet the legitimate demands of business, whether normal or abnormal, in accordance with the spirit and provisions of the Federal reserve act.

Fourth. The fair and equitable division of the available capital for the Federal reserve banks among the districts created.

Fifth. The general geographical situation of the district, transportation lines, and the facilities for speedy communication between the Federal reserve bank and all portions of the district.

Sixth. The population, area, and prevalent business activities of the district, whether agricultural, manufacturing, mining, or commercial, its record of growth and development in the past, and its prospects for the future.

In determining the several districts the committee has endeavored to follow State lines as closely as practicable, and wherever it has been found necessary to deviate the division has been along lines which are believed to be the most convenient and advantageous for the district affected.

The 12 districts and the 12 cities selected for the locations of the Federal reserve banks are as follows:

DISTRICT NO. 1—*The New England States: Maine, New Hamp-*

shire, Vermont, Massachusetts, Rhode Island, and Connecticut, with the city of Boston as the location of the Federal reserve bank.

This district contains 445 national banks which have accepted the provisions of the Federal reserve act. The capital stock of the Federal Reserve Bank of Boston, on the basis of 6 per cent of the total capital stock and surplus of the assenting national banks in the district, will amount to $9,924,543.

DISTRICT NO. 2—*The State of New York, with New York City as the location of the Federal reserve bank.*

This district contains 477 national banks which have accepted the provisions of the Federal reserve act. The capital stock of the Federal Reserve Bank of New York, on the basis of 6 per cent of the total capital stock and surplus of the assenting national banks in the district, will amount to $20,621,606; and if there be added 6 per cent of the capital stock and surplus of the State banks and trust companies which have applied for membership up to April 1, 1914, the total capital stock will be $20,687,606.

DISTRICT NO. 12—*The States of California, Washington, Oregon, Idaho, Nevada, and Utah, and all that part of Arizona not included in district No. 11, with the city of San Francisco, Cal., as the location of the Federal reserve bank.*

This district contains 514 national banks which have accepted the provisions of the Federal reserve act. The capital stock of the Federal reserve bank of San Francisco, on the basis of 6 per cent of the total capital stock and surplus of the assenting national banks in the district, will amount to $7,825,375; and if there be added 6 per cent of the capital stock and surplus of the State banks and trust companies which have applied for membership up to April 1, 1914, the total capital stock will be $8,115,494.

The committee was impressed with the growth and development of the States of Idaho, Washington, and Oregon, but on the basis of 6 per cent of the capital stock and surplus of national banks and State banks and trust companies which have applied for membership, that section could not provide the $4,000,000 minimum capital stock required by the law. With the continued growth of that region it is reasonable to expect that in a few years the capital and surplus of its member banks will be sufficient to justify the creation of an additional Federal reserve district, at which time application may be made to the Congress for a grant of the necessary authority.

It is no part of the duty of the organization committee to locate branches of the Federal reserve banks. The law specifically provides that "each Federal reserve bank shall establish branch banks within the Federal reserve district in which it is located." All the material collected by the committee will be placed at the disposal of the Federal reserve banks and the Federal reserve board when they are organized and ready to consider the establishment of branch banks. . . .

> W. G. McAdoo,
> D. F. Houston,
> Jno. Skelton Williams,
> Reserve Bank Organization Committee

Washington, D.C., April 2, 1914

26. Regional War Industries Boards and Districts

FROM Grosvenor B. Clarkson, *Industrial America in the World War,* Boston, 1923, pp. 241–242, Appendix V.

C. A. Otis, president of the Chamber of Commerce of Cleveland, and a banker of that city, was placed at the head of the Section of Resources and Conversion. His selection was another instance of how men with ideas made their niches in the War Industries Board. Mr. Otis had taken the lead in Cleveland, even before the United States entered the war, in a successful endeavor to concentrate in the Cleveland district the making of all parts and accessories of the characteristic manufacturing products of that part of the country. This work had been prompted by the confusion encountered in responding to the demands of the Allies. The object was to cut out wasteful and time-consuming cross-hauling, and generally to integrate industrial processes not domiciled in a single plant.

Such an experience met the requirements of the War Industries Board, for in connection with unit conversion Mr. Baruch was planning to meet the problem of regional congestion of production with territorial decentralization. In a way Mr. Otis and his associates had been building up a little war industries board of their own in Cleveland. Like nuclei all over the country were what the Board needed—not only to promote the diffusion of war industry, but to break up the jam of administration that was overwhelming the central offices. Under the new organization authority, being definitely placed in the hands of the chairman in the first instance, was by him conveyed to division and section heads. A step further would be to project authority, not only functionally, but territorially. Thus arose the regional system under Mr. Otis's direction.

"I'm sold," said Baruch at the conclusion of his first interview with Otis.

The latter then suggested that some great organizer, such as President Farrell of the United States Steel Corporation, be put in charge of the new enterprise.

"No, you have the idea, and I think you are the fellow to carry it out," was Baruch's answer. "You get your winter clothes and come to Washington."

Otis and Peck worked out the plan of nineteen (later twenty-one) industrial regions with an "adviser," representing the War Industries Board, in each. These advisers were usually men associated with local chambers of commerce and fully conversant with industrial facilities and personnel in their district. They knew men and facilities. They knew what was feasible and what was possible. They had a commendable local interest, but it was remarkable how completely they subordinated the local to the general. If the full story were ever told of how these local men sometimes prevented their home-town plants or business men from getting Government patronage that they were not competent to handle, a number of gentlemen would find it desirable to seek new habitats. On the other hand, they developed and encouraged worthy local enterprises of conversion or new organization that might never have got a hearing in Washington.

Should regional patriotism, however, advocate a steel plant in Salt Lake City or in Maine because there happened to be some convertible buildings on hand or some idle labor available, it collided with the watchful Otis in Washington. Regional integration of industry was one of his great purposes—the territorial concentration of the final form of manufacture, with the production of materials, massed labor, ample power, and adequate transportation with a minimum of long hauls and the elimination of cross-hauls.

With the coming of regional organizations the day was gone forever when smooth persons armed with a roll of blue-prints could talk themselves into contracts they were not competent to perform. If they came to Washington, a few minutes' telephone talk between Otis and Trigg in Philadelphia or McAllister in Cleveland indicated the way for them. But if the men and the project were genuine, the same quick intelligence started them immediately on their way to business. . . .

REGIONAL WAR INDUSTRY CENTRES

Region	Territory
No. 1, Boston, Mass.	Maine, New Hampshire, Vermont, eastern Massachusetts, Rhode Island.
No. 2, Bridgeport, Conn.	Western Massachusetts, Connecticut.
No. 3, New York, N.Y.	Nine southeastern counties of New York, Long Island, and northern New Jersey.

No. 4, Philadelphia, Pa.	Eastern Pennsylvania, southern New Jersey, Delaware.
No. 5, Pittsburgh, Pa.	Western Pennsylvania, except Erie, Crawford, and Mercer counties; Jefferson and Belmont Counties of Ohio; Allegany, Garrett, and Washington Counties of Maryland; West Virginia.
No. 6, Rochester, N.Y.	New York State, except Metropolitan district New York City.
No. 7, Cleveland, Ohio	Erie, Crawford, and Mercer Counties of Pennsylvania; northern Ohio, excepting Jefferson and Bolmont Counties.
No. 8, Detroit, Mich.	Southern Michigan.
No. 9, Chicago, Ill.	Iowa, northern Illinios, and northern Indiana.
No. 10, Cincinnati, Ohio	Southern Ohio, southern Indiana, and Kentucky.
No. 11, Baltimore, Md.	Eastern Maryland, Virginia.
No. 12, Atlanta, Ga.	North Carolina. South Carolina, Georgia, and Florida, excepting western tier of counties.
No. 13, Birmingham, Ala.	Tennessee, Missippi, Alabama, western tier of counties in Florida, and southern Louisiana.
No. 14, Kansas City, Mo.	Utah, Wyoming, Colorado, northern New Mexico, northern Oklahoma, Kansas, Nebraska, and western strip of Misouri.
No. 15, St. Louis, Mo.	Missouri, Arkansas, and southern Illinios.
No. 16, St. Paul Minn.	Montana, North Dakota, South Dakota, Minnesota, and northwestern Michigan.
No. 17, Milwaukee, Wis.	Southern Wisconsin.
No. 18, Dallas, Tex.	Texas, northern Louisana, southern Oklahoma, southern New Mexico, and southeastern Arizona.
No. 19, San Francisco, Cal.	California, Nevada, and Arizona, except southeastern counties in Dallas District.
No. 20, Seattle, Wash.	Washington, Oregon, and Idaho.
No. 21, Denver, Colo.	Colorado, Utah, Wyoming, and Northern New Mexico.

H. The Metropolis in Prosperity and Depression

It was not until the late 1930s that a major study of cities and their role in the nation's history was made by the National Resources Committee. That comprehensive study, made at the request of the U.S. Conference of Mayors and other urban bodies, first clearly depicted the city as "the workshop of our industrial society and the nerve center of our vast and delicate commercial mechanism." A few brief quotes from the Foreword of its report aptly place the city in the national economy (Doc. 27). The efforts of various core cities to achieve a federal union with their suburbs prompted the *National Municipal Review* to devote its entire issue in August 1922 to one long article by Professor Charles C. Maxey on this subject (Doc. 28). Among other dynamic metropolises, Cincinnati and Detroit experienced a dramatic upsurge of civic spirit in the twenties and, on the onset of the depression, each made heroic efforts to counteract its hardships. The Detroit program was compared by William P. Lovett in the *National Municipal Review* (Doc. 29) with that of Cincinnati; both were of keen interest to the leaders of many cities and helped to prepare the way for the assumption of federal responsibility for welfare programs under the New Deal. The direct relation between the urban needs, as recognized by the mayors who took the lead in forming the U.S. Conference of Mayors, and the federal response of Roosevelt's advisors is clearly evident in several brief articles appearing in *The American City* in 1933 and 1934 (Doc. 30).

27. Cities in the Nation's Economy

FROM National Resources Committee, *Our Cities: Their Role in the National Economy*, Washington 1937, pp. V-VII.

The modern nation finds in its cities the focal point of much that is threatening and much that is promising in the life of its people. Scanning the troubled horizons of the past few years for these symptoms of national strength and national strain, we find first of all that the city has become not only one of the fundamental supports but also one of the primary problems of the Nation's economy.

N*

As America pitches back and forth between alternate depression and recurrent prosperity, it is in the Nation's cities that the shadow of economic insecurity is darkest. For in the city will be found the workshop of our industrial society and the nerve center of our vast and delicate commercial mechanism. In 1935 one-fifth of all the employable persons on relief in the country were to be found in our 10 largest cities. Subject to continuing unemployment, lacking the rural reserves of shelter and subsistence, the city worker is seriously handicapped in the struggle for existence.

In a time of national stress the task of relief and recovery falls not merely upon a single community or segment of the Nation, but upon the Nation as a whole. It is the Federal Government that has had to assume the major burdens of providing emergency relief for the city as well as the farm, of stimulating public works in the Nation's urban centers, and even of reviving insolvent municipal finances. Of the billions of dollars devoted to public emergency relief during the period 1933 to 1936, a large percent was contributed by the Federal Government.

The Nation's task has now become not only one of relief and recovery but of reconstruction, and this also has been recognized as in part the Federal Government's responsibility. Confirmed by the regulations and decisions of the highest tribunals in the land, there has been launched, along with an agricultural and fiscal plan, a Nation-wide program of social security and rational labor relations, principally designed to reduce the insecurities of the mass of city workers and thereby of the system of national production and consumption which rests in large part upon their welfare and their prosperity. . . .

In looking at the urban problems, therefore, we consider it not as the concern of the city alone, but as a problem of the farmer as well, in that it is a problem of all the American Nation. From the point of view of the highest and best use of our national resources, our urban communities are potential assets of great value, and we must consider from the point of view of the national welfare how they may be most effectively aided in their development. . . .

The city has seemed at times the despair of America, but at others to be the Nation's hope, the battleground of democracy. Surely in the long run, the Nation's destiny will be profoundly affected by the cities which have two-thirds of its population and its wealth. There is liberty of development in isolation and wide spaces, but there is also freedom in the many-sided life of the city where each may find its own kind. There is democracy in the scattered few, but there is also democracy in the thick crowd with its vital impulse and its insistent demand for a just participation in the gains of our civilization. There is fertility and creation in the rich soil of the broad countryside, but there is also fertility and creativeness in forms of industry, art, personality, emerging even from the city streets and reaching towards the sky.

The faults of our cities are not those of decadence and impending decline, but of exuberant vitality crowding its way forward under tremendous pressure—the flood rather than the drought. The city is both the great playground and the great battleground of the Nation— at once the vibrant center of a world of hectic amusement lovers and also the dusty and sometimes smoldering and reddened arena of industrial conflict. It is the cities that must meander the ambiguous and shifting boundaries between recreation and vice, not only for their own citizens but for some of their visitors as well. It is the cities that must deal with the tragic border lines of order and justice in bitter industrial struggles. On these two problems alone many a "good government" has been wrecked. . . .

It is the purpose of this inquiry to indicate some of the emerging city problems in which the Nation as a whole has an interest and in which the National Government may be helpful. . . . The sanitation, the education, the housing, the working and living conditions, the economic security—in brief, the general welfare of all its citizens— are American concerns, insofar as they are within the range of Federal power and responsibility under the Constitution. In the report which follows, the National Resources Committee, following the report of its committee on urbanism, takes stock of these urban conditions and calls the Nation's attention to a wide range of relevant subjects, including urban population trends, urban and rural ways of life, industrial centralization and decentralization, model cities, urban planning and housing, urban growth, transport facilities, land policies, urban government, unions of cities, and Federal-city relations.

28. The Greater Boston Movement

FROM 'The Political Integration of Metropolitan Communities,' by Chester C. Maxey, *National Municipal Review*, January 1922, XI 245–248.

The federal census of 1920 gives Boston a population of 748,060 and ranks Boston as the seventh city of the United States, but Boston newspapers and civic organizations insist that the true magnitude and importance of their city are not indicated by the census figures. It is pointed out that outside of the corporate limits of Boston but within a radius of fifteen miles of the state house in Boston there dwells a further population of over 700,000; and it is contended that Boston proper is but the torso of a great metropolitan community of about 1,500,000 inhabitants constituting an organic entity in all respects except political organization. At present this vast community is a morass of co-existent, overlapping, conflicting, and competing units of local government, there being in all fourteen cities, twenty-six towns, five counties, and five state boards or agencies functioning within the metropolitan area.

What this condition means is well set forth in "An Appeal for the Federation of the Metropolitan Cities and Towns," issued in 1919 by Mayor Peters of Boston. In urging the political unification of the metropolitan district Mayor Peters incidentally points out that the absence of political unity has had the following results: (1) It has rendered the metropolitan community incapable of co-operating effectively to secure freight rates favorable to the upbuilding of export trade and the establishment of regular steamship service with foreign ports; (2) it has been one of the major causes of the failure of the metropolitan community to provide terminal facilities conducive to shipping and trade; (3) it is responsible for the failure of the metropolitan district to develop adequate factory sites because of inability to provide street connections and housing facilities; (4) it is responsible for the decline of real estate values in many sections of Boston owing to the want of intelligent control of suburban developments; (5) it is responsible for Boston's falling under the domination of political organizations whose strength lies in control of the votes of the foreign population; (6) it is to blame for the failure to provide for police and fire protection and for street improvements on a metropolitan basis; (7) it has prevented the enactment of uniform health and housing laws which would relieve congestion in Boston and promote the growth of the less densely populated suburbs; (8) it has unduly inflated the cost of local government owing to duplication of services and overhead organization.

The question of merging the governmental agencies of the metropolitan area has been under discussion in Boston for many years. In 1896 a special commission was appointed by the legislature to study the problem of municipal administration in Boston and the adjoining municipalities, and it prepared a report recommending the federation of the various towns and cities as a single county which should have the functions of a municipal corporation. In 1911 the Boston Chamber of Commerce reported a plan of federation through the creation of a metropolitan council consisting of representatives of the various municipalities. In the same year the state legislature created a second commission to consider the metropolitan problem, and this body recommended a plan to loose federation similar to the plan of the Chamber of Commerce. In 1919 at the instance of Mayor Peters of

Boston a bill was introduced in the state legislature authorizing the outright annexation of the suburban municipalities by Boston. The idea of a loose federation of municipalites was abandoned by the mayor in the hope that by pressing the movement for annexation he could precipitate discussion which would result in the crystallization of public opinion on the subject of unification, and also in the hope that if the bill should pass, some progress toward unification might be made by piecemeal annexation. It is needless to say that the bill did not succeed, and that unification at the present juncture seems as remote as ever.

Unification Proposed for Cleveland

The same anomalies of local government that have been observed in other metropolitan centers are to be found in Cleveland and Cuyahoga county. The population of Cleveland is 796,841, but in the contiguous suburban communities of East Cleveland, Cleveland Heights, Lakewood, West Park, Shaker Heights, Bratenahl, and Euclid Village, there is a combined population of 101,820 which in every practical sense is a part and parcel of the city of Cleveland. This integrated metropolitan population is ninety-five percent of the population of Cuyahoga county and could be readily governed as one municipal corporation; but Cuyahoga county is overlaid with ninety-three detached and disconnected units of local self-government, these being largely cities, villages, townships, and school districts in the metropolitan area.

The disadvantages of disintegration and the corresponding advantages of unification have not received adequate consideration in Cleveland and her suburban satellites, and consequently the movement for consolidation has made little progress. Two civic organizations—The Civic League and the County Charter Government Association—have given the matter some attention, but have felt unable to undertake an intensive and persistet campaign. In 1919 a resolution proposing an amendment to the state constitution, which would provide for a consolidated form of city and county government, was introduced in the state senate, but it was shelved in committee, no opportunity being given for its consideration. In 1921 Representative Davis of Cuyahoga county introduced a bill to facilitate consolidation of local governments in Cuyahoga county, but this likewise received scant consideration by the legislature. In the spring of the present year movements for annexation developed in West Park and Lakewood, and commissions are now at work preparing terms of annexation to be later submitted to the voters.

29. *Detroit Battles the Depression*

FROM 'Detroit Feeds Its Hungry,' by William P. Lovett, *National Municipal Review*, July 1931, XX: 402–406.

If one learns best by doing, Detroit's past hectic year of struggle must have left the city a rich experience, at least. Beginning with Mayor Charles Bowles, who was recalled from office by popular vote July 22 last, the year has been kaleidoscopic indeed. Mayor Frank Murphy took hold last September, after making unemployment relief practically his entire platform. Since then we have had the benefit of the Cincinnati plan and all the other municipal plans. Yet our mayor told his Unemployment Committee as late as May 12, "We must bend all our efforts towards getting federal aid to relieve our current emergency caused by unemployment; meantime we must organize ourselves in preparation for this aid."

On the credit side the record shows a major city tackling without hesitation a situation filled with perils, difficulties, and impossible problems. To do this we made no new decision. The city has always furnished welfare relief most generously to its unemployed. This situation differed in size, and in its unexpected duration. But even when the stringency of the general depression was aggravated by a municipal welfare deficit of $15,000,000 and still mounting, the city continued to believe in its ability to find a way out.

In December, 1929, when the effects of the national crash in the stock market were beginning to be appreciated, alarm was sounded by our United States Senator, James Couzens, former mayor. Before the annual meeting of the powerful Michigan Manufacturers' Association he pictured the acute problem of seasonal unemployment in Detroit's automobile industry. He challenged the industrial leaders to show "a will to do," and to make an attempt to solve this and related problems, if they would avoid the disagreeable alternative of action by the government. It developed later that certain few plants had made sincere efforts to stabilize employment, but without significant results. . . .

While the city faced financial deficit and unemployment, Judge Murphy thrilled thousands of voters with ringing emotional appeals for recognition of the human values. He forecast "the dew and sunshine of a new day,"—a phrase frequently echoed more recently to his apparent discomfiture. He demanded old-age pensions, unemployment insurance, and insisted that no human being would be without food or shelter if he were elected mayor.

On that program Mayor Murphy was elected. That has been the program since he took office last September. (That always was

Detroit's program.) Nobody has gone without food or shelter. But with the state legislature in session almost five months, the bills for old-age pensions and unemployment insurance were among the missing.

The basic problem of the city budget for the year beginning July 1 next has been handled with amazing success by city officials and citizen agencies working in close cooperation; this includes the deficit in current expenses, the varying welfare fund deficit of millions, and certain borrowings. But the only thing we have proved, as to unemployment relief by the city government, is that conditions made the problem too big for the city alone to solve in any ideal fashion.

Perhaps Cincinnati showed superior wisdom by preparedness. Or Cincinnati, like all the others, could not equal Detroit in the number and size of its difficulties. When has any American city past or present appropriated more than $1,500,000 a month, over a period of many months, to public relief? (No wonder Mayor Murphy called it a famine!) Is it not a new record for a city to carry 45,000 families on its relief rolls for most of a year?

Mayor Murphy began by naming a large citizens' committee, more than a hundred men and women from all groups and classes—industry, labor, business, religion, society and civic affairs. Numerous sub-committees were formed. Other committees were added and multiplied, till the count was lost. In May the five latest committees were: for investigation of welfare food budgets, for study of the milk problem for indigent families, committee on pre-natal and infant care, labor committee, and committee on old-age pensions. . . .

Our community chest, running annually above $3,000,000, secures funds for the maintenance of eighty organizations but emergency relief customarily is handled through the city or county governments; hence public appeals for private gifts were neither made nor expected. Like snow removal, the city fathers have put into the budget each year a nominal amount for welfare relief, later granting over-drafts and creating deficits according to needs. Thus the city always has been prepared yet unprepared, generous but quite unscientific in its methods. Like our industrial growth and financial prosperity we always had enough to go around—so, why worry?

For the unemployment committee the city council appropriated $35,000; city employees added as much more by their personal donations. A flock of secretaries were engaged and things hummed, chiefly in the office of the mayor. The natural procedure was followed: to list the unemployed men and their families, see that necessary food, lodging, fuel, shelter and clothing were provided, locate workingmen in jobs, private or municipal, wherever possible, weed out non-residents and unworthy, care for the sick, etc.

Granting his sincerity, good intentions, and enthusiasm, the mayor's obvious lack of any definite plan, in dealing with tasks so many and so great, opened wide the doors of controversy and criticism. "The whole mess might have been prevented, or vastly changed, if more good judgment had been exercised at the beginning"—so affirm those who "never liked Murphy anyway, and didn't vote for him." Naturally the political winds have blown cold or hot, here or there, with guesses as to whether this history, in the mayoralty election next fall, will become to Mr. Murphy an asset or a liability.

"Surely," it is said, "he never can find jobs for all, and the jobless will be mad." "He got hold of a bear by the tail." But it is retorted, "Dew and sunshine always win with the masses." Or, "Soak the rich, for they pay the most taxes anyway."

Early meetings of the general committee revealed that it was too big for effective service, and highly charged with elements of industrial and social controversy. The factions met and wrangled. Only the mayor's official authority on many occasions prevented dissolution. The press of course stirred the pot, and secret meetings were hard to arrange.

Leaders of capital and labor often locked horns, then separated in disgust. The labor union faction, a distinctly minority group under questionable leadership, hung to the mayor's coattails and demanded acceptance of some fundamental theories, forcing questions as to labor conditions and seeking to raise the bars against any employment of Canadians. Mayor Murphy openly or covertly sided with this group; he declared "the emergency must not be made the excuse for lowering wage or other labor standards."

The chief trouble arose from criticism of the manifest exploitation of the whole system, or lack of system. Large numbers of men and families have received help who neither needed nor deserved it, who had no real residence in Detroit, or who might have been supporting themselves here or elsewhere at honest work if they had not been too lazy or dishonest. The facts on this point simply cannot be known. Opening of free lodging houses for men aggravated the condition, which was not helped by the fact that a large percentage—perhaps a fifth—of those receiving aid had been employed in the past by factories in Detroit suburbs, including Ford's, which do not pay taxes to Detroit.

When there was talk of "men in good clothes, driving up in automobiles to get their dole," Mayor Murphy replied, "No one has said our specific method of welfare was wrong, and no one has suggested a better one." His answer to opponents of unemployment insurance has been, "The city has been paying this insurance for years, through its welfare department."

But why not let the city find jobs in city employ for those who are helped? There have not been enough jobs to satisfy a tenth of the needs, and trial of this plan showed a heavy loss in labor efficiency.

In March the welfare expense ran to $1,800,000. The industrial and social tide was at its lowest ebb. Since then it has been slowly rising. The April appropriation was $1,344,000, still surpassing that of New York. With the backing of the Citizens' Committee on City Finance, which thought out the city budget plans accepted by the mayor and council, Mayor Murphy and his associates began to accept also that cooperation in solving the relief problem which previously he either had not wanted or was unwilling to accept. . . .

On principle the mayor was more sympathetic with union labor than with employers. This always has been an open-shop town, but the past year has notably strengthened the prestige and political influence of the organized labor minority. Efforts, early and late, to procure friendly conference, privately or in public, between the mayor and "big business" men, were fruitless of results. The employing class were in a critical mood, especially after the heckling of union leaders in committee meetings. A further irritation was the issue of the public speech for the radicals, on which the mayor won a well-deserved victory by establishing a public forum.

Why did not Mayor Murphy save months of time and effort by utilizing, at the start, the services of trained social workers, ready to step from the ranks of the community chest group? "He did use them," is the local reply. But he, or others, far too long kept them too far in the background, lacking in authority or responsibilities.

"City agencies and professional welfare workers," it was said, "by virtue of their training are rendered incapable of handling the current emergency problem. We are not dealing with tramps and paupers, but with respectable citizens temporarily out of employment. Only volunteer workers, with the community's social problems close to their hearts and their viewpoint unobstructed by the formalism of the professional worker, are fit to handle the situation."

Mayor Murphy's "dew and sunshine" policy received its body blow June 9, when Detroit was amazed to learn, quite by accident, that frauds in administration of the welfare department had mulcted the city of $200,000 or more, while one clerk, who confessed to the theft of $60,000 by manipulating grocery orders, loomed with a sensational police and penitentiary record. Thus was proved the folly of operating a huge relief program by volunteer workers, instead of demanding from the start a leadership of trained, trustworthy experts.

That point of view explains much of the municipal failure, to the time when John F. Ballenger and Stuart Queen, of the Community Union group, really became directors of the program. Now Mr. Ballenger publicly states his belief that the welfare department of the city never was organized to face a problem such as 48,000 families constituted. Within the past two months the trend has been from hit-or-miss relief, inspired by heart-throbs, to an increasing degree of system and efficiency, from listing and investigations to the final link in the chain. Whatever next winter may bring, apparently we shall be prepared for it. There is a cooperation all down the line, in plans and activities, which formerly had been impossible. . . .

But Detroit's experience indicates the further need of deep thinking on broad lines and coordinated planning of a sort which avails itself of general experimentation, even on state and national lines. Somehow business and government must work together, must give authority to social and industrial experts, and must not expect such a city as Detroit, with its excessive emergency burden, to operate its government aid in complete isolation.

30. United States Conference of Mayors Sponsors Federal Legislation

FROM *The America City*, May 1933, p. 5, January 1934, p. 5.

Certain measures of Federal legislation which are deemed essential for the continued stability and functioning of the larger cities of the country are being actively sponsored by the United States Conference of Mayors, organized by the mayors of more than fifty important cities at a meeting in Washington, D.C., on February 17 last. National measures to which special consideration is being given by the Conference relate to municipal debt, loans by the Reconstruction Finance Corporation, and unemployment relief. Local financial problems are also being studied, and the Conference issued last month mimeographed reports on "License Taxes as a Source of Municipal Revenue" and on "Municipal Notes and Warrants."

For a number of reasons the Conference asked for and received the cooperation of the American Municipal Association (the Federation of some twenty-five state leagues of municipalities), and that organization now serves as the secretariat for the Conference. Paul V. Betters, therefore, has the double title of Executive Director of the American Municipal Association, and Secretary of the United States Conference of Mayors, with headquarters at Drexel Avenue and 58th Street, Chicago.

Mayors Ask Additional Two Billions or More for Local Public Works
Deploring the fact that the great majority of the funds already allotted out of the $3,300,000,000 PWA appropriation have been for strictly

Federal projects, the Executive Committee of the United States Conference of Mayors on December 15 adopted a resolution reading in part as follows:

"If people are to be put to work where the need for work exists, it is apparent that local projects offer the greatest opportunity in this direction. . . . Unless a new appropriation is made, hundreds of needy projects now before the Public Works Administration will of necessity be abandoned, since the funds now remaining are only sufficient for a small number of additional allotments. Under the stimulation of the national recovery measures many communities have gone forward in developing useful public projects, with these same communities fulfilling their responsibilities by pledging their own funds and resources to help defray the cost. If an additional appropriation is not provided, all of these projects will be nothing more than idle plans for giving people work.

"In 1932, when the United States Conference of Mayors was the first national agency to sponsor a public works program, it was recommended that a five-billion-dollar appropriation be made. At this time, we believe, at least two billion dollars should be provided with most of this new fund to be used for local public works. The stringent tax and financial situation confronting practically all cities dictates the need for liberalization of the existing statute."

o

I. The Metropolis in War and Peace

As in the First World War, the cities performed vital tasks for the nation in the early forties, but this time, under the leadership of Mayor LaGuardia as president of the U.S. Conference of Mayors, they were determined to secure an effective post-war cooperation between the cities and the federal government (Doc. 31). The crucial problem, as Mayor LaGuardia clearly saw, was housing, and the progressive steps taken by the federal government in this field during the forties and fifties are briefly summarized by one of the leading workers in this field, Catherine Bauer Wurster (Doc. 32). But even after many urban leaders had begun to grapple with their problems and secured a promise of federal assistance, the disproportionate voting weight of the rural opposition frequently checked the passage of the necessary appropriations, as Senator John F. Kennedy candidly declared in an address to the U.S. Conference of Mayors in 1958 (Doc. 33). The problem of financing urban construction was enormously complicated by the rapid migration of Negroes to the cities and the transformation of decaying residential areas into racial ghettos. Some of the baffling aspects of these problems are discussed in the summary report of a Presidential Commission on Race and Housing edited by Davis McEntire (Doc. 34).

31. The Work of the U.S. Conference of Mayors

FROM 'The Presidential Address' of Mayor F. H. LaGuardia, *City Problems of 1945/46*, Washington 1945, pp. 4–12.

The task of a Mayor is going to be extremely difficult in the immediate future. Of course, I am addressing myself particularly to the Mayors of cities in the United States because I know our conditions. I believe we are going into a period as difficult as that in the peak of the depression. . . .

Most of the trouble centers in the urban areas, particularly the larger cities. . . .

When war was thrust upon us in 1941, the thinking men and women of the country gave considerable thought to studying these economic factors that brought about the depression and unemployment. A great deal of time has been given by Congress. As your representative, I have appeared since 1941 some fifteen or sixteen times before committees of the Senate and the House on postwar problems. I appeared in my individual capacity at least nine additional times, since I was not sure that I was reflecting the viewpoint of this Conference.

As I say, there were hearings after hearings. In all, I have appeared some twenty-five or twenty-six times. Others have, too. . . .

There is one matter before all others, with which we are concerned, and that is taxation. Some years ago—I think it was in 1941—I called a regional conference here, right in this hall, and I suggested then that we should make a thorough study of the whole tax structure of the country because the cities fit right into the complete tax structure.

We cannot possibly finance the cost of city government unless we get some order in our chaotic tax situation in this country. . . .

We must impress upon Congress and the Congress upon the states that we must have uniformity of taxation throughout the country and a separation of the fields of revenue in order to put an end to the overlapping of taxes, the multitudinous tax collection agencies, the inequalities that exist, and the confusion that prevails.

I talked to the President of the United States about this. He has had experience in local taxation, for he, too, was a local official at one time. He sees the necessity of it. I have not had an opportunity to talk with the present Secretary of the Treasury, with whom I served in Congress many years, Mr. Fred Vinson; but I have had several discussions with Mr. Morgenthau. Everyone slightly familiar with the problem of taxation recognizes the necessity of a complete reformation. . . .

Among the very many subjects on which I have appeared in your behalf before the committees of the Senate and the House is that of the postwar public works program. There are two distinct schools of thought on that. I think most of us follow the thought that it is necessary, particularly in the reconversion period, to keep our heavy industries going—our mines, transportation, our steel mills, our forests, our lumber mills, hardware, brickyards.

Unless we have a tremendous and a gigantic public works program, it will be difficult to create the impact that is so necessary to absorb the hundreds of thousands of these displaced workers in plants and yards and factories previously employed on war production.

The committees seem to be sympathetic, but somehow or other we have not proceeded very far. Through the efforts of your Conference, many of the mayors have appeared before the committees—Mayor Kelly, Mayor Chandler, and others. Congress did appropriate funds to be advanced to municipalities for the preparation of plans. They at least recognized the need.

It is true under the present law the bill provides that the advance must be repaid if the work is constructed without any Federal grant. That is purely academic inasmuch as very little of these works will be constructed unless there is a Federal grant. There is no loss, and if there is a Federal grant, it all comes out in the wash.

Every municipality is in need of Federal grants from the public works program. Billions of dollars of necessary, needed public works in the cities have been filed in Washington. Some cities have proceeded to prepare their own plans. My city has spent in the neighborhood of 30 million dollars for plans. We are ready to go. We have the land, we have the plans, we have the money. Nothing is started yet.

We advertised for bids on the first housing unit some three weeks ago. I received no bids. We advertised again and received bids that were 68 per cent over the estimated costs based on 1940 prices. We cannot build that way.

I wish you had time to see the new airport at Idlewild. It is a 200 million dollar project. You will find the first three runways completed. You will find the temporary administration building 90 per cent completed. You will find the approach road completed. We have spent some 30 or 40 million dollars there already. Yet we cannot operate. The plumbers and the diggers are having a quarrel.

I have appealed to the union here and they agreed and it was adjusted, but nobody went to work. I went to Washington to the Building Trades Department of the American Federation of Labor, and we settled it there within an hour. Instructions came to New York. Nobody has gone to work.

There it is. We are ready to go, 99 per cent. We have no telephones. We cannot get telephones. The electrical union demands the right to pull the wires through the conduit. The Telephone Company Union says, "No, that is our job." I said, "All right, we will do it." The Telephone Company said, "We won't sell you the cable." If we let the telephone company union do it, all of the trades will walk out. If we let the trades do it, the telephone company won't give us the service.

Gentlemen, we cannot reconvert that way. That is not going back to work. Suppose those squabbles and quarrels had existed in our armed forces. What would we have done?

We had other difficulties. We wanted to build a post office at LaGuardia Airport. That is part of the contract with the Government; we must provide all the services. The first advertising—no bids. Naturally during the plastering we have to provide heat. That is a very simple matter. We just connected with our heating plant. We have to provide $66 a day to pay men on three shifts that would have been employed if we did not have our own heating.

That is not creating wealth. That is not producing. All these matters must be ironed out. As you gentlemen know, I have given my life to labor. I have burned all my bridges ahead of me for labor. I have a right to talk. I am going to continue to talk. I am going to protect legitimate labor. We must have an opportunity to work, to earn good wages, and to live properly. When they are wrong, some of them haven't the guts to say that they are wrong.

We had a great deal of amusement, let us say, in appearing before the departments of the Government and the Congress on the disposition of surplus supplies. We have appeared repeatedly, many of the Mayors.

Everything is simply fine and grand. The law is all right. The Administration agrees with us in the interpretation of the law. They are all in favor of giving the municipalities priorities as intended and provided in the law. Everything is fine, except we do not get anything.

I shall not bore you with many of the incidents and the method employed to advise the municipalities of available supplies and by the time we are ready, the supplies are not there, or how they help us by offering us tires in 70-ton lots, regardless of size. You have to buy what is in the 70 tons, regardless of size and quality. Imagine the Mayor or the purchasing agent of a city buying that way. That is a typical instance.

I really believe that the Surplus Property Administrator wants to be helpful, but he is just a policy-making agency and the decision of declaring supplies surplus rests with the various departments, such as Army, Navy, Treasury, Shipping Board, and so on. It is moving a little better but not quite unsatisfactorily.

The other day a circular came to my office advertising for sale a complete building, machine shops, and land located on our airport. It belongs to us. That is a hot one, isn't it?

I wish they would give us some hospital supplies and some of the things that we need, but I want you to know your Conference is right on it, and we keep on it and shall keep on it until it will be possible to get some system whereby we may have the advantage of getting the priority intended in the law. . . .

There is one of the President's policies that is very attractive to all who have made a study and which concerns the cities a great deal. That is the President's health insurance plan. I know some people are shocked when they hear about that, but I remember back—I think it was our first Regional Conference in San Francisco; if not, the one in 1934 in Chicago—when we first talked housing. Many of our colleagues were quite shocked then and they said, "Well, if you have a resolution, be sure to put into that resolution that only those who want it are interested."

I do not know a Mayor in this country who is not interested in housing. In fact, on the floor of the House, it was designated as socialistic. The word communistic had not become so popular at the time, so they called it socialistic.

So today a great many people who take a snap judgment on this great problem of health are rather shy on the President's national health insurance plan. I commend to you the study of the plan and a careful analysis of what it means to the people of the city and to the city government.

We recognize that the health of the people is a concern of the government and that health is a function of government. Great strides and great work have been accomplished by the United States Public Health Service. Cities vie with each other in providing health service, in preventive medicine, in keeping people healthy.

What we do today would be considered as fantastic twenty-five years ago or thirty years ago. We start with prenatal care of the young mother and provide proper maternity care, also baby health stations for the baby and guidance to the mother. All through the period of the rearing of the child, there is ample provision for his protection in health, if the parents cannot otherwise afford to obtain it.

We do the same in contagious and infectious disease, and nobody objects to that. The great work that is going on in tuberculosis is going to wipe out the dreaded disease within a generation. We were interrupted because of the war and we were prevented from carrying on and were pushed back somewhat, but that work is being picked up now, by the United States Government, the state, the municipality. I am quite certain that tuberculosis will be wiped out within the next generation.

We are all concerned with the study of cancer, and science is working at it. We have two or three large institutions in this city. New York City has provided a cancer research institute and a cancer hospital attached to that institute. The foundations are completed. We were interrupted because of the war. We are going to resume.

The research will be carried on at Presbyterian Hospital, which is a branch of the Medical School at Columbia University. There is another cancer institute at Memorial Hospital, and there the city is constructing a 300-bed custodial hospital for cases that seem hopeless, where they may get relief, and at the same time afford opportunity for scientific study on such cases.

We are doing the same on tropical disease and middle-age diseases. What we are doing is being done in other cities throughout the country, and you know if we could apply all of the progress of medicine and surgery as well as preventive medicine, with the knowledge that we have, it is going to be a disgrace to be sick. . . .

I really ask an impartial approach and a careful study of the national health insurance plan. It does not provide a subsidy. It provides the service which is so needed, not only care in your home but the proper care of the sick in the hospitals where they belong. It also provides the clinics for checkups, to keep one healthy and prevent him from becoming sick. . . .

Of course, the problem that we all want to meet is that of the returning veteran. . . . We must provide in our community the proper setup to give him the services that he requires.

We have done that in New York City, and if you have time, I should like to have you visit 500 Park Avenue. It is devoted entirely to service. We have the cooperation of the United States Government. We have the Veterans Bureau there, the Compensation Bureau. We will have the United States Employment Service there. We have the United States Civil Service there, the city Civil Service, the city Public Health Department, a panel of employees, consultants on the educational privileges of the G.I. Bill.

In this way, the veteran can get the information and the service then and there. The thing the veteran hates is to get the run-around, to be sent from one referral to another. We try to avoid that.

32. Renewal: Battleground against Slums

FROM 'Framework for an Urban Society' by Catherine Bauer Wurster, in President's Commission on National Goals, *Goals for Americans,* New York 1960, p. 229.[1]

In any list of goals, renewal of our older cities must be near the top. There is a great deal of seriously substandard housing in American communities, and spreading "gray areas" in various stages of actual or potential decay, plus commercial and industrial blight. It is quite evident that economic progress alone does not cure these evils, and that local governments cannot do the necessary job alone. Congress has therefore enacted successive measures granting substantial aid; for low-rent public housing since 1937; for broader slum clearance and private redevelopment programs since 1949; and for comprehensive renewal efforts, including rehabilitation and conservation of marginal poverty, since 1954. A social goal was clearly established more than a decade ago in the preamble to the 1949 Act," "A decent home in a suitable living environment for every American family." The economic goal is to revitalize the old centers, strengthening property values, and the tax base. To achieve the latter ends, cities hope

[1] Reproduced with the permission of Columbia University Press.

to gain more middle- and upper-income residents than they have at present, and they also seek new business and industry.

33. 'The Shame of the States'

FROM 'Time for an Urban Magna Carta' by Senator John F. Kennedy, City Problems of 1958, pp. 33–37.

Since your very able Executive Director, Harry Betters, had that article (prepared from the speech I was unable to deliver last year) reprinted and circulated among your membership, I will not repeat the details of it here. Its main thesis as you will recall, was to describe the gross discrimination against our cities which results from the unjust apportionment of legislative seats in the House of Representatives and particularly in our state legislatures. This continued discrimination may have resulted in part from that period of a half century ago when Lincoln Steffens and his fellow muckrakers described municipal corruption and graft as "the shame of the cities." But to continue that discrimination and denial of fair representation, I maintain, ought to be called "the shame of the states. . . ."

This is a matter about which I feel very strongly—not only as a former Congressman from an urban district, or as a Senator from a largely urbanized state—but also as a proud citizen of a proud city. I think it is high time that this nation eliminated the written and unwritten restrictions on the influence of urban politicans in our public life which have resulted largely from ancient prejudices and unwarranted suspicions. I think it is high time that the overwhelming majority of Americans who live in our cities—and their needs, their problems, and their spokesmen—were accorded the consideration they deserve in our legislative bodies—instead of being regarded as second-class citizens who must come to those legislative bodies to beg with hat in hand for the fair treatment they deserve to help solve their own problems. . . .

But on top of these difficult problems, the progress of our cities is further handicapped by the discriminatory attitude—reflecting discriminatory representation—of our state and Federal legislative bodies.

Consider, for example, the single issue of housing—where this organization has played such an important and constructive role. Few other problems are of such concern to our nation's cities. The latest national housing inventory conducted last year by the Bureau of Census showed that nearly five million urban homes were in such poor condition as to need replacement today. Yet urban redevelopment projects initiated as far back as 1950 are still incomplete. The entire urban-renewal and slum-clearance program is bogging down from a lack of funds, a lack of authority and a lack of effective re-location programs for families displaced by these projects.

The 85th Congress gave its attention to this program of such importance to more than 125 cities with redevelopment programs—and the Senate passed a bill which would have added $400 million for this program, established a more effective approach to relocation, and in other ways attacked the blight which has plagued our cities. Unfortunately, this bill was killed in the House of Representatives—and the hard facts of the matter are that it was killed by the disproportionate voting strength of Congressmen from non-urban areas.

These are not the only bills of interest to urban areas which met defeat in the House of Representatives this year. A measure to assist municipal government in the financing and construction of community facilities was also cut down in the House. A labor reform measure, sponsored by Senator Ives and myself to end the labor rackets that are of primary concern in our cities, met with a similar fate. In these and other cases, members of both parties from urban areas—members familiar with urban problems and urban needs—supported these bills. But their support was not enough.

The Congress votes this way because the Congress is constituted this way—because our urban citizens are grossly shortchanged in their representation in the House of Representatives. Supposedly, the Connecticut Compromise in the Constitution gave small and rural states a disproportionate influence in the Senate, in the electoral college and in the amending process—so that less than 3 per cent of our population now has 16 Senators, just as 50 per cent of our population has only 16 Senators—but the House of Representatives was supposed to be the other end of the compromise.

Yet in one state, a city of over 800,000 people has only one spokesman in Congress, though it is nearly 4 times as large as a rural district in the same state—which also has one Congressman. In another state, the Congressional districts within the large metropolitan area contain on the average 404,000 people—but outside the city, the average Congressional district contains only 322,000 people. In at least seven states, a Congressman from a sparsely settled area represents less than half as many people as his colleague from the state's major urban area. In at least 18 states, the city dweller's vote is in effect worth less than his rural neighbor's. . . .

I suggest, therefore, that it is time for an urban Magna Carta—a statement of our principles in this battle for equality—a statement of our goals and ideals, not to be implemented instantly, not perhaps to be agreed upon unanimously, but to restate in positive terms the rights which were demanded of King John so many centuries ago.

34. *Metropolitan Areas: Central Cities versus Suburbs*

FROM David McEntire, *Residence and Race,* Berkeley 1960, pp. 17–19, 165, 169–170.[1]

Negro migration since 1940 has been directed overwhelmingly toward the central cities of metropolitan areas, whereas the white population has been shifting outward from the cities into surrounding suburban territory. The result is a steadily increasing prominence of Negro and other minorities in the population of the larger cities.

In the 1940–1950 decade, the 168 standard metropolitan areas (SMA's) as defined by the Census,[2] accounted for three-fourths of the national increase in white population but 110 per cent of the total non-white increase, reflecting a net decline of nonwhite population in non-metropolitan territory. The fourteen SMA's with populations of more than a million received 32 per cent of the total white increase, but nearly 75 per cent of the national increase in nonwhite population. Within the metropolitan areas, more than two-thirds of the added white population but less than one-fifth of the nonwhite increase found residence outside the central cities, but in the fourteen largest areas this disparity was even more pronounced.

In the years since 1950 the movements of population to metropolitan areas and from central cities to suburbs have been running even more strongly than during the 1940s. Of the increase in the civilian population of the United States between 1950 and 1956, an estimated 85 percent was accounted for by the growth of population in standard metropolitan areas, and more than 80 percent of this growth occurred outside the central cities. In many cities the white population is stationary or declining while the number of nonwhites continued to mount. In New York City, for example, the nonwhite gain of 206,000 persons in the period 1950–1957 was overbalanced by a decline of 302,000 in the white population, leaving the city with a net loss in excess of 96,000 persons. Since the Puerto Rican group, mostly white, increased by nearly a half million in the same period, the loss of white population other than Puerto Rican must have been in the magnitude of three-quarters of a million or more.

Studies in Chicago, Philadelphia, Cleveland, Atlanta, and other large cities show similar disparate trends in population growth. In Los Angeles, with much more space for growth than most large cities, the

[1] Reproduced with the permission of the University of California Press.

[2] The Census defines a standard metropolital area as a country or a group of contiguous countries socially and economically integrated with a central city of at least 50,000 inhabitants.

rate of white population increase accelerated after 1950 in the metropolitan area but slowed down in the city. Almost two in every five
persons added to the Los Angeles population during 1950–1956 were
nonwhite, as compared with one in four during 1940–1950.

To see these population changes in proper perspective, it must be
noted that growing metropolitan populations, of necessity, have been
housed largely outside the central cities because these cities, especially
the older ones, are filled up. Short of extensive rebuilding for higher
densities in the central cities, there has been no alternative to building up the outlying areas.

The shift of population to the suburbs, moreover, is essentially a
continuation of historic trends. American cities have always grown outward from their centers. As the metropolitan population has spread
over a wide area, the political boundaries of the city have been left
far behind. But, if the automobile and the superhighway have permitted enlargement of the metropolitan area, they have also served to
tie the parts of the area more closely together. The functioning city
of the present day is the metropolitan area and not just the territory
within certain political boundaries. Hence the outward movement of
population within the metropolitan area and the expansion of the
metropolitan area itself are to be seen realistically as city growth in
the traditional pattern, modern phase.

Movement of minority groups into the central parts of metropolitan
areas is equally an historic process. In an earlier time, immigrant
groups thronging into American cities found living space in the older
areas abandoned by others moving outward to newer districts. As the
immigrants and their children became assimilated and improved their
economic position, they in turn moved away from the areas of their
first settlement in search of better living elsewhere. The in-migrant
Negroes and Puerto Ricans have been housed in much the same
manner as the immigrant predecessors. Given time and opportunity,
these latest newcomers to the city will undoubtedly also move to more
desirable residence areas. Indeed, there is evidence that this process
is already underway.

Housing Demand in Racially Mixed Areas
A racial transition zone is commonly pictured as one where whites
are leaving and nonwhites coming in. The Philadelphia study found
the process to be considerably more complex. Among some two thous-
and home buyers, 443 or more than one-fifth were whites. Although
outnumbered more than three to one by Negroes, the presence of
white buyers in substantial numbers is, nevertheless, a significant fact
from several points of view. It refutes the notion that whites will not
buy in an area once entered by Negroes, and calls for inquiry into the

conditions under which whites will continue to buy in such areas. As discussed previously, whether any area can maintain a racially mixed composition depends, of course, on its ability to attract new white residents.

Investigation of the trend of house prices in one area (good housing, rapid transition) revealed a substantial price advance from 1948 through 1955, of approximately the same magnitude as occurred in the city as a whole. The rise appeared most pronounced in the sections of heavy Negro entry and rapid departure of whites. This is further evidence that racial change is not necessarily associated with depressed prices.

Mortgage lenders often take a dubious view of racially mixed areas, but this was not true in Philadelphia. Financing was liberal and played a key role in sustaining demand and price. Ninety percent of the white buyers and practically all the Negroes depended on mortgage financing to acquire their homes. The loans came almost entirely from established institutional sources. . . .

During the time period covered by the present studies, surging Negro demand, supported by growing availability of mortgage credit and concentrated at certain points, was sufficient to maintain and to strengthen house prices in many areas of racial transition. Market stability was helped by the apparently changing attitudes of white property owners which led them generally to refrain from flooding the market with houses on the appearance of Negroes. To an appreciable extent, whites continued to buy into some racially mixed areas, and this too, helped to keep prices up. . . .

The increasing market freedom which minorities are gaining, together with the growing social differentiation of the groups, means undoubtedly that their housing demand will be more dispersed and more varied in the future than in the past. Nonwhites are apt to enter more areas than the nonwhite population can fill, and for some areas complete racial transition will be impossible. As noted, this is already true in some higher-priced neighborhoods. Hence there is likely to be an increasing number of neighborhoods where the maintenance of a sufficient market for houses will require white as well as nonwhite buyers in adequate numbers.

J. The Metropolis and the Federal Government

As the problems of its cities became the primary concern of the nation, the relationships between the mushrooming metropolises and the state and federal governments emerged as the basic urban problem. The several unsuccessful attempts by the Eisenhower administration to check the growth of federal power are reviewed by Morton Grodzins in an article on 'Attempts to Unwind the Federal System' published by the President's Commission on National Goals (Doc. 35). One enduring contribution of the Eisenhower years was the creation of the Advisory Commission on Intergovernmental Relations and among its numerous studies is one on *Metropolitan America: Challenge to Federalism* in which it describes with great clarity the current development of metropolitan interdependence and its implications for the federal system (Doc. 36). But it was the convergence of still another historic movement—the migration of Negroes to the cities and their mounting demands for civil rights and economic equality—that aggravated the metropolitan crisis and pushed these problems into the mainstream of American life as the report of the Advisory Commission of Civil Disorders clearly demonstrates (Doc. 37).

35. *Attempts to Unwind the Federal System*

FROM Morton Grodzins, "The Federal System,' in The Report of the President's Commission on National Goals, *Goals for Americans,* New York 1960, pp. 267–268. Published by The American Assembly, Columbia University, New York. Reprinted by permission of Prentice-Hall, Inc., Englewood Cliffs, N.J.

Within the past dozen years there have been four major attempts to reform or reorganize the federal system: the first (1947–49) and second (1953–55) Hoover Commissions on Executive Organization; the Kestnbaum Commission on Intergovernmental Relations (1953–55); and the Joint Federal-State Action Committee (1957–59). All four of these groups have aimed to minimize federal activities. None of them has recognized the sharing of functions as the characteristic way

American governments do things. Even when making recommendations for joint action, these official commissions take the view (as expressed in the Kestnbaum report) that "the main tradition of American federalism [is] the tradition of separateness." All four have, in varying degrees, worked to separate functions and tax sources.

The history of the Joint Federal-State Action Committee is especially instructive. The committee was established at the suggestion of President Eisenhower, who charged it, first of all, "to designate functions which the States are ready and willing to assume and finance that are now performed or financed wholly or in part by the Federal Government." He also gave the committee the task of recommending "Federal and State revenue adjustments required to enable the States to assume such functions."[1]

The committee subsequently established seemed most favorably situated to accomplish the task of functional separation. It was composed of distinguished and able men, including among its personnel three leading members of the President's cabinet, the director of the Bureau of the Budget, and ten state governors. It had the full support of the President at every point, and it worked hard and conscientiously. Excellent staff studies were supplied by the Bureau of the Budget, the White House, the Treasury Department, and, from the state side, the Council of State Governments. It had available to it a large mass of research data, including the sixteen recently completed volumes of the Kestnbaum Commission. There existed no disagreement on party lines within the committee and, of course, no constitutional impediments to its mission. The President, his cabinet members, and all the governors (with one possible exception) on the committee completely agreed on the desirability of decentralization-via-separation-of-functions-and-taxes. They were unanimous in wanting to justify the committee's name and to produce action, not just another report.

The committee worked for more than two years. It found exactly two programs to recommend for transfer from federal to state hands. One was the federal grant program for vocational education (including practical-nurse training and aid to fishery trades); the other was federal grants for municipal waste treatment plants. The programs to-

---

[1] The President's third suggestion was that the committee 'identify functions and responsibilities likely to require state or federal attention in the future and . . . recommend the level of state effort, or federal effort, or both, that will be needed to assure effective action.' The committee initially devoted little attention to this problem. Upon discovering the difficulty of making separatist recommendations, i.e., for turning over federal functions and taxes to the states, it developed a series of proposals looking to greater effectiveness in intergovernmental collaboration. The committee was succeeded by a legislatively-based, 26-member Advisory Commission on Intergovernmental Relations, established September 29, 1959.

gether cost the federal government less than $80 million in 1957, slightly more than two per cent of the total federal grants for that year. To allow the states to pay for these programs, the committee recommended that they may be allowed a credit against the federal tax on local telephone calls. Calculations showed that this offset device, plus an equalizing factor, would give every state at least 40 per cent more from the tax than it received from the federal government in vocational education and sewage disposal grants. Some states were "equalized" to receive twice as much.

The recommendations were modest enough, and the generous financing feature seemed calculated to gain state support. The President recommended to Congress that all points of the program be legislated. None of them was, none of them has been since, and none is likely to be.

The American federal system has never been a system of separated governmental activities. There has never been a time when it was possible to put neat labels on discrete "federal," "state," and "local" functions. Even before the Constitution, a statute in 1785, reinforced by the Northwest Ordinance of 1787, gave grants-in-land to the states for public schools. Thus the national government was a prime force in making possible what is now taken to be the most local function of all, primary and secondary education. More important, the nation, before it was fully organized, established by this action a first principle of American federalism: the national government would use its superior resources to initiate and support national programs, principally administered by the states and localities.

36. Metropolitan Interdependence and the Federal System

FROM Advisory Commission on Intergovernmental Relations, *Metropolitan America: Challenge to Federalism*, Washington 1966, pp. 5–9.

Underlying many metropolitan problems is the failure of governmental institutions to come to grips with the growing interdependence of people and communities within metropolitan areas. As urban settlements spread across lines of local jurisdiction, the cities and suburbs together came to comprise a single integrated area for living and working. People look for housing and employment within a broad region circumscribed more by the convenience of commuting and by personal preference than by local government boundaries. The existence of a metropolitanwide housing and job market is, in fact, the basis for defining metropolitan areas. In the definition of the U.S. Bureau of the Budget and the Bureau of the Census, "the general concept of a metropolitan area is one of an integrated economic and social unit with a recognized large population nucleus."

The detailed criteria used in defining "standard metropolitan statistical areas" (SMSA's) provide further insight into the integrated character of these areas. Each area must contain at least one city of 50,000 inhabitants or more, or "twin cities" with a combined population of at least 50,000. The metropolitan character of the county containing the central city or cities is established by determining that the county is a place of work or residence for a concentration of non-agricultural workers. The specific conditions that must be met include a requirement that at least 75 percent of the labor force must have nonagricultural occupations, and other tests concerning population density and job concentrations. In New England, the componets of metropolitan areas are cities and towns rather than counties. Outlying counties (cities and towns in New England) are considered part of the metropolitan area if they meet either of the following tests:

(1) If 15 percent of the workers living in the county work in the county where the central city is located, or

(2) If 25 percent of those working in the outlying county live in the county where the central city is located.

If the information concerning these two requirements is not conclusive, other kinds of information are considered: reports of newspaper circulation, the extent to which residents of outlying areas maintain charge accounts in central city retail stores, official traffic counts, and other indicators of central city-suburban interaction.

Metropolitan areas are integrated in other ways, as well. Local communities share many kinds of natural resources used for urban living: water supplies, drainage basins, recreation areas. They also share many man-made facilities that cut across local boundaries, such as highway and utility systems, and many other facilities that serve large segments of the metropolitan population, such as airports and commercial centers. These forms of interaction, together with the metropolitan character of housing and employment markets, create a broad area of common interest. The otimum use of shared facilities and resources calls for a high level of cooperation and for coordinated action by interdependent communities.

The policies of any one community typically have considerable impact in the other parts of the metropolitan area. If one locality fails to control air or water pollution, its neighbors suffer. This principle was illustrated recently when Nassau County, which borders New York City, demanded that New York put its mosquitoes under surveillance. The public works commissioner of Nassau County charged that swarms of mosquitoes from the city had been invading Nassau territory: "Mosquitoes have no respect for boundary lines or home rule," he complained.

The effects of local action (or inaction) that spread into other communities have come to be known as "spillovers." They are very common in metropolitan affairs and often consist of indirect effects. Thus, suburban communities that succeed in excluding the poor impose considerable burdens on other communities where the poor are concentrated. Spillovers can also be beneficial to neighboring localities. Effective traffic control or public health measures benefit people outside a city or town as well as local residents. Spillovers usually imply disparities between tax and service boundaries. Thus the residents of central cities may be taxed to provide services that are important to the suburbs as well as to themselves. Or suburbanites may be taxed to clean up polluted streams that flow into neighboring territory. In all these cases, people who do not live in a particular jurisdiction nevertheless have a strong interest in its performance of government functions.

The prevalence of spillovers constitutes a strong case for cooperation in metropolitan areas. Metropolitan service needs also provide compelling arguments for joint action. In such fields as water supply and sewage disposal, the cost of service per household can be reduced dramatically in large-scale operations by joint agreement of local governments. Similarly transportation systems—highways, public transit—require joint planning if they are to provide needed service at reasonable cost.

Despite the evident and important benefits of cooperative action in metropolitan areas, many local governments continue to go it alone. The realities of functional interdependence in metropolitan areas are in conflict with concepts of home rule that predate the age of metropolitan growth. Home rule in the contemporary metropolitan setting has often led to local isolation and conflict, to the detriment of the metropolitan population at large. Each community, in pursuing its own interests, may have an adverse effect on the interests of its neighbors. A major task for government in metropolitan areas is to develop policies consistent with the integrated character of the modern metropolitan community. Federal policies are guided increasingly by an awareness of this need, as President Johnson emphasized in his message on the cities:

> The interests and needs of many of the communities which make up the modern city often seem to be in conflict. But they all have an overriding interest in improving the quality of the life of their

people. And they have an overriding interest in enriching the quality of American civilization. These interests will only be served by looking at the metropolitan area as a whole, and planning and working for its development.

The fundamental metropolitan problem is not that there are difficulties in supplying public services or ameliorating social and economic disparities. It is that governments in metropolitan areas are often unable to cope with these issues. The system of local government in the United States has many achievements to its credit, but, like any social system, it also has its disadvantages. Within metropolitan areas, many important issues of public policy can no longer be handled by local communities acting alone; their small areas of jurisdiction are inadequate for either administering areawide services or resolving areawide problems.

The close ties of people and businesses to one another in metropolitan areas have no parallel in government. While social and economic relationships have shifted to an enlarged metropolitan scale, governments and the loyalties they inspire have remained local. As Roscoe Martin has put it:

> The metropolitan area has no capital, courthouse, or city hall, no corporate existence, no body, no soul, no sense of being, indeed no being in any concrete meaning of the term. Al Smith was from the sidewalks of New York, not from the sidewalks of the New York-Northeastern New Jersey standard consolidated area.

Metropolitan areas are governed not only by traditional cities, towns, and counties, but also by a wide variety of special districts that overlap other boundaries. The complexity of local government can be illustrated by listing the array of local jurisdictions responsible for Park Forest, a suburb of Chicago, as of 1956: Cook County, Will County, Cook County Forest Preserve District, village of Park Forest, Rich Township, Bloom Township, Monee Township, Suburban Tuberculosis Sanitarium District, Bloom Township Sanitary District, Non-High School District 216, Non-High School District 213, Rich Township High School District 227, Elementary School District 163, South Cook County Mosquito Abatement District.

Fragmentation of this kind may appear to bring government "closer to the people," but it compounds the difficulties of achieving coordination within metropolitan areas. Political responsibility for government performance is divided to the point of obscurity. Public control of government policies tends to break down when citizens have to deal with a network of independent governments, each responsible for highly standardized activities. Even where good channels are developed for registering public concern, each government is so circumscribed in its powers and in the area of its jurisdiction that important metropolitan action is virtually impossible for local governments to undertake. If a few governments are prepared to agree on joint measures or coordinated programs, their efforts can be blocked by others that are unwilling to cooperate.

Local governments, fragmented as they are, nevertheless keep the metropolis running. They operate the schools, maintain the streets, take care of police and fire protection. But when issues of metropolitan-wide importance arise—such as commuter transportation, water supply, or racial and economic segregation—people must turn to other channels for action. As Robert Wood has pointed out, an "embryonic coalition" of metropolitan leaders tends to emerge to tackle areawide problems. These leaders—politicians, editors, businessmen, labor leaders—operate informally and outside the regular structure of government, as they attempt to prod government into action. They lack the requirements for effective policymaking: an adequate institutional base, legal authority, direct relationships with the metropolitan constituency, and established processes for considering and resolving issues as they emerge.

When important public issues can only be handled informally and outside government channels, it is time to review the system of government in metropolitan areas and to regard the shortcomings of this system as major problems in themselves. Norton Long has set the problem of metropolitan areas in this political context:

> The problems of the metropolis are important, but not because of flooded cellars or frustrated motorists, nor because they seriously threaten the viability of the metropolitan economy. They are important because they are symptomatic of the erosion of the competence of local government. The threat of the eroded central city and the crazy-quilt triviality of suburbia is the threat to destroy the potential of our maintaining and reconstructing meaningful political communities at the local level. What has been treated as a threat to our physical well-being is in reality a threat to our capacity to sustain an active local civic life.

With local governments often unwilling or unable to meet metropolitan needs, the Federal and State Governments have taken on increasing responsibilities for metropolitan welfare. The State role ranges from financial aid to direct State operations in metropolitan areas, such as highway building, and State establishment of special metropolitan authorities responsible for such functions as water supply and port development. The Federal role consists mainly of financial assistance for programs administered by State or local government. The number and size of Federal-aid programs have been growing at a striking rate: there are now more than 70 Federal-aid programs that directly support urban development, as well as a number of other kinds of Federal aid available to local governments in metropolitan areas.

State and Federal programs are helping to cope with many metropolitan needs, but they also raise troublesome political and governmental issues. Federal and State participation in metropolitan affairs greatly complicates the already fragmented governmental scene. Activities of all three levels of government now function in close juxtaposition, subject to an extremely complicated web of Federal, State, and local laws and administrative regulations. In the course of supplying needed help, Federal and State programs threaten to push the confused governmental situation closer to a state of chaos. Coordination of efforts is a prime requirement for effective government action in metropolitan areas; yet the problems of coordination are compounded by the addition of higher levels of government to the fragmented local scene.

There is an implicit danger that greater reliance on Federal and State action in metropolitan areas may be a form of political abdication in which local governments wash their hands of difficult responsibilities and pass the buck to higher levels. This approach would lead waning local influence over policies and programs that have significant local impact. Thus it is important to find ways of administering State and Federal programs within a system of democratic control in which metropolitan citizens can shape the programs that operate in their own areas.

Local communities in search of financial aid have turned mainly to the Federal Government rather than the States. The rural orientation of State legislatures has been well documented, and is only now changing to reflect recent reapportionments. For a number of reasons, the cities have found a more sympathetic hearing in Washington than in the State capital. In seeking Federal aid for urban problems, cities have tended to bypass the State and deal directly with Washington. A pattern of intergovernmental relations has developed in which cities and towns in metropolitan areas pursue largely independent policies, with a minimum of interlocal cooperation, but many engage in numerous direct dealings with the Federal Government. The State role has been lagging far behind both local and Federal activity. Yet the States occupy critical positions within the America federal system, and possess the power and resources to strengthen local capacities and stimulate greater cooperation within metropolitan areas.

The new intergovernmental relationships also pose more fundamental issues for the future of the American federal system. Minimizing State participation in urban affairs is tantamount to removing State influence from a critical range of domestic issues. The federal system of the United States involves a division of powers between the States and the Federal Government. The States have created a further division by delegating powers to the local governments they have established. If the State role in this partnership is weakened, the ramifications may be far reaching. Without active State participation, it is doubtful whether local government can be reorganized to perform more effectively in metropolitan areas; the localities derive their powers from the State and need State authorization for structural reforms. More broadly, the State role in metropolitan affairs must be considered in terms of the philosophy of the federal system. The division of authority between the States and the Federal Government has served the county well in the past and has helped to safeguard the values of representative and responsible government. Basic changes in the system of intergovernmental relations should not be undertaken lightly or permitted to occur by default.

37. Race Riots and their Causes

FROM The Report of the National Advisory Commission of Civil Disorders, Washington 1968, pp. 147–149, 229–230.

The racial disorders of last summer in part reflect the failure of all levels of government—Federal and state as well as local—to come to grips with the problems of our cities. The ghetto symbolizes the dilemma: a widening gap between human needs and public resources and a growing cynicism regarding the commitment of community institutions and leadership to meet these needs.

The problem has many dimensions—financial, political and institutional. Almost all cities—and particularly the central cities of the largest metropolitan regions—are simply unable to meet the growing need for public services and facilities with traditional sources of municipal revenue. Many cities are structured politically so that the great numbers of citizens—particularly minority groups—have little or no representation in the processes of government. Finally, some cities lack either the will or the capacity to use effectively the resources that are available to them.

Instrumentalities of Federal and state Government often compound the problems. National policy expressed through a very large number of grant programs and institutions rarely exhibits a coherent and consistent perspective when viewed at the local level. State efforts, traditionally focused on rural areas, often fail to tie in effectively with either local or Federal programs in urban areas.

Meanwhile, the decay of the central city continues—its revenue base eroded by the retreat of industry and white middle-class families to the suburbs, its budget and tax rate inflated by rising costs and increasing numbers of dependent citizens and its public plant—schools, hospitals, and correctional institutions deteriorated by age and long-deferred maintenance.

Yet to most citizens, the decay remains largely invisible. Only their tax bills and the headlines about crime or "riots" suggest that something may be seriously wrong in the city.

There are, however, two groups of people that live constantly with the problem of the city: the public officials and the poor, particularly the residents of the racial ghetto. Their relationship is a key factor in the development of conditions underlying civil disorders.

Our investigations of the 1967 riot cities establish that:

> Virtually every major episode of urban violence in the summer of 1967 was foreshadowed by an accumulation of unresolved grievances by ghetto residents against local authorities (often, but not always, the police). So high was the resulting underlying tension that routine and random events, tolerated or ignored under most circumstances (such as the raid on the "blind pig" in Detroit and the arrest of the cab driver in Newark), became the triggers of sudden violence.
>
> Coinciding with this high level of dissatisfaction, confidence in the willingness and ability of local government to respond to Negro grievances was low. Evidence presented to this Commission in hearings, field reports and research analyses of the 1967 riot cities establishes that a substantial number of Negroes were disturbed and angry about local governments' failures to solve their problems.

Several developments have converged to produce this volatile situation.

First, there is a widening gulf in communications between local government and the residents of the erupting ghettos in the city. As a result, many Negro citizens develop a profound sense of isolation and alienation from the processes and programs of government. This lack of communication exists for all residents in our larger cities; it is, however, far more difficult to overcome for low-income, less educated citizens who are disproportionately supported by and dependent upon programs administered by agencies of local government.

Consequently, they are more often subject to real or imagined official misconduct ranging from abrasive contacts with public officials to arbitrary administrative actions. . . .

Second, many city governments are poorly organized to respond effectively to the needs of ghetto residents, even when those needs are made known to appropriate public officials. Most middle-class city dwellers have limited contacts with local government. When contacts do occur, they tend to concern relatively narrow and specific problems. Furthermore, middle-class citizens, although subject to many of the same frustrations and resentments as ghetto residents in dealing with the public bureaucracy, find it relatively easy to locate the appropriate agency for help and redress. If they fail to get satisfaction, they can call on a variety of remedies—assistance of elected representatives, friends in government, a lawyer. In short, the middle-class city dweller has relatively fewer needs for public services and is reasonably well positioned to move the system to his benefit.

On the other hand, the typical ghetto resident has interrelated social and economic problems which require the services of several government and private agencies. At the same time, he may be unable to identify his problems to fit the complicated structure of government. Moreover, he may be unaware of his rights and opportunities under public programs and unable to obtain the necessary guidance from either public or private sources. . . .

Third, ghetto residents increasingly believe that they are excluded from the decision-making processes which affects their lives and community. This feeling of exclusion, intensified by the bitter legacy of racial discrimination, has engendered a deep seated hostility toward the institutions of government. It has severely compromised the effectiveness of programs intended to provide improved services to ghetto residents. . . .

Finally, these developments have coincided with the demise of the historic urban political machines and the growth of the city manager concept of government. While this tendency has produced major benefits in terms of honest and efficient administration, it has eliminated an important political link between city government and low-income residents.

These conditions have produced a vast and threatening disparity in perceptions of the intensity and validity of Negro dissatisfaction. Viewed from the perspective of the ghetto resident, city government appears distant and unconcerned, the possibility of effective change remote. As a result, tension rises perceptibly; the explosion comes as the climax of a progression of tension-generating incidents. To the city administration, unaware of this growing tension or unable to respond effectively to it, the outbreak of disorder comes as a shock. . . .

The Commission has already addressed itself to the need for immediate action at the local level. Because the city is the focus of racial disorder, the immediate responsibility rests on community leaders and local institutions. Without responsive and representative local government, without effective processes of interracial communication within the city, and without alert, well-trained and adequately supported local police, national action—no matter how great its scale—cannot be expected to provide a solution.

Yet the disorders are not simply a problem of the racial ghetto or the city. As we have seen, they are symptoms of social ills that have become endemic in our society and now affect every American— black or white, businessman or factory worker, suburban commuter or slumdweller.

None of us can escape the consequences of the continuing economic and social decay of the central city and the closly related problem of rural poverty. The convergence of these conditions in the racial ghetto and the resulting discontent and disruption threaten democratic values fundamental to our progress as a free society.

The essential fact is that neither existing conditions nor the garrison state offers acceptable alternatives for the future of this country. Only a greatly enlarged commitment to national action—compassionate, massive and sustained, backed by the will and resources of the most powerful and the richest nation on this earth—can shape a future that is compatible with the historic ideals of American society.

It is this conviction that leads us, as a commission on civil disorders, to comment on the shape and dimension of the action that must be taken at the national level. . . .

The spectacle of Detroit and New Haven engulfed in civil turmoil despite a multitude of federally aided programs raised basic questions as to whether the existing "delivery system" is adequate to the bold new puposes of national policy. Many who voiced these concerns overlooked the disparity between the size of the problems at which the programs are aimed and the level of funding provided by the Federal Government.

Yet there is little doubt that the system through which Federal programs are translated into services to people is a major problem in itself. There are now over 400 grant programs operated by a broad range of Federal agencies and channeled through a much larger array of semiautonomous state and local government entities. . . .

In recent years serious efforts have been made to improve program coordination. During the 1961–1965 period, almost 20 Executive Orders were issued for the coordination of Federal programs involving intergovernmental administration. Some 2 dozen interagency committees have been established to coordinate two or more Federal aid programs. Departments have been given responsibility to lead others in areas within their particular competence—OEO, in the poverty field; HUD in Model Cities. Yet, despite these and other efforts, the Federal Government has not yet been able to join talent, funds, and programs for concentrated impact in the field. Few agencies are able to put together related programs to meet priority needs.

There is a clear and compelling requirement for better coordination of federally funded programs, particularly those designed to benefit the residents of the inner city. If essential programs are to be preserved and expanded, this need must be met. . . .

Just as Lincoln, a century ago, put preservation of the Union above all else, so should we put creation of a true union—a single society and a single American identity—as our major goal. Toward that goal, we propose the following objectives for national action:

Opening up all opportunites to those who are restricted by racial segregation and discrimination, and eliminating all barriers to their choice of jobs, education, and housing.

Removing the frustration of powerlessness among the disadvantaged by providing the means to deal with the problems that effect their own lives and by increasing the capacity of our public and private institutions to respond to these problems.

Increasing communication across racial lines to destroy stereotypes, halt polarization, end distrust and hostility and create common ground for efforts towards common goals of public order and social justice.

ACKNOWLEDGMENTS

Document 21, page 181, Reprinted by permission of the Macmillan Co., New York, N.Y.

Document 23, page 185, Reprinted by permission of Charles Scribner's Sons, New York, N.Y.

Document 27, page 195, Reprinted by permission of the New Republic Publishing Company, New York, N.Y.

Document 32, page 211, Published by the American Assembly, Columbia University, New York, N.Y. Reprinted by permission of Prentice-Hall, Inc., Englewood Cliffs, N.J.

Document 34, page 214, Reprinted by permission of the University of California Press, Berkeley, Calif.

GEORGE ALLEN & UNWIN LTD

Head Office
40 Museum Street, London W.C.1
Telephone: 01-405 8577

Sales, Distribution and Accounts Departments
Park Lane, Hemel Hempstead, Herts.
Telephone: 0442 3244

Athens: 34 Panepistimiou Street
Auckland: P.O. Box 36013, Northcote Central N.4
Barbados: P.O. Box 222, Bridgetown
Beirut: Deeb Building, Jeanne d'Arc Street
Bombay: 103/5 Fort Street, Bombay 1
Buenos Aires: Escritorio 454-459, Florida 165
Calcutta: 285J Bepin Behari Ganguli Street, Calcutta 12
Cape Town: 68 Shortmarket Street
Hong Kong: 105 Wing On Mansion, 26 Hancow Road, Kowloon
Ibadan: P.O. Box 62
Karachi: Karachi Chambers, McLeod Road
Madras: 2/18 Mount Road, Madras
Mexico: Villalongin 32, Mexico 5, D.F.
Nairobi: P.O. Box 30583
Philippines: P.O. Box 157, Quezon City D-502
Rio de Janeiro: Caixa Postal 2537-Zc-00
Singapore: 36c Prinsep Street, Singapore 7
Sydney N.S.W.: Bradbury House, 55 York Street
Tokyo: C.P.O. Box 1728, Tokyo 100-91
Toronto: 18 Curlew Drive, Don Mills

No. 1 Anti-Catholicism in Victorian England

E. R. NORMAN

Victorian 'No Popery' agitations were in fact almost the last expressions of a long English tradition of anti-Catholic intolerance. During the nineteenth century, the legal and social position of the Catholics was in reality greatly improved, and outbursts against them were inspired by a public opinion which clung to theories of the Constitution and to social habits which were changing faster than might otherwise have been supposed. On certain occasions, however, anti-Catholic agitations became one of the more important religious and political catalysts of the nineteenth century.

No. 2 Germany in the Age of Bismarck

W. M. SIMON

This is the first time that a comprehensive selection of documents on Germany in the Age of Bismarck has been made available to students and other readers in the English language. As the title indicates, the documents have been chosen to illuminate not only Bismarck's own personality and policies but also the nature of the problems he faced and the reactions of his contemporaries. The same is true of Professor Simon's Introduction: he has here taken the opportunity of writing a thorough and searching essay, whereas in his recent *Germany: a Brief History* space allowed only a much more compressed consideration of the period under discussion here.

No. 3 Problems of Empire: Britain and India 1757-1813

P. J. MARSHALL

This book is a study of the impact made on Britain by the conquest of large parts of India in the second half of the eighteenth century. The sudden success of the East India Company in subjugating a vast population with a sophisticated civilization created problems of an unprecedented kind for Britain. It raised in an acute form questions about the scope and limits of state action, the rights of chartered bodies, the duties of conquerors to subject peoples, the appropriateness of exporting western ideals and concepts of law and government to Asia, and the manner in which the resources of the East could best contribute to Britain's power and wealth.

LONDON: GEORGE ALLEN AND UNWIN LTD